PENSIONS AT WORK:
SOCIALLY RESPONSIBLE INVESTMENT OF
UNION-BASED PENSION FUNDS

Pension funds have come to play an increasingly important role within the new economy. According to Statistics Canada, in 2006 the assets of Canadian trusteed pension plans alone were about $836 billion and represented the savings of 4.6 million Canadian workers. *Pensions at Work* builds on scholarship, both Canadian and international, about socially responsible investment and on the Canadian labour movement's growing interest in joint trusteeship of pension plans that represent deferred wages of its members. The essays, by a distinguished group of experts from a variety of backgrounds, address the different manifestations of socially responsible investment – social screens, economically targeted investment, and shareholder activism. The volume also discusses the concept of fiduciary responsibility as it pertains to trustees of pension funds, and matters related to the preparation of trustees nominated by unions for the boards of pension funds. Although there is a growing literature on socially responsible investment, this study directs that discussion to pension funds and even more so to pension funds in which union representatives are trustees, a relatively recent phenomenon.

Addressing an array of important issues, such as trustee education, the impact of human capital criteria on shareholder returns, the influence of employee engagement on corporate performance, and the nature of public-private partnerships, *Pensions at Work* is an essential resource for anyone with an interest in the labour movement and for institutional investors in general.

JACK QUARTER is a professor and co-director of the Social Economy Centre at the Ontario Institute for Studies in Education, University of Toronto.

ISLA CARMICHAEL is the Director of Policy for the Ontario Expert Commission on Pensions, and a sessional lecturer at the Department of Adult Education and Counselling Psychology at the Ontario Institute for Studies in Education, University of Toronto.

SHERIDA RYAN is a doctoral candidate and a Social Sciences and Humanities Research Council fellow with the Department of Adult Education and Counselling Psychology at the Ontario Institute for Studies in Education, University of Toronto.

Pensions at Work

Socially Responsible Investment of Union-Based Pension Funds

Edited by

Jack Quarter, Isla Carmichael, Sherida Ryan

UNIVERSITY OF TORONTO PRESS
Toronto Buffalo London

© University of Toronto Press Incorporated 2008
Toronto Buffalo London
www.utppublishing.com
Printed in Canada

ISBN 978-0-8020-9310-3

Printed on acid-free paper

Library and Archives Canada Cataloguing in Publication

Pensions at work : socially responsible investment of union-based
pension funds / edited by Jack Quarter, Isla Carmichael, Sherida Ryan.

ISBN 978-0-8020-9310-3

1. Pension trusts – Investments – Canada.   2. Labor unions – Canada.
3. Investments – Moral and ethical aspects.   I. Quarter, Jack, 1941–
II. Carmichael, Isla   III. Ryan, Sherida, 1949–

HD7105.45.C3P48 2008   332.67'2540971   C2007-907471-5

University of Toronto acknowledges the financial assistance to its
publishing program of the Canada Council for the Arts and the
Ontario Arts Council.

University of Toronto Press acknowledges the financial support for its
publishing activities of the Government of Canada through the Book
Publishing Industry Development Program (BPIDP).

To the many unionized workers who are members of pension funds with investments that form the financial backbone of our society

Contents

Figures and Tables

Tables

Figures

Appendixes

Foreword

The concentrated nature of share ownership on the world's capital markets means that large institutional investors – insurance companies, mutual funds, and pension funds – own the bulk of the world's listed companies. In many countries, a significant portion of these shareholdings is held in workers' retirement savings, pension funds, and other investment vehicles – workers' capital.

As beneficial owners of these deferred wages, workers are the *indirect* owners of a substantial portion of the world's equities. According to a 2002 estimate, workers' retirement savings and pension funds total more than US$11 trillion globally, and it has been estimated that pension fund holdings account for about one-third of the world's total share capital.

The investment of worker retirement savings is meant to provide long-term financial returns to pension fund beneficiaries. However, the opposite is sometimes the case. Corporate concentration, excessive executive pay, and the privatization of public services demonstrate the need for unions to mobilize to save both jobs and pension funds in the face of the lack of diligence on the part of mainstream investment managers, analysts, and auditors, and the sometimes blatant self-interest of corporate executives and controlling shareholders. Many companies are involved in human rights and international labour standards violations, the privatization of public-sector jobs, or pollution of the environment. With companies typically focused on short-term returns, long-term social, corporate, and environmental challenges go unaddressed, with ensuing collateral damage for pension funds and their members as well as the general public. High-profile scandals have highlighted the need for legal frameworks for corporate governance and an oversight role for workers and their unions in both pension fund and corporate governance structures.

Almost all research on pension fund investment is dominated by a business perspective. It is refreshing, therefore, to see a book on pension fund investment that has a labour perspective. The Canadian Labour Congress and its affiliates were active participants in the SSHRC-funded research alliance that led to this book, and therefore we are pleased to see these studies come together in this single collection. This book provides a 'toolbox' that should help create a better understanding of pension fund investment from a labour perspective. It should help inform the actions that pension trustees and their unions can undertake to increase the long-term value of pension funds. In order to be success-ful, however, worker capital requires effective coordinated action. A key challenge is helping workers' capital find its local as well as its global 'voice.' With some concerted efforts, appropriate strategies, and effec-tive coordination, mobilizing workers' capital in solidarity can make a difference to the world around us, simply because workers own much of the world – however indirectly – through their invested retirement savings.

Ken Georgetti
President, Canadian Labour Congress

Preface

In 2006, trusteed pension funds in Canada had $836 billion of assets and represented the savings of 4.6 million Canadian workers. Even in the world of high finance, $836 billion is a staggering sum! It is widely acknowledged that the investment of these pension funds forms the underpinning of the Canadian economy and has an international impact. Many of the 4.6 million Canadian workers who have trusteed pension plans are covered by collective agreements negotiated by their unions. The Canadian labour movement, therefore, has developed policies on the management and investment of pension funds, as reflected in resolutions adopted at the Canadian Labour Congress in 1986 and 1990.

Pension capital and its relationship to organized labour is the starting point of this book, which focuses on socially responsible investment and its link to pension capital and labour studies. There has been a growing body of research on socially responsible investment – research that accompanies a burgeoning investment practice of socially responsible and ethical mutual funds. There are also large bodies of research on pensions and labour studies, but the key feature of this book is that it involves a unique synthesis of three themes. To the best of our knowledge, this book is unique in that regard.

This book is derived from a three-year research alliance funded by the Social Sciences and Humanities Research Council of Canada (SSHRC).* This initiative, originally saddled with the cumbersome but descriptive title, A University–Union Research Alliance on the Socially Responsible Investment of Pension Funds in the New Economy, was shortened to a more manageable Pensions at Work. In fact, the website that became the repository for the project's many initiatives signified the renaming – www.pensionsatwork.ca.

The original name, while difficult to repeat and even more difficult to recall, reflected the many components of this initiative. It was not simply one project, but rather a grouping of nine projects, called a research alliance. Moreover, the participants were not simply from universities, as is the case with most research projects in the social sciences, but involved community partners, or what SSHRC labels a community–university research alliance. In our case, the participants were from eight universities and 17 partner organizations, primarily the Canadian Labour Congress and its provincial affiliates. This research alliance gave the CLC and its affiliates an opportunity to participate in research that reflected the concern of its members for how pensions were being invested. Throughout this three-year research initiative, we had the ongoing assistance of Bob Baldwin, the CLC's then director of social and economic policy, kindly enabled by Ken Georgetti, president of the Canadian Labour Congress; Michel Lizée, coordonnateur au service aux collectivités de l'Université du Québec à Montréal (UQAM); and Denise Gagnon, education officer, Fédération des travailleurs et travailleuses du Québec. We are particularly indebted to the support that they and other labour partners provided.

This book consists of chapters based upon the nine projects that formed the research alliance. These projects are clustered around three primary themes: the impact of socially responsible investment of pensions, the barriers to the socially responsible investment of pension funds, and education for union trustees of pension funds.

The book consists of the following chapters:

1. 'Socially Responsible Investment of Pensions: Issues and Debates,' the opening chapter by the editors of this collection, Jack Quarter, Isla Carmichael, and Sherida Ryan, provides an overview of the issues in this field and an introduction to the book.
2. 'Just Having It Is Not Enough: Labour's Voice on Pension Boards,' by Johanna Weststar and Anil Verma, carefully demonstrates the gaps in education of union trustees of pension funds.
3. 'Fiduciary Duties, Investment Screening, and Economically Targeted Investing: A Flexible Approach for Changing Times,' by Gil Yaron, addresses the bugbear of socially responsible investment: Is it contrary to the fiduciary responsibility of trustees?
4. 'Human Capital–Based Investment Criteria for Total Shareholder Returns,' by Jane Thomson Comeault and David Wheeler, addresses a thorny question: What is the impact of human capital criteria on shareholder returns?

5. 'Corporate Governance and Environmental Risk Management: A Quantitative Analysis of "New Paradigm" Firms,' by Gordon L. Clark and James Salo, presents a careful analysis of the impact of corporate engagement upon corporate performance.
6. 'Social Accounting and Reporting for Economically Targeted Investments: The Expanded Value Added Statement,' by Laurie Mook, moves the research on economically targeted investment forward by creating a new accounting format – an adaptation of a value added statement called the expanded value added statement.
7. 'Economically Targeted Investments, Union Pension Funds, and Public–Private Partnerships in Canada,' by John Loxley, undertakes a critical analysis of public–private partnerships from a labour perspective, reinforcing the need for investment criteria that are socially responsible.
8. 'Economically Targeted Investing: Financial and Collateral Impact,' by Kathryn Manley, Tessa Hebb, and Edward T. Jackson, presents a comprehensive analysis of the impact of economically targeted investments in Canada and also a comparison to those of the huge pension plan, the California Public Employees Retirement System.
9. 'Pension-Fund Management and Socially Responsible Investment,' by Ran Goel and Wes Cragg, addresses a difficult question: Is there a case for socially responsible investment based upon ethics alone?
10. 'Training for Effective Action: Evaluation of the Quebec Federation of Labour Training Program on the Bargaining and Administration of Pension Plans,' by Alain Dunberry, discusses the author's formative evaluation of Canada's leading education program for labour trustees of pension funds.

All chapters address socially responsible investment in its various manifestations, and how it is perceived and practised by different pension funds and unions. We are pleased to say that for seven of the ten chapters, the author or co-author was a graduate student at the time the research was undertaken, though several of them have since graduated. Indeed, one editor of this collection, Sherida Ryan, is in that circumstance, and another editor, Isla Carmichael, who was the Pensions at Work manager, was a postdoctoral researcher.

While this book, like many others, raises as many questions as it answers, it is a unique collection of materials about socially responsible investment of union-based pension funds in Canada. We are proud to have put this collection together and thank all contributors to the book and the larger group of participants in the research. As noted, all of the materials associated with this research alliance are available at our now archived website – www.pensionsatwork.ca

Note

* We wish to thank SSHRC for its generous support of this research under project number 538-2003-1003.

Contributors

Isla Carmichael is director of policy for the Ontario Expert Commission on Pensions. She was previously a postdoctoral fellow at the Ontario Institute for Studies in Education of the University of Toronto (OISE/UT) and project manager of Pensions at Work, funded by the Social Science and Humanities Research Council of Canada. She is the author of *Pension Power: Unions, Worker Control, and Social Investment in Canada* (2005) and co-editor (with Jack Quarter) of *Money on the Line: Workers' Capital in Canada* (2003). She completed her doctorate at the OISE/UT in 2000. Her research was recognized through the Graduate Prize for Outstanding Research by the Policy Research Initiative of the Government of Canada. She is a labour appointee to the Investment Committee of the Canada Post Pension Plan and for seventeen years occupied senior posts with the Ontario Public Service Employees Union, specializing in social and economic policy. She has extensive experience teaching at both graduate and undergraduate levels.

Gordon L. Clark, FBA, DSc (Oxford), was appointed the Halford Mackinder Professor of Geography at the University of Oxford in 1995. He is also affiliated with the Institute of Ageing and St Peter's College, Oxford. Prior to his appointment at Oxford, he taught public policy at Harvard University, the University of Chicago, Carnegie Mellon University, and Monash University. An economic geographer with continuing interest in the nature and practice of decision making, he is researching the governance, organization, and investment management of pension and retirement institutions around the world. This research has also been linked to a more general concern with the role of institutional investors in the long-term accountability, governance, and performance of global corporations. His most recent book is *The Geography of Finance* (2007) with Dariusz Wójcik.

Wes Cragg is director of the Schulich School of Business Ethics Program and professor of philosophy at York University, where he is responsible for encouraging and coordinating research and curriculum development in business ethics. He is a graduate of the University of Alberta and the University of Oxford, where he studied as a Rhodes Scholar. He recently concluded a major interdisciplinary study entitled *Ethics Codes: The Regulatory Norms of a Globalized Society?* examining the effectiveness of codes and self-regulation in international business transactions. Wes was recently awarded a $2.1 million Social Science and Humanities Research Council grant to support the development of a Canadian Business Ethics Research Network and a second SSHRC grant to study ethics at the intersection of business and health care. He is published widely in Canadian and international journals and other academic publications on topics in business ethics, corporate citizenship, corporate social responsibility, corporate governance, bribery and corruption, and applied ethics. He is a member of the editorial boards of *Business Ethics Quarterly*, the *Journal of Business Ethics*, and *Interchange*, and a former president of the Canadian Philosophical Association. Wes is the founding president and chair of Transparency International Canada (1993–2006). He is vice-chair of Mining and Sustainability, a recently formed Canadian NGO.

Alain Dunberry is a professor of the Department of Specialized Education and Training at the Université du Québec à Montreal. He has been a consultant in international cooperation for more than 25 years with the Canadian International Development Agency, the World Bank, and the United Nations Educational, Scientific, and Cultural Organization. He teaches program evaluation and adult education and is involved in social development projects.

Ran Goel graduated with a juris doctor degree from the University of Toronto in 2007. He holds a master's with distinction from the London School of Economics and Political Science, where he studied under a Commonwealth Scholarship, and a business degree from the Schulich School of Business, York University. Ran has been involved with corporate responsibility and responsible investment issues for the past six years. He founded the Responsible Investment Working Group at the

University of Toronto. His related publications include 'Guide to Instruments of Corporate Responsibility' (2005), and 'Responsible Investment at the University of Toronto' (2006, co-author). Ran is an associate in the pooled investment practice of an international law firm in New York City.

Tessa Hebb is the director of the Carleton (University) Centre for Community Innovation (3ci), a leading knowledge producer on social finance. Her research focuses on the financial and extra-financial impact of pension fund investment in Canada and internationally. She is also a senior research associate at the Labor and Worklife Program, Harvard University, and the University of Oxford Centre for the Environment. She is researching the role of U.S. public-sector pension funds and urban revitalization as lead investigator on a three-year Rockefeller and Ford Foundation grant. She was awarded the prestigious William E. Taylor Fellowship (2003) from the Social Sciences and Humanities Research Council, Government of Canada. Tessa Hebb has published many articles on pension fund investing policies and is the co-editor of *Working Capital: The Power of Labor's Pensions*.

Edward Jackson is associate dean (Research and Graduate Affairs) in the Faculty of Public Affairs at Carleton University. He also serves as chair of the Carleton Centre for Community Innovation, which carries out research on financing civil society, and is active on foundation and government committees on social finance. Co-founder of the Community Economic Development Technical Assistance Program, his other research interests include CED impact assessment and community–university engagement.

John Loxley is professor of economics in the University of Manitoba, advisor to the Manitoba minister of finance, and economic consultant to the Credit Union Central of Manitoba. He has been researching public–private partnerships for the last 10 years.

Kathryn Manley works for the Canadian Food Inspection Agency. She recently completed an MBA at Carleton University, where she submitted a thesis entitled *Formal and Informal Venture Capital and Networking: The Effect of Clusters*. She has been awarded numerous scholarships including the Carleton Senate Medal for Outstanding Academic Achievement. She previously worked at the Canadian International

Development Agency for 12 months. She also holds a Bachelor of Commerce from Carleton University, with concentrations in finance and information systems.

Laurie Mook has degrees in accounting, international development, educational policy studies, and adult education. She was a Social Science and Humanities Research Council of Canada doctoral fellow at the Ontario Institute for Studies in Education of the University of Toronto, where she developed the expanded value added statement model for economic, social, and environmental accounting. She is co-author (with Jack Quarter and Betty Jane Richmond) of the recent book, *What Counts: Social Accounting for Non-profits and Cooperatives*, second edition (2007).

Jack Quarter was the principal investigator for the SSHRC-funded Research Alliance on Socially Responsible Investment of Pension Funds in the New Economy that led to this book. He is a professor at OISE/University of Toronto and co-director of the Social Economy Centre. His recent books include: with Laurie Mook and Betty Jane Richmond, *What Counts: Social Accounting for Non-profits and Cooperatives*, second edition (2007); as co-editor and contributor with Isla Carmichael, *Money on the Line: Workers' Capital in Canada* (2003); and *Beyond the Bottom Line: Socially Innovative Business Owners* (2000).

Jane Thomson Comeault, PEng, MES, is a visiting research fellow at the Faculty of Management, Dalhousie University, and a freelance sustainability consultant based in Vancouver, BC. She has worked with several organizations, including the International Finance Corporation, the United Nations Development Programme, the World Business Council for Sustainable Development, and Canada's National Roundtable on the Environment and the Economy (NRTEE). She has co-authored a number of publications, including 'Creating Sustainable Local Enterprise Networks' (2005) in *MIT Sloan Management Review*, and *Comparative Study of UK and Canadian Pension Fund Transparency Practices* (2004) for the NRTEE Capital Markets and Sustainability Program. Her interests include sustainable finance, sustainability and management strategy, and the role of the private sector in development. Jane has a Masters of Environmental Studies, specializing in business and sustainability from York University, and a bachelor of science in mechanical engineering from the University of Manitoba.

Sherida Ryan is a doctoral candidate in adult education and community development at the Ontario Institute for Studies in Education of the University of Toronto and a Social Sciences and Humanities Research Council of Canada fellow. Her research examines the relationship between information and communication technology and participation in the online non-profit sector. Sherida's particular interest is online community development and she has studied online social action networks, human rights organizations, health support groups, and social economy enterprises. 'Don't Trust Anyone Outside Your Pack: Initial Trust Formation in an Online Social Activist Network' was published in the *Internet Research Annual*, volume 2, of the Association of Internet Researchers.

James Salo is a graduate of the University of Oxford, where he earned his DPhil from the University of Oxford Centre of the Environment, where he holds the position of research associate. His thesis was titled *Corporate Environmental Performance: Governance, Intangibles, and Financial Markets.* James previously attended Clark University, located in Worcester, MA, where he completed a combined BA/MAin Environmental Science and Policy. He is an environmental research analyst at Trucost Plc in London and has spent time working as a summer analyst for Credit Suisse (London) and for the Coalition for Environmentally Responsible Economies (Ceres) (Boston).

Anil Verma is professor of industrial relations and human resource management at the University of Toronto, where he holds a joint appointment at the Rotman School of Management and the Centre for Industrial Relations. He has taught at the University of California, Los Angeles, the University of British Columbia, and the University of Saskatchewan, and worked in the steel industry as an engineer for five years. His primary research interests are in management responses to unionization, participative forms of work organization, wage and employment outcomes, and the contribution of workplace innovations to organizational effectiveness and performance. He has served as president of the Canadian Industrial Relations Association and on the executive board of the International Industrial Relations Association, Geneva. Anil consults with a wide range of businesses, unions, governments, and international agencies, including the Advisory Committee on Labour and Income Statistics, Statistics Canada. He serves on the Independent Board of Examiners for the Canadian Council of Human

Resource Associations and the Board of Directors of COSTI Immigrant Services, the largest such organization in Canada.

Johanna Weststar recently joined the Management Department at the Sobey School of Business at Saint Mary's University in Halifax as an assistant professor. She completed her PhD at the Centre for Industrial Relations and Human Resources at the University of Toronto in 2007 and her master's in industrial relations at Queen's University in 2003. In addition to pensions, Johanna's research interests include the interconnections of learning and work, as well as workers in high-tech industries such as information communications technology, electronic games, and new media.

David Wheeler is dean of the Faculty of Management, Dalhousie University, NS. The Faculty of Management comprises four schools – the School of Business Administration, the School of Public Administration, the School of Information Management, and the School of Resource and Environmental Studies – as well as the Marine Affairs Program. The Faculty of Management at Dalhousie has a holistic and values-based approach to management education and research. The faculty is also home to five centres of research and learning: the Eco-Efficiency Centre, the Centre for Management Informatics, the Norman Newman Centre for Entrepreneurship, the RBC Centre for Risk Management, and the Centre for International Trade and Transportation. David has published more than 70 articles and book chapters in a wide variety of academic journals, books, parliamentary inquiries, and popular journals, and has delivered speeches to numerous conferences and events. He has been an adviser to the United Nations for more than 20 years and has been a frequent adviser to the World Bank (International Finance Corporation) on the role of the private sector in international development.

Gil Yaron is past-director of Research, Law, and Policy for the Shareholder Association for Research and Education. SHARE is a national not-for-profit organization helping pension funds to build sound investment practices, to protect the interest of plan beneficiaries, and to contribute to a just and healthy society. Gil holds a master's of law from the University of British Columbia and has been a member of the bar of British Columbia since 1998. He is the author of numerous articles on pension trustee fiduciary duties and socially responsible investment. Gil is the owner of Frogfile Office Essentials, an office-supply company specializing in environmentally responsible office products.

PENSIONS AT WORK:
SOCIALLY RESPONSIBLE INVESTMENT OF
UNION-BASED PENSION FUNDS

1 Socially Responsible Investment of Pensions: Issues and Debates

JACK QUARTER, ISLA CARMICHAEL,
AND SHERIDA RYAN

Although there is an extensive body of research on social investment and its impact, little of that research applies to pension funds, and even less to Canadian pension funds. The primary purpose of this book is to synthesize the research on social investment with the growing interest in pension investment – particularly from unions as they respond to concern about how their members' savings are being invested. This book synthesizes three typically distinct themes – socially responsible investment, pensions, and labour studies – as they apply to the role of unions in investment. In this chapter, we shall address each of these themes, starting with the changing role of unions in relation to pension fund investment.

Unions and Investment

The active interest of trade unions in the administration of pension funds represents a departure from tradition. After the Second World War, the industrial labour movement refused to accept involvement in the administration of pension funds on the grounds that such a strategy would undermine the strength of collective bargaining and would, essentially, be concessionary (Mosher, 1952). The latter concern was based on years of labour and community campaigns, which focused on trying to win universal state pensions, rather than workplace-based pensions. In the immediate post-war period, the struggle for universal pensions appeared to be lost. Instead, post-war unions bargained a 'flat' pension benefit for their members, just like bargaining a wage rate. Members did not pay contributions to the plan. This practice was common in the auto and manufacturing industries during this period, and it was only later, in the 1960s, that the Canada Pension Plan was introduced.

In contrast, the construction, retail, and needle trades had a tradition of sole-trusteed pension (and often welfare) plans, with the union taking sole responsibility for administering its members' contributions. The tradition stemmed from the tendency of employees to move from one contractor to another rather than maintaining a stable employment relationship with one company (O'Grady, 1993). Clearly it was too difficult to get employers jointly or individually to take any responsibility for providing their employees with a pension or welfare benefits. In some cases, employers were prepared to take some collective responsibility and make contributions, and as a result multi-employer pension plans (MEPPs) were established, with employers being 'negotiated in,' agreement by agreement. These plans were often created trade by trade in the construction industry. Sometimes the employer allowed the union to manage the plan, although, technically, the plan was jointly trusteed, as was the case with the Carpenters' Pension Plan in British Columbia.

Over the past 30 years, there has been a change of approach, driven by the growth of public-sector unionism, the dominance of large public-sector pension plans funded by employee as well as employer contributions, and the decline of the practice of bargaining 'flat' pension benefits. During the same period, the economy has been marked by such factors as increasingly high unemployment in public and private sectors, stagnant wages, the decline of manufacturing and the rise of the service sector, the internationalization of finance and the rise of the institutional investor, employer pension contribution holidays, and the irrationality of the stock markets (Shiller, 2000). In response to these conditions, a resolution by the 1986 convention of the Canadian Labour Congress 'endorse[d] the goal of organized Canadian workers achieving greater control and direction of the investment of pension funds' (Baldwin, Jackson, Decter, & Levi, 1991, p. 10). This was followed by a similar resolution at the 1990 convention (Carmichael, 2005).

These resolutions signalled an active interest from the labour movement in pension-fund management. The movement was now dominated by large public-sector unions, whose members made pension contributions to their pension plans. Their interest was driven largely by a concern to protect the pension monies by moving them out of the consolidated revenue funds of provincial governments across Canada and into trusteed pension funds and, in particular, into joint trusteeship. In Ontario, the Ontario Federation of Labour argued for co-determination of pension funds in a brief to the Rowan Commission (Task Force on the Investment of Public Sector Pension Funds, 1987). The Ontario Public Service Employees' Union (OPSEU) achieved joint trusteeship of its major plans (Carmichael, 1996, 1998). The Canadian Union of Public Employees (CUPE), the largest public-sector union, with more than half a million members across Canada and representing the employees of 30 of the top 100 plans in Canada, succeeded with other unions in gaining joint trusteeship of the large Hospitals of Ontario Pension Plan in the early 1990s. CUPE has had a consistent strategy ever since in all provinces across Canada. It is now estimated that 18 of the top 23 unions in Canada have either achieved some form of trusteeship of their members' pensions or are negotiating it (Carmichael & Quarter, 2003).

In the 1990s, this change was not without controversy (Gindin, 1997; Stanford, 1999), with the Canadian Auto Workers Union (CAW) – one of Canada's largest unions – still reflecting the traditional stance of the labour movement. Organized labour, the CAW argued, should focus on its traditional role of representing the 'labour' rights of workers and exclude itself from pension-fund management. The essence of the CAW critique was that union involvement in pension-fund management reduced union bargaining strength.

This critique of labour's involvement in issues of capital was much broader than pension-fund investment. It included such practices as buyouts of firms threatened with closure and labour-sponsored investment funds, which have become a major form of venture capital in Canada since the 1984 launch by the Quebec Federation of Labour of the Solidarity Fund (Hebb & Mackenzie, 2001). Bob White, former director of the CAW, referred to worker buyouts as 'lemon socialism' (personal communication, September 1991).

However, economic realities have outstripped these arguments as labour-sponsored investment funds have foundered in volatile stock markets, and the manufacturing and aerospace sectors of the economy have been marked by mergers, buyouts, and the end of the Auto Pact. Just as significantly, the CAW has diversified and now has a sizeable public-sector membership. As a result, it has lobbied alongside CUPE and other public-sector unions for changes to the Ontario Municipal Employees Retirement System to have a more equitable stakeholder representation in pension governance (CAW, 2006). Up against a more powerful lobby from the police and firefighters, CUPE and the CAW

won the right to a review within three years of the pension-fund governance structure.

Pension promises have not been fulfilled in the hardest-hit manufacturing and aerospace companies of the economy – such as Stelco, Air
Canada, Nortel, Canadian Pacific, and United Airlines – where unions
traditionally have not been involved in pension governance. Conversely, the dismal record of governance practices of corporate pension
plans in Canada has led to renewed calls for multi-stakeholder governance. In an editorial in the *Financial Post*, Keith Ambachtsheer (2006, p.
FP15), a leading pension industry consultant, referred to the pension
crisis of low returns and 'ineffective' governance and management.
Among several best practice suggestions, Ambachtsheer recommended
that company pension plans restructure their boards to be more representative of 'stakeholder interests.'

There are also calls for more involvement by plan members based on
the Quebec model of pension regulation, the most notable coming from
the Canadian Association of Pension Supervisory Authorities (CAPSA,
2004). The more recent mandate of CAPSA has been to harmonize pension laws across Canada, which are now both federal (for some feder-
ally regulated companies) and provincial. Almost 3,000 pension plans –
almost a quarter of all private-sector plans – had members in more than
one pension jurisdiction in 2002. This regulatory nightmare results in
costly administration and may even hinder the development of pension plans.

The Quebec governance model favoured by CAPSA consists of
pension committees with employer and employee representation. Employee representation is not equal, but employee representatives are
chosen by employees themselves, and may include in-house unions,
likely at the local level. The *Quebec Supplemental Pension Plans Act* also
provides for a system of alternates so that representation can be maintained in the event that a trustee is unable to attend meetings. This
model is not as strong as some joint-trusteeship models in other parts of
Canada but is much envied by many unions whose members are in corporate plans.

Union Trustee Education

Critics and proponents of labour trusteeship of pensions question the
preparedness of labour trustees to assume this role. The hegemonic
control exerted by the financial industry over investment practice (and

often over investment education as well) may be exercised in the absence of any alternative frameworks proposed by trustees' unions. But coercion and undermining of 'lay' trustees by fund managers should also not be underestimated. As it becomes clear that more union members want joint trusteeship and some control over investment of their pension funds, opposition has mounted to union trustees. Senator Kirby, as chair of Canada's standing Senate Committee on Banking, Trade, and Commerce, has called for 'the quality of direction and over-sight needed in today's complex world' through 'highly knowledge-able people' to 'effectively monitor fund managers' (Kirby, 1998, p. 41). The model often cited is that of the Ontario Teachers' Pension Plan Board, which always appoints members of its board of directors on the basis on their financial expertise. Rarely are they teachers.

For these reasons, there has been considerable pressure on the trade union movement to provide trustee education as a complement to its campaigns to win joint trusteeship. We wanted to investigate how the trade union movement was responding and undertook a survey of phone interviews of the major unions in Canada. We were already aware of some education strategies: the 10-year program of the Quebec Federation of Labour for labour trustees of pension funds, the biennial pensions conference of the Canadian Labour Congress (CLC), the edu-cational initiatives organized by the CLC through the Vancouver-based, non-profit Shareholder Association for Research and Education (SHARE),[1] and the work of the International Foundation of Employee Benefits and Pensions, an American-based educational institution. However, we wanted to learn what forms of education and educational infrastructure major labour federations and unions were putting in place for their members.

The results are summarized in Table 1.1. As can be seen, among the large labour federations and unions, it is commonplace to have a pen-sion specialist and related committee; however, it is not common prac-tice to have a newsletter related to pensions, a pensions section on a website, or a pensions conference. About half of the unions surveyed have some form of pension education for members, but only one cov-ered joint trusteeship. Surprisingly, three-quarters reported covering social investment in their member education. Pension education for trustees was undertaken in-house by only a quarter of those surveyed, and most referred their trustees to external programs, including the Advanced Trustee Management System (ATMS) program offered by the International Foundation of Employee Benefit Plans; the Canadian

Table 1.1. Summary of Pension Education by Unions in Canada.

Organization	Pension specialist	Pension committee	Pension newsletter	Pension section on Web	Organized pension conference	Pension education for members	Joint trusteeship (covered)	Social investment (covered)	Pension education for trustees
CLC unions and federations	6/7	5/7	0/7	2/7	3/7	3/7	1/7	6/7	2/7
Other public sector large unions	1/1	1/1	0/1	0/1	0/1	0/1	0/1	0/1	0/1
Teachers' unions	3/3	3/3	2/3	3/3	1/3	3/3	0/3	3/3	1/3
Other unions	1/1	1/1	0/1	1/1	0/1	0/1	0/1	0/1	0/1
Totals	11/12	10/12	2/12	4/12	4/12	6/12	1/12	9/12	3/12

Note. CLC unions and federations include BC Federation of Labour, Ontario Federation of Labour, Quebec Federation, Saskatchewan Federation of Labour, Alberta Federation of Labour, Ontario Public Service Employees Union, and Alberta Union of Public Employees. Other public-sector large unions include Public Service Alliance of Canada. Teachers' unions include BC Teachers' Federation, Alberta Teachers' Federation, and Ontario Teachers' Federation. Other unions include Canadian Auto Workers.

Securities Course offered by CSI; Pension Investment Management Services offered by Mercer's and the Schulich School of Business at York University; or the courses offered by Humber College's Centre for Employee Benefits. The SHARE/Canadian Labour Congress program undertook some of the trustee education.

Although the lack of preparedness of labour trustees for their role is a topic of discussion at union conferences (for example, the Canadian Labour Congress Pensions Conference in 2004), there is surprisingly little research on this topic. Chapter 2, by Weststar and Verma, specifically discusses labour trustee preparedness for their role. This study is one of a kind in Canada in that it is based upon a national survey, conducted in both English and French, of labour trustees of pension funds. Although there is no comprehensive list of labour trustees (a matter that in itself is of great interest), Weststar and Verma, through working with labour federations, were able to compile 231 names, of which 117 returned their survey. One of their central findings was that 'only 29% reported that they were prepared for their role as a labour trustee when they took up the position for the first time. Almost half reported that they were not prepared, and 27% indicated that they were not sure – this in itself indicates less than complete preparation' (p. 51). Of their sample, 14% claimed no exposure to pension issues, 17% learned through self-study, and 23% gained knowledge through their own pension. As one trustee in their study states,

> I suspect that even though we talk often, as a union, about bargaining issues and pension benefits the union is fighting for, many people don't really understand the basics of the plan. I've learned a lot on the job because our plan has had some funding issues that have made us deal with the federal regulator and that has taught us all a great deal about solvency and funding liabilities. We've replaced several fund managers and that has taught us a lot about what to watch for and how to track our investments. But it has all been a bit ad hoc. (p. 51)

To function in their role, many of the trustees took courses, but, with the exception of Quebec, relatively few courses were offered from a labour perspective. These data address the question of whether the role of labour trustee is distinctive. Interestingly, the trustees in the sample were predominantly on pension boards with more than one labour trustee representative, and, on 56% of the boards, labour trustees constituted at least half of the representation.

Therefore, even though there is growing interest among unions in achieving greater control over the investment of pension funds through having trustees from the labour movement on pension boards, it appears that there is a need for greater investment in the education of union trustees. But what does this mean? First, it is by no means clear that any one affiliate or union has the capacity or financial resources to design and deliver the ongoing education necessary to fully train its own union trustees. Second, there is little history of collaborative effort in ongoing education among trade unions, except those initiatives delivered (often on a one-off basis) through the federated affiliates. As Bob Baldwin, pensions consultant and previous director of social and economic policy at the CLC, pointed out at the most recent Pensions at Work conference (2006), while union members at all levels need more and regular opportunities to learn about pensions, there needs to be an 'honest appraisal' of whether unions can commit to delivering the education internally (Baldwin, 2006). If some can and some cannot, are unions willing to share their programs?

The Quebec Federation of Labour has agreed to share its pension programs in both English and French via the Pensions at Work website. It had little choice but to create a program when the Quebec pension law was passed 10 years ago. Since elections or selections of trustees happened at the local level, the central organization not only had to develop materials but also had to keep track of trustees. The program development is impressive and includes education for members, trustees, staff representatives, and negotiators. Programs are available at the beginning (about 12 three-day sessions a year) and advanced level (about two residential five-day sessions) in trusteeship as well as collective bargaining of pensions. To enable networking and exchange of ideas, skills, and experience, there is also a yearly conference of on average 100 participants as well as train-the-trainer courses. As part of the Pensions at Work research program, Alain Dunberry, an evaluation specialist at Université du Québec à Montréal, worked with the Quebec Federation of Labour to evaluate its trustee education program (see chapter 10 for this innovative work).

Pensions Funds

Pension funds represent the savings or deferred income of plan members, the capital of which is invested in a cycle to generate the necessary income to pay pension benefits. Therefore, pension funds are huge pools of capital that form the financial underpinnings of the economy both domestically and internationally. In the first quarter of 2006, trusteed pension funds in Canada had assets of $836.8 billion and represented the deferred earnings of 4.6 million Canadian workers (National Union of Public and General Employees, 2006). The retirement savings of millions of Canadian workers enrolled in trusteed pension plans have steadily recovered from the downturn in the early 2000s. Since the first quarter of 2003, when pension fund assets hit a four-year low of $532.4 billion, they have increased in value by 57.1%.

Worldwide, the picture is similar. Pension-fund assets in the OECD countries, by the end of 2005, amounted to US$17.9 trillion – up from US$13 trillion in 2001 (OECD, 2006). As Minns (2003) points out, pension-fund assets are greater than the combined total market value of all the world's industrial, commercial, and financial corporations quoted on the three largest world stock markets (New York, Tokyo, and London).

In addition, Registered Retirement Savings Plans (RRSPs), set up by individuals to save for their own retirement, are a major form of savings, with assets in 2003 of $403.2 billion (Statistics Canada, 2006). The contributions and the investment gains of registered pension plans and RRSPs are both tax exempt.

The gains in pension funds tend to mirror those of stocks traded on the world's stock exchanges, since a large portion of pension assets are invested in stock markets. In Canada, in the first quarter of 2006, nearly 40% of the value of all fund assets was held in stocks. Within the OECD countries, Finland invested 41.3% of pension assets in equities, the Netherlands 49.8%, the United Kingdom 40.1%, and the United States 41.3%. This is an increase over the preceding year (OECD, 2006).

Among the largest pension plans in Canada is the Ontario Teachers' Pension Plan, with assets of $96 billion in 2005 (Ontario Teachers Pension Plan, 2006), its holdings including $20.2 billion in Canadian equities and $25.8 billion in non-Canadian equities. Quebec's Caisse de dépôt et placement du Quebec (CDP), founded by an act of the Quebec Assembly in 1965, is the largest Canadian investment-management company, managing the Quebec Pension Plan, public-sector occupational pension plans, and the assets of other organizations in Quebec, and its net depositor assets at the end of 2005 were $122 billion (Caisses de dépôt et placement du Québec, 2006). The Ontario Municipal Employees Retirement System had assets of $41 billion in 2005 and was another major investor in Canadian corporations (OMERS, 2006). The Canada Pension Plan, referred to above, had $53 billion of assets in

2003, of which the $17.5 billion not required for payments to beneficia-
ries was heavily invested in equities, 63% in Canadian public equity
markets (Government of Canada, 2006). Moreover, this fund is projected to increase to $246 billion within the next decade, making it
among the world's larger institutional investors (CPP Investment
Board, 2006).

Politics of Pension Funds

Yet workers, for the most part, have no control over the investment or
accumulation of these funds. Pension funds are invested in the market
primarily through fund managers employed by the major financial
institutions and retained by the pension fund. In its survey of 146 fund
managers, Benefits Canada (Bak, 1997) reports that pension assets
under management in 1997 were $339.3 billion. This figure represents
approximately 70% of all pension assets in Canada at the time. Furthermore, the top 10 money managers controlled almost 44% of these
assets.

The larger funds tend to hire their own investment staff, but 60% of
pension funds use external investment managers. Professional fund
managers have almost total discretion over the investment of funds
(Deaton, 1989; Minns, 1996; Rifkin & Barber, 1980; Roe, 1991). For the
most part, pension-fund managers retain the privileges of capital trusteeship, and, through their exercise of voting rights for shares held by
the fund, influence decisions on the purchase of companies, on takeovers, on corporate policies including downsizing, on privatization of
government assets, on corporate behaviour such as health and safety
and environmental standards, and finally, on corporate structures and
compensation (Carmichael, 2005).

This privilege of trusteeship does not include the increasing role of
pension funds in international markets, as well as their role in foreign
currencies, national debts, and other economic policies (Davis, 1995;
Minns, 2003). The CLC has stated that 'the largely private nature of the
investment process makes workers, communities and governments the
hostages of those who control the investment process' (Canadian
Labour Congress, 1990, p. 3).

These investment managers often have a direct financial interest in
takeovers and privatization. In 1994, in the United Kingdom, eight out
of the top ten pension-fund management companies were involved as
advisers in takeovers. Of the eight U.K. banks involved in privatization

sales, four were among the top ten pension-fund managers. Financial institutions involved in the management of pension funds have a 'clear commercial interest' in the takeover business and the privatization of public services and state pension systems (Minns, 1996, p. 386).

Arguably more significant than the recent growth of pension funds is the underfunding of many pension plans following the stock market slump in the early 2000s and, subsequently, lower interest rates. This was preceded by a period of stock market gains, increased pension benefits, and employer contribution holidays. According to one report in the *Globe and Mail*, in 2002 only 23 of 104 companies surveyed showed pension surpluses, and the collective pension-funding shortfall was more than $18.7 billion (Church, 2003). The Office of the Superintendent of Financial Institutions (OSFI), the federal pensions regulator, introduced new policies that include the imposition of a timetable for companies under its jurisdiction to fund underfunded plans (Stewart, 2003). Class action suits have sprung up in the United States, and a number of similar cases in Canada, all relating to pension management and employer liability when pension plans are underfunded.

Pension Fund Management

As noted earlier, fund management is a contested arena. The most common model is that of the corporate pension plan, otherwise called a sole trusteeship, in which the company board of directors is also the board of trustees of the plan. This model clearly constitutes a conflict of interest (CAPSA, 2004; Carmichael, 2005). However, sometimes the plan has no trustees at all. These are often smaller pension plans in the private sector. Management of the funds is essentially contracted out to an insurance or investment-management company. Oversight of the funds may (or may not) be provided by the benefits person in the company's Human Resources Department. This model, by no means uncommon, betrays an equally shocking failure of governance (Stromberg, 2005).

Another example of a plan without trustees is a pension arrangement covering government employees and teachers that remains in the consolidated revenues of the state. It was only in the 1990s that provincial employee and teacher unions rebelled successfully against this model. Copps Coliseum, in Hamilton, had its biggest demonstration when teachers and public employees travelled from across Ontario to protest against the Liberal government of Premier David Peterson and to save their pensions. No teachers' or public-service unions in the country at that time had collective bargaining rights over pensions or the right to information from governments; therefore, they could not allay their fears that their pension monies, and in particular their members' contributions, were drifting into government expenditures. The lack of transparent accounting procedures was appalling. The Ontario Teachers' and the Ontario Public Service Employees' Union were the first to get their pension funds into separately managed entities, with other provincial unions following. Similar steps were taken within the Canada Pension Plan when, in 1997, it was put under the control of its own investment board appointed by government and the funds were moved into a separate entity. In 1999 the Public Sector Investment Board took control of pension funds for the Canadian Forces and Royal Canadian Mounted Police.

Types of Pension Plans

Another contested arena is the type of plan. For the purposes of this discussion, there are two types of plans: defined benefit (DB) and defined contribution (DC). In defined benefit plans, employers – and, more often than not, employees – make contributions into a plan that has a defined benefit upon retirement. The pension benefit is 'defined' on the basis of plan financing, including the investment gains of the fund. However, until recently, it has been widely assumed, particularly by plan members, that the 'pension promise' is immutable (unless benefits are improved). The defined benefit plan has been the prevailing model for occupational pension plans, but is now precarious (Clark & Monk, 2006). Lack of stakeholder governance, mentioned previously, has had an enormous impact on the viability of DB plans, as have short-term factors such as regulatory time limits on capital accumulation (which is tax-exempt, up to a certain limit), lower interest rates, employer contribution holidays, and increased employee benefits. Pension plans are ideally suited to a long-term program, matching their assets with their liabilities, but this point has not always been recognized in either financial-management practice or regulatory regimes.

We have discussed the flat benefit plan, which is a subset of the defined benefit plan and in which unions negotiated only the amount of the pension benefit, often regardless of plan financing. While this model worked well for those private-sector unions with bargaining strength and with the right to bargain pensions, it has long outlived its usefulness. In fact, some would argue that this lack of union responsibility for the long-term financing and governance of pension plans has contributed to the weakening of the defined benefit model.

An employer response has been to wind up defined benefit plans to avoid the associated risk and convert to defined contribution plans, where the risk rests with the individual employee. This has happened to some extent in all OECD countries. Some notable examples in Canada are Air Canada and Nortel. In other cases, employers have shifted to a blend of defined benefit and defined contribution, where employees have a choice of plan. In yet other cases, there have been reductions in benefits based on unfunded liabilities, such as the British Columbia Carpentry Workers' Pension Plan.

Nevertheless, Statistics Canada reports that over 88% of pension-plan members still belong to defined benefit plans, and this figure climbs to 95% for public-sector workers. On the other hand, in Canada nearly 90% of defined contribution plans had fewer than 100 members, reflecting the fact that in Canada these plans are still a primary option for employers of small workplaces, where defined benefit plans are too costly (Statistics Canada, 2003).

In defined contribution plans, the individual employee absorbs the risk of his or her own savings and the amount of the final retirement benefit. The total amount of money accumulated in an individual's account is used on retirement to 'purchase' a monthly retirement income (e.g., an annuity). No one knows what this monthly income will be, and the cost of annuities may fluctuate dramatically each year.

The discussion of risk has been a difficult one for unions and their members, particularly in the historic absence of transparency. Winning a place at the table when, quite possibly, the cupboard is bare is a no-win situation for many union leaders. Yet the alternative scenario of watching the employer unilaterally reduce pension benefits or, worse still, wind up defined benefit plans, is not palatable either.

Given the support for broader stakeholder representation on pension boards, it is possible that pension laws will eventually accommodate employee representation in some form and, consequently, distribute risk more evenly among employers and plan members than is presently the case in either defined contribution or defined benefit plans.

Another option that unions have pursued has been to form multi-employer pension plans (MEPPs). MEPPs have been traditional in the manufacturing and construction sectors but are not always jointly trusteed. Public-sector unions have been taking the MEPP model to the bargaining table on behalf of predominantly female workers in nursing homes and group homes. When workers in smaller workplaces in the service sector – the majority of whom are women – are unionized, pension and benefit plans are often far more difficult to negotiate because of the high costs associated with small DB plans. Group RRSP arrangements, or defined contribution plans, have been their only option, leaving them vulnerable to market fluctuations.

In response to these circumstances, unions like CUPE and the Service Employees International Union have negotiated to include employers within jointly trusteed pension plans where the unions and employers have a 50% partnership, or even sole trusteeships where the unions are the only sponsors and assume full risk for the plan. As well, the Quebec government has recently introduced a member-funded pension plan (MFPP), financed by members with a fixed contribution from the employer. The cost of the pension plan's commitments, less the employer's fixed contributions, will be the sole responsibility of the plan's active members. There are a number of regulatory features built into this model to contribute to its sustainability, including fully indexed benefits only with plan solvency, financing of shortfalls and deficits from member benefits, and a prohibition on benefit formulas based on the member's highest earnings during a specified number of years.

These last types of plans retain the best feature of defined benefit plans – they are essentially financial collectives in which benefits to all members are spread out over the long term. Plan members acknowledge the risk to their benefits but get control through trusteeship to mitigate the risk. In contrast, defined contribution plans have none of these features. Plan members rarely form a collective in any meaningful sense, and their benefits depend solely upon the performance of their investment. They may be given 'choice' over their investment, but in practice the money is likely entrusted to a financial manager who gains from managing the portfolio.

Pensions and Social Impact

Given the size of these funds, there have been mixed views about the potential power that may be exercised by workers and their organizations over the economy. Peter Drucker coined the term *pension socialism* as early as 1976, with some concern. Yet he was also critical of the financial industry: 'Global bankers ... have introduced not a single major innovation in 30 years,' he said. 'Rather, the financial industry has turned inward to perfecting supposedly scientific derivatives in a shortsighted hope of wringing the risk out of financial speculation, like Las Vegas gamblers futilely trying to devise systems to beat the house' (cited in Andrews, 1999, p. B19). Richard Deaton (1989), faced with the inadequacies of public and occupational pensions to meet the needs of citizens, criticized the corporate sector and the state for appropriating pension funds as a source of investment to meet their own financial requirements. Robert Monks, shareholder activist, says that pension funds can control corporate America and make them responsible for their social and environmental impacts (Monks, 2005). Carmichael (2005) describes the contested terrain of pension administration and investment but shows the potential for a more democratic economy through a more equitable distribution of pension power.

In other words, there is broad recognition of the power associated with the large pools of pension capital and their potential for social impact, but the sine qua non in any reform agenda is plan-member interests. The trustees of pension plans, it is widely agreed, have an obligation to manage the plan in the interests of its members. Although the meaning of *member interests* has been disputed in the courts, as discussed in chapter 3 by Gil Yaron, the common denominator in all legal rulings on this matter is that the trustees must engage in a process that attempts to uphold member interests, a primary aspect of which is member financial interests. This obligation, of course, constrains the freedom available in pension-fund investment, but as discussed below and in Yaron's chapter, the debate surrounding fiduciary responsibility ranges from one in which rate of return is the exclusive criterion, to others in which criteria in addition to rate of return can be considered. This perspective is frequently referred to as *socially responsible investment*.

Although research on socially responsible investment is often viewed as a unique line of scholarship, it is also part of a growing body of knowledge that challenges market autonomy and situates the economy within a social framework that emphasizes the reciprocal relationship between society and the economy. The theoretical roots of this work can be found in Polanyi's concept of the economy as an 'instituted process' (Polanyi, 1957), in Granovetter's subsequent elaboration upon 'embeddedness' (1985), and in the more recent development of the social capital concept (Putnam, 1995, 1996, 2000). Each of these formulations addresses a unique set of issues, but all view the economy within a social context.

Although this viewpoint may seem self-evident to some, it does fly in the face of tradition that tends to view the economy as an end in itself and parts of society not specifically within the economy as an 'external-ity' – to apply a label commonly utilized by economists. An extreme expression of this viewpoint is Friedman's (1970, p. 32) oft-quoted pro-nouncement: 'There is one and only one social responsibility of busi-ness – to use its resources and engage in activities designed to increase its profits so long as it stays within the rules of the game, which is to say, engages in open and free competition without deception or fraud.'

Modern accounting also follows this tradition and limits itself to the financial transactions of an organization, not its broader impact. The cri-tique of this practice has led to the field of social accounting (Mathews, 1997) and the creation of alternative accounting frameworks that take social and environmental impact into consideration (Mook, Quarter, & Richmond, 2007). Chapter 6 by Laurie Mook presents a framework for analysing the social and environmental impact of an economically tar-geted investment.

Social accounting is but one of the many new fields of inquiry that, like socially responsible investment, challenge the concept of market autonomy and focus on the society/economy nexus. First, there is scholarship that explores the social impact of corporate behaviour, including corporate social responsibility (Carroll, 1979, 1991, 1999; Drucker, 1984), corporate social performance (Asmundson & Foerster, 2001; Roman, Hayibor, & Agle, 1999), virtue theory and other theories of business ethics (Arjoon, 2000; Martin, 2002), multiple bottom-line management (Conway, 2001; Roberts & Cohen, 2002; Waddock, 2000), and stakeholder theory (Clarkson, 1995; Wheeler & Sillanpää, 2000). Although these lines of inquiry are distinct, they share an effort to broaden the framework for evaluating corporate performance, to embed performance within an explicit value framework, and to create methods of accounting for corporate social performance that go beyond financial accounting.

Second, there is a related line of inquiry, widely known as alternative economics, that presents a more fundamental critique of conventional economics, particularly its impact upon human society – or to quote the book subtitle of Schumacher (1973), 'Economics as if people mattered.' Among the alternative economists are critics of environmental exploi-tation (Ekins, Hillman, & Hutchinson, 1992; Henderson, 1991; Sachs, Loske, & Linz, 1998; Schumacher, 1973), of the exploitation of women (Mies, 1986; Milani, 2000; Shiva, 1989; Waring, 1996, 1999), of the inad-equacy of conventional methods of growth, and of the need for alterna-tives (Daly & Cobb Jr, 1994; Ekins, 1986), including new methods of accounting for social value (Gray, Owen, & Adams, 1996; Mathews, 1997; Mook et al., 2007).

Third, there is a line of inquiry known as the social economy or économie sociale, which applies primarily to organizations that are part of neither the private nor the state sectors of the economy. In Canada, the bulk of this scholarship is from Quebec, such as Lévesque and Ninacs (2000), Shragge and Fontan (2000), and Vaillancourt and Tremblay (2002); however, there is some from other parts of Canada (Browne & Welch, 2002; Mook et al., 2007; Quarter, 1992). The social economy framework has been applied to a subset of organizations with a social mission, but it also proposes that even though these organizations are set up for a social purpose, they generate economic value. As Shragge and Fontan (2002, p. 9) argue, 'A social economy implies a basic reorientation of the whole economy and related institutions.'

Socially responsible investment can be viewed as part of a broad set of intellectual traditions, and although each has distinct features, all situate the economy, including the business sector, within a social context that in part colours our interpretation of corporate behaviour and related issues such as investment policies. Socially responsible investment is but one manifestation of these intellectual traditions that are reinterpreting the economy–society relationship.

Socially Responsible Investment of Pension Funds

Socially responsible investment involves huge amounts of capital. In the United States, a 10-year study by the Social Investment Forum estimates the number of socially screened mutual funds increased from 55 in 1995 to 201 in 2005, and the total assets under management by these funds increased from US$12 billion to US$179 billion (Social Investment Forum, 2006). This report 'identified $2.29 trillion in total assets under management using one or more of the three core socially responsible investing strategies – screening, shareholder advocacy, and community investing. Nearly one out of every ten dollars under professional management in the United States today, or 9.4 percent of the $24.4 trillion in total assets under management tracked in Nelson Information's Directory of Investment Managers, is involved in socially responsible investing' (Social Investment Forum, p. iv).

And the trend in the United States is not unique. In Canada, the assets managed according to social responsibility guidelines as of June 2004 reached $65.46 billion (Social Investment Organization, 2005). Moreover, a 2003 report of eight Western European countries by the European Sustainable and Responsible Investment Forum (Eurosif) states that 'Social Responsible Investment has undergone tremendous developments in Europe in the last few years' (European Sustainable and Responsible Investment Forum, 2003, p. 6). This report indicates further that in these countries assets of €336 billion are subject to some form of screening, and indicates that the United Kingdom and the Netherlands are the strongest in this regard.

Socially responsible investment (also referred to as social investment) has different manifestations, but all involve the inclusion of social standards in investment decisions (Bruyn, 1987; Carmichael, 2000, 2005; Carmichael & Quarter, 2003; Ellmen, 1989). In other words, investment decisions are not based simply on the rate of return (the usual practice) but also on non-financial criteria (for example, impact on the community) that may interact with the rate of return. The problem with this definition is that it also allows for the inclusion of criteria that discriminate against the rights of particular groups (such as anti-gay screens used by some U.S. funds). Therefore, this book utilizes the additional criterion suggested by some researchers (Bruyn, 1987; Carmichael, 2000, 2005; Lowry, 1991; Zadek, Pruzan, & Evans, 1997) that socially responsible investment should challenge conventional corporate behaviour and improve society.

In its earliest formulation, socially responsible investment was used interchangeably with ethical investment, and provided an ethical critique of corporate behaviour. However, over time, socially responsible investment and ethical investment have become distinct, the latter emphasizing an ethically appropriate course of action, and in its purest formulation not heeding the rate of return (Ellmen, 1989). By comparison, socially responsible investment does emphasize the rate of return, but argues that by applying social criteria the rate of return is not hindered, and may be enhanced. This viewpoint underlines chapter 4 by Thomson Comeault and Wheeler, which builds upon earlier work by members of that research team showing that removing the worst social performers from the TSX60 Index did not harm the rate of return (Milevsky, Aziz, Goss, Thomson, & Wheeler, 2004). Indeed, that argument is a theme that runs through many of the chapters in this collection (Clark and Salo; Manley, Hebb, and Jackson; Thomson Comeault and Wheeler).

In chapter 9, Goel and Cragg present the argument for ethical investment. The difference between socially responsible and ethical investment is probably greater in theory than in practice, as no one promoting an ethical standard would completely ignore the rate of return of an investment, and at the opposite extreme, even the staunchest proponents of the bottom line might balk at investments with extreme socially destructive consequences. Therefore, the difference in practice is in degree rather than as categorical as the arguments would lead one to believe. Goel and Cragg actually look at the prevalence of global standards and their impact on institutional investment, a topic also examined by Clark and Hebb (2005) in a study supported by this project. Clark and Hebb argue that adoption of corporate and environmental standards by firms in the global marketplace may mitigate risk and therefore act as a driver of value.

There are at least three distinct forms of socially responsible investment that shall be discussed in turn – investment screening, corporate engagement or shareholder action, and economically targeted investment. All approaches to socially responsible investment involve a variation in the way that investment assets are handled and combine financial objectives with non-financial objectives about social, environmental, ethical, or corporate governance (SEE/CG) issues.

Investment Screening

As the name implies, screening involves the application of either negative or positive investment screens or indicators to investment choices. A negative screen or sanction is the simplest in that it involves the prohibition of a particular class of investments. South Africa under apartheid was subject to negative investment screens by pension funds and other investment vehicles, and arguably was a relatively successful example of the application of a negative screen. The tobacco and armament industries are more current campaign targets of negative sanctions. The United Church of Canada Pension Plan, whose members are current employees and retirees of the church, including its clergy, has a longstanding tradition of applying an array of social screens for 'sin' stocks related to alcohol, tobacco, gambling, and armaments. It does this directly and also through investment in other funds (for example, the Domini 400 Social Index). Negative screens can lend themselves to effective boycotts, as in the case of South African apartheid, where a worldwide campaign led to legislation in several countries banning investment in that country.

It is not often acknowledged by fund managers that indices of stocks are routinely screened, and undesirable stocks are pulled with no harm to returns. For example, an income trust index may be screened to pull out the riskier income trusts with less reliable cash flow; indices may be screened to pull particular stocks that may create a reputational risk. Moreover, as mentioned, the research undertaken in association with the Pensions at Work project provides additional supportive evidence of this practice in relation to a passive index, TSX60 (Milevsky et al., 2004).

Positive screens are those that normally involve a fund with a group of investments that have been screened on a set of indicators – for example, to encourage the quality of the environment. There are many leading funds focusing on the environment, such as Middlefield Alternative Energy Fund, Sentry Select Alternative Energy Fund 2001, and the Desjardins Environment Fund. However, the trend among socially screened funds is to utilize a broader set of criteria over a variety of sectors of the economy, to diversify the portfolio and reduce the risk. The reasoning behind this approach is derived from modern portfolio theory, which analyses investments for their risk–reward relationship and whether the return is justified by the average level of risk in the fund (Harrington, 1987; Markowitz, 1952; Sharpe, 1963). There is a large research literature on the financial impact of socially responsible investment, with studies overwhelmingly indicating that returns are not adversely affected (Orlitsky, Schmidt, & Rynes, 2004).

The 'best of sector' approach guarantees that no single industry will be excluded because of its poor social, environmental, or governance performance. This approach attempts not to narrow the universe of potential investments but, instead, to simply choose the best SEE/CG performers within a particular sector. There are agencies – increasingly larger investment companies – that rate corporations on social indicators, as a service to investment funds. There is much variability in rating techniques to be considered in investing in a particular company, country, or market.

Perhaps the most interesting example of positive screening has been developed by the California Public Employees' Retirement System (CalPERS). After intensive lobbying by the union trustees, led by Service Employees' International Union, CalPERS instituted a comprehensive screen for international investment (emerging markets) based on the Global Sullivan Principles (Sullivan, 1999) and the ILO Declaration on Fundamental Principles and Rights at Work (1998). In this screen, all factors are weighted, and country and market factors each account for 50% of the total score. Country factors are political stability, transparency of government, and productive labour practices. Market factors are market liquidity and volatility, market regulation, legal system, investor protection, capital market openness, settlement proficiency, and transaction costs. An underlying sentiment is that these principles contribute to economic growth (and economic growth is equated with high returns). Considerable interest in the CalPERS screen has developed because it may provide a complementary strategy to global activism in challenging corporate behaviour and setting labour standards.

Shareholder Action and Corporate Engagement

The second form of social investment is shareholder action, of which corporate engagement is a subset. Pension funds use this investment strategy in order to remedy or improve a corporation's behaviour. The most usual strategy, particularly among large pension funds, is to establish proxy-voting guidelines, to guide the vote for or against management resolutions being forwarded to annual meetings. The pressure to exercise proxy votes comes from the prevailing legal view that votes are assets of the fund and as such are to be used with an eye to their value. Corporate engagement may range from a phone call or letter, to a meeting with management of a company – strategies designed to press for a change in corporate behaviour. The problem with corporate engagement is often a lack of transparency or, in other words, secrecy, particularly in Canada where companies are closely held (Hebb, 2006). William Dimma, a director of several public companies, believes that the preferred way is 'quiet and private.' Indeed, he maintains that this is the 'Canadian way ... the way to get things done' (Canada Senate Standing Committee on Banking, 1998, p. 9).

Further shareholder actions are drafting and circulating shareholder resolutions to be voted on by all shareholders. In Canada, the early impetus for corporate engagement as well as other types of shareholder action has come largely from religious organizations (Hutchinson, 1996), including the United Church of Canada Pension Plan, that formed the Task Force on Churches and Social Responsibility. The U.S. counterpart to this organization is the Interfaith Center for Corporate Responsibility, representing 275 faith-based institutional investors with a combined portfolio of US$110 billion. This organization sponsors, on average, more than 200 shareholder resolutions per year.

The Canadian labour movement became involved in shareholder action when, in 2000, it was a founding member of the Shareholder

Association for Research and Education (SHARE). SHARE is a national non-profit organization 'dedicated to improving institutional investment practices that protect the long-term interests of pension plan members, beneficiaries and society in general. It focuses particularly on the governance and investment of workers capital, the funds set aside in pension funds for workers' retirement' (Shareholder Association for Research and Education, 2006). SHARE is a very active participant in shareholder resolutions, as both leader and supporter, and its database provides a listing of upcoming resolutions as well as the results of past actions. SHARE may also be retained to create proxy-voting guidelines and issue proxy alerts bimonthly to highlight upcoming votes. SHARE is active in the international movement on corporate social responsibility.

Most large pension funds have developed proxy-voting guidelines as part of their investment policy statements. They employ rating agencies to track votes and post their guidelines on their websites. The Ontario Public Service Employees' Union Pension Trust has taken an unequivocal position on using its proxy votes, where possible. Colleen Parrish, manager of the plan, describes the process for instructing fund managers on how to vote proxies:

> We instruct all our investment managers and our custodian to bring forward issues that we then screen for those that should receive the attention of the Board of Trustees ... Well, when a lot of pension plans do that, then there's a real sense out there that corporate governance matters. Slowly you start to have an impact because it changes the way the capital markets work. (Carmichael, 2005, p. 56)

A significant barrier to institutional investor involvement in governance is the control of funds by the financial industry. Where assets are pooled into larger funds, individual pension funds rarely have control over the share votes. This restriction affects a large proportion of smaller pension funds, where fund management is contracted out. For example, the Carpentry Workers' Pension Plan of British Columbia was unable to join in the shareholder action on child labour, organized by the BC Federation of Labour.

Fund managers, on the other hand, seek to influence the behaviour of corporations in which they invest pension funds. Douglas Grant, chair of Sceptre Investments, which is the fifth largest pension fund manager in Canada, explains:

We have private meetings with companies ... These meetings are valuable to us, in part, because we control the agenda and, in part, because it is important to us to know the character of the people managing the companies that we invest in. It is important to the companies, and they agreed to do it because they need to keep in touch with their shareholders and we are, typically, a big shareholder. (Canada Senate Standing Committee on Banking, 1998, p. 8)

The Ontario Municipal Employees Retirement System (OMERS) has registered its interest in actually pursuing active corporate governance strategies beyond proxy voting, and the Ontario Teachers' Pension Plan board of trustees has face-to-face meetings with management. The board considers these meetings as 'an integral part of our due diligence in selecting companies for major investment and managing those investments in the long term' (Canada Senate Standing Committee on Banking, 1998, p. 9).

In the United States, CalPERS established a reputation for using this practice (Smith, 1996), and devotes a section of its website to shareholder initiatives in which it has been involved. Some of the issues that CalPERS has highlighted are executive compensation, accountability and disclosure to shareholders, and links between compensation and performance (CalPERS, 2006). In addition, CalPERS employs a corporate engagement strategy for underperforming companies with poor governance practices in which the fund has invested. CalPERS seeks to engage the companies' executives and to reform the governance.

Corporate engagement may lead to other forms of shareholder action such as boycotting, or screening out a particular investment. For example, Talisman sold its 25% stake in the Greater Nile oil concession in 2003 in response to the public criticism and negative screens imposed upon its stock. Talisman undertook to improve its image by publishing a *Corporate Responsibility Report* and participating in the United Nations Global Compact (Talisman Energy, 2006). Nevertheless, the corporation recently was subject to a $1-billion U.S. class action lawsuit alleging that 'Talisman willingly aided the Sudanese government in a campaign of genocide and human rights abuses against the civilian population' (CanWest News Service, 2006, p. 3).

Boycotting a company is an extreme form of shareholder action when the more usual processes of persuasive meetings and shareholder resolutions have not yielded the desired result. However, the cost of withdrawing shares may be high. Therefore, pension funds tend to make their presence felt and bring value to their investments through engagement and exercising their proxy votes, rather than exiting. Given the size of their investments and the limited range of market alternatives, Canadian pension funds have little choice but to maintain and improve their corporate engagement.

Another issue that arises in corporate engagement is its impact upon the performance of the targeted company. A comprehensive review of the U.S. literature on pension-fund activism and firm performance suggests that there was no substantial effect (Wahal, 1996). That review suggests that the firms targeted by CalPERS experience a small increase in stock values, whereas non-CalPERS targets do not change significantly. The problem with such studies is that they often lack a long-term view of the potential value to be drawn from corporate engagement. Indeed, some theorists say that corporate engagement is being more widely used, given the costs of exit, and is acknowledged as contributing to stock value (Clark & Hebb, 2004; Wahal & McConnell, 2000). To avoid the higher costs, another solution may be to act in concert with other pension funds in which case corporate engagement may become a more potent force (Becht & Mayer, 2001). Securities laws internationally are increasingly allowing shareholders to communicate with one another (Monks, 2001).

Chapter 5 by Gordon Clark and James Salo addresses the interrelationship of drivers of corporate performance. Most pension funds undertaking corporate-engagement campaigns do so through corporate governance. Their primary finding is that so-called new paradigm firms that rely on intangibles such as corporate reputation and brand image make the management of their governance and environmental performance a greater priority than other corporations. This chapter is part of an elaborate line of research on corporate engagement by Clark and Salo, and Tessa Hebb.

Economically Targeted Investment (ETI)

Economically targeted investments are defined as 'investments designed to produce a competitive rate of return commensurate with risk as well as create collateral economic benefits for a targeted geographic area, group of people, or sector of the economy' (Bruyn, 1987, p. 6). This may cover real-estate development or funds, responsible contractor requirements, regional development, investment in socially responsible investment (SRI) funds, union-friendly investment vehicles, worker buyouts, or privatization alternatives (Barber, 1997).

Economically targeted investment (ETI) is categorized for the most part as a form of private equity and bears a greater degree of risk and uncertainty, unless – as in the United States – government, as an implicit recognition of its role in the economy, underwrites the risk. ETIs, therefore, have a long history in the United States (Calabrese, 2001; Zanglein, 2001), but in Canada there are fewer examples of this type of investment by pension funds (Carmichael, 2005; Quarter, Carmichael, Sousa, & Elgie, 2001). In this volume, Yaron's chapter 3 addresses the impact of American regulation on Canadian ETI practice and fiduciary responsibility. Yaron points out that ETIs are supported by an interpretative bulletin from the Department of Labor, provided that they are 'carefully screened and selected to meet the prevailing rate of return' (Watson, 1995, p. 4). This reduces the pressure on trustees if a particular investment performs poorly, as is inevitably the case in a proportion of higher-risk ventures.

Real estate is a primary target for economically targeted investments, and agencies of the U.S. federal government reduce the risk by providing guarantees. Another risk-reducing factor is the pooling of these investments and their management by specialists, thereby relieving pension funds and other investors of this burden (Carmichael, 2005). There are some outstanding examples of pooled investment vehicles organized by the labour movement, targeted to real estate and involving pension funds. The prototype is the AFL-CIO Housing Investment Trust involving about 400 investors, including major pension funds in the United States. The trust, with investments of more than $5 billion, touts itself as 'a national leader in the investment of union capital for the financing of housing,' having created 'over 80,000 units of housing, approximately half of which are affordable to low- or moderate-income households' (AFL-CIO Housing Investment Trust, 2007). The trust invests in mortgage securities that finance the housing development, but adds the condition that the developer must employ union labour – an important collateral benefit for the sponsors.

Another example is the Union Labor Life Insurance Company, which began operations in 1925 as a union-owned insurance company that would provide affordable insurance for union workers and their families. The company diversified in 1977 to form the J for Jobs program to invest in commercial mortgages and to create union construction jobs. As of 2005, J for Jobs had investments in 61 projects representing $8.8 billion total project value (ULLICO, 2005). Similarly, the Multi-Employer Property Trust, initiated in 1982, pools the investments of 287 pension plans to provide equity for real-estate developments such as office buildings, retail centres, and warehouses. In 2006, this fund was the owner of 173 properties across the United States with net assets of $5.71 billion (Multi-Employer Property Trust, 2006). These investment vehicles emphasize the collateral benefit that union labour must be employed.

In Canada, the outstanding example of a real-estate development company organized by pension funds (26 union and management funds) is Concert Properties, headquartered in Vancouver, but now operating in Toronto as well (Carmichael, 2000, 2005). Since 1989, Concert has built 6,000 rentals and condominiums and has assets in excess of $800 million (Concert Properties, 2006). One of its recent developments in Toronto involved a partnership with the Ontario Municipal Employees Retirement System (OMERS). In 1992, some of the pension funds involved in Concert established a fund, Mortgage Fund One, and since that time have created additional products, such as Mortgage Fund Two and Three, operating under the umbrella of ACM Advisors Ltd (ACM Advisors Ltd, 2006). As of mid-2006, these funds had $835 million in assets under management, and like their U.S. counterparts, Concert and the related mortgage funds promote the hiring of union labour (OMERS, 2006).

In addition to real-estate development, economically targeted investments by pension funds also involve regional and social targeting. CalPERS targets a portion of its investments for California (11% by 2004), and in 2002 CalPERS began to target underserved areas of the state, a program that is discussed in detail in chapter 8 by Manley, Hebb, and Jackson. Through the California Initiative, CalPERS targeted $500 million to small businesses in parts of the state where capital is more difficult to access and where there generally is a lower standard of living. By 2005, the California Initiative led to investments in 83 companies whose eligibility included that the principals in the company meet equity criteria, that the company employ persons with relatively low incomes, and that it be located in an area with challenges in accessing investment capital.

In Canada, the best example of regional and social targeting by a pension fund is the large Caisse de dépôt et placement du Québec, the organization that manages the province's public pension plans. The government act approved in 2005 with respect to the Caisse specifically states that part of its objective is 'contributing to Québec's economic development' (Caisses de dépôt et placement du Québec, 2006). The Caisse has pursued its commitment to Quebec through investing in venture capital, financing for small- and medium-sized enterprises through a working arrangement with the National Bank, and succession financing for family businesses. In 2005, about 45% of the Caisse's private equity portfolio was invested in Quebec, including a major investment in infrastructure projects (Caisses de dépôt et placement du Québec). Interestingly, the annual report of the Caisse has a substantial section detailing its impact upon Quebec's economy.

A distinctive feature of economically targeted investment is the emphasis on collateral benefits and the ability to justify the additional benefit from a values framework. This issue is discussed by John Loxley in chapter 7, on public–private partnerships involving pension funds, in particular the OMERS pension fund that has invested in these partnerships through its company Borealis. Loxley questions whether these public–private partnerships should be considered economically targeted investments, as the collateral effect is to displace jobs in the public sector. Private companies, financed in part by pension funds, are undertaking infrastructure development projects that might be financed through the public sector. The Canadian labour movement has strongly opposed these arrangements, arguing that the projects should be undertaken through the public sector (Carmichael, 2005).

Arguably, all investments have collateral effects (that is, broader social and economic impacts). Values determine whether these broader effects represent collateral benefits or collateral damage. From a labour perspective, the public–private partnerships are harmful, whereas from a business perspective the argument may be presented differently. Measuring collateral effects presents a challenge for pension funds, because, as mentioned, financial accounting considers these matters as externalities that normally are excluded from income statements. Externalities such as environmental and health-care costs typically are excluded from accounting statements. Chapter 6 by Laurie Mook presents a demonstration of how a value added statement could be adapted (an expanded valued added statement) to include collateral benefits for an economically targeted investment. Her study, based upon the Collingwood community developed by Concert in Vancouver, presents not only the financial value added derived from Concert's transactions but also the social and environmental value added, as estimated from appropriate indicators. Without appropriate accounting frameworks, it is difficult to make headway with calculating collateral effects. As long as these calculations are not made, it is likely that trustees and managers of pension funds will be very cautious about entering into economically targeted investments that bear a higher risk than investments in bonds and large publicly traded corporations – the usual menu for pension funds.

Conclusion

Is socially responsible investment a viable strategy to be endorsed by the labour movement and by the trustees that the labour movement nominates to the boards of pension funds? In part, the answer depends upon expectations. If expectations are for a major, transformative change of society, then clearly the answer to the question is 'no.' If the expectation is for slow reform, then the answer is 'possibly.' Pension funds, whether unions appoint their trustees or whether their trustees are appointed by corporate or government sponsors, are cautious about socially responsible investment. The trustees are responsible for huge amounts of capital upon which the plan's beneficiaries rely for their retirement income, and they are justifiably apprehensive and very dependent upon investment managers.

Of the different forms of socially responsible investment, corporate engagement appears to be the most widely embraced by pension funds, as it is simply a variation of a long-time practice of large investors pressuring corporations in which they have a stake. As large investors, pension funds cannot exit quickly without depressing the price and thereby hurting their return. Corporate engagement permits them to attempt to shape corporate behaviour with the hope that this effort will result in better financial results. If the pressure extends to so-called externalities like human rights issues and the environment – for example, the Talisman campaign – this represents a departure from conventional pressure tactics. The risk in corporate engagement for pension funds is that they might damage the reputation of a corporation in which they have a major stake, and they are reluctant to do that, as it could hurt their investment.

Possibly an indirect effect of corporate engagement is the more stringent enforcement of law against corporate executives. There has been a string of high-profile prosecutions of corporate leaders in recent years and increased scrutiny of accounting practices. Possibly, this would not have happened without the vigorous campaign by activist shareholders to reform corporate governance.

Economically targeted investment is arguably the riskiest form of socially responsible investment in that, unlike investments in publicly traded corporations, there is a shorter track record for predicting outcomes. Pension funds that engage in targeted investment limit their participation to 1–2% of their assets. Overexposure is risky, as was discovered by the Carpentry Workers' Pension Plan of British Columbia (2006), which had over-invested in real-estate development as a means of creating union jobs for its members, but was caught in a downturn of real-estate prices and was forced to restructure the pension plan. This is not a typical story, but is a stark reminder that economically targeted investments bear increased risk. They also appear to bear the greatest benefits, if done well, in that they can target relatively small amounts of pension investments to innovative projects and projects that could serve economically poorer areas. In the United States, this has been done with government support.

Social screens might be the most questionable strategy of socially responsible investment, if results are the criterion. Negative social screens, or boycotts, appeared to be successful in putting pressure on the apartheid system in South Africa, and have mobilized antipathy to the so-called sin products. However, it is not clear how badly these screens have hurt the targeted producers, as the companies find markets in economically poorer countries and diversify their production. Positive screening, or the application of a set of social criteria to a basket of investments, has a compelling logic to it, but this strategy is unlikely to shake the commanding heights of the economy. The best-of-sector approach, while logical from an investment point of view, means that the difference between those at the top and bottom of the list is just noticeable, if noticeable at all.

Nevertheless, even though the social screening of investments may not produce a transformative impact on society, there is evidence that it puts pressure on corporations in that good scores on social screens create favourable publicity and may attract investors. For example, *Business Ethics* issues a Corporate Social Responsibility Report that ranks the 100 best corporate citizens according to their financial performance (as taken from a data file from the magazine *Business Week*) and six social criteria (employees, the community, overseas stakeholders, minorities, women, and customers), as taken from ratings by the KLD Research and Analytics of Boston (Miller, 2002). Companies are invited to prepare information packets about their performance on social criteria such as diversity, which looks at treatment of women and minorities, including the percentage in management, equity policies, and formal complaints. The firms that receive a high ranking in this report typically advertise the results. IBM issued a special press release announcing that it 'Takes Top Spot Among 650 Leading U.S. Public Companies' (IBM, 2002).

Interestingly, screening limited to equity investments in corporations does not include government bonds, even though a compelling case could be made that investment in these forms of securities is socially responsible in that they represent in part an investment in the social infrastructure of a nation – an obvious collateral benefit, and a benefit for public-sector workers. Pension funds have a substantial portion of their portfolio in government bonds, but, over the years, there has been a shift to equity investments in publicly traded corporations as pension funds seek higher returns. Bonds, on the other hand, have a more predictable return, and they represent an investment in the national well-being, arguably a greater social investment than that in publicly traded corporations. Interestingly, this is not a position that the labour movement, including the large public-sector unions, has embraced. Interestingly too, the organizations rating corporations on social indicators do not promote government bonds as a form of social investment. Government bonds represent debt, and, from a political point of view, debt has become a dirty word, even if it is used to finance social infrastructure.

For corporate executives, what matter are their financial results, and unless they believe social behaviour affects financial results, social considerations are unlikely to be of interest. The accounting profession is a key partner in this thinking in that its statements limit the performance assessment of the organization to a narrow set of financial variables and exclude social and environmental impacts. Social-rating agencies perform ersatz forms of accounting, and they could be characterized as a gentle countervailing force that cannot begin to match corporate power. Without broader accounting frameworks, as advocated in social and environmental accounting, the likelihood of a significant change in corporate behaviour is small. There is some indication that the Canadian Institute of Chartered Accountants is reviewing the matter of accounting for externalities, but this is a highly conservative body that initiates alterations of practice at a glacial pace.

There are some hopeful signs, such as the agreement of large pension funds to sign onto the UN principles on responsible investing. However, as Eugene Ellmen, president of the Social Investment Organization cautions, 'It is possible for these signatories to sign on to these principles – backed by the integrity and credibility of the UN – and actually not change one dollar of their investment portfolios' (Ellmen, 2006, p. 3).

Legislation passed in 2000 by the British government is another hopeful sign in that it requires pension plans to disclose annually how social, ethical, and environmental policies are taken into account in their investment and proxy strategies. There is evidence that, since this legislation was approved, there has been a sharp increase in corporate engagement and negative screening by pension funds. Similar legislation has been enacted in Australia, France, Germany, and Italy (Ellmen, 2006). While the disclosure legislation lacks the influence of accounting, it is a form of reporting that can be a basis for performance evaluation. Canada, of course, does not have such legislation.

For organized labour, a role at the table of their members' pension plans is difficult to bypass. However, it is not evident that their trustees are having a significant impact upon investment policy. As suggested above, if unions put more into trustee education, perhaps it would enhance the impact of their trustees. That said, trustees recognize that their primary priority is ensuring that their plan meets its obligation to beneficiaries regarding their retirement income, and this greatly constrains their freedom with these large pools of capital. There does not appear to be an ideal solution, but the opportunity associated with trusteeship of pension plans seems too great to forego. Whether that opportunity will realized remains to be seen.

Note

1 Both the Quebec Federation of Labour and SHARE were involved in the Pensions at Work Research Alliance.

References

Ambachtsheer, K. (2006, 29 March). One sick system: Pension Revolution I: Pension expert Keith Ambachtsheer says neither defined benefit nor defined contribution plans protect workers' retirements. *Financial Post*, p. FP23.

ACM Advisors Ltd (2006). *Company overview.* Retrieved 2 October 2006 from http://www.acma.ca/company-overview.asp

AFL-CIO Housing Investment Trust. (2007). *About us.* Retrieved 18 January 2007 from http://www.aflcio-hit.com/wmspage.cfm?parm1=674

Andrews, F. (1999, 18 November). Drucker disdains corporate myopia. *Globe and Mail*, p. B19.

Arjoon, S. (2000). Virtue theory as a dynamic theory of business. *Journal of Business Ethics, 28*(2), 159–78.

Asmundson, P., & Foerster, S. (2001). Socially responsible investing: Better for your soul or your bottom line [Electronic version]. *Canadian Investment Review* (Winter), 1–12.

Bak, L. (1997). The top 40 money managers. *Benefits Canada, 21*(10), 36–45.

Baldwin, B. (2006). Workplace pensions challenges for Canadian trade unionists. *Conference 2006: Pensions at Work.* Retrieved 17 February 2007 from the Pensions at Work website: http://www.pensionsatwork.ca/english/conference_06.php

Baldwin, B., Jackson, T., Decter, M., & Levi, D. (1991). *Investment funds: Issues and prospects.* Ottawa: Canadian Labour Congress.

Barber, R. (1997). *Retirement, pension and capital strategies: An inventory of major issues confronting labor.* Washington, DC: Centre for Economic Organizing.

Becht, M., & Mayer, C. (2001). Corporate control in Europe. In F. Barca & M. Becht (Eds.), *The control of corporate Europe* (pp. 149–73). Oxford: Oxford University Press.

Browne, P., & Welch, D. (2002). In the shadow of the market: Ontario's social economy in the age of neo-liberalism. In Y. Vaillancourt & L. Tremblay (Eds.), *Social economy: Health and welfare in four Canadian provinces* (pp. 101–28). Halifax: Fernwood.

Bruyn, S. (1987). *The field of social investment.* Cambridge: Cambridge University Press.

Caisses de dépôt et placement du Québec. (2006). *Caisse de dépôt et placement du Québec: Summary.* Retrieved 23 September 2006 from the Google website: http://finance.google.com/finance?cid=11777694

Calabrese, M. (2001). Building on success: Labor-friendly investment vehicles. In A. Fung, T. Hebb, & J. Rogers (Eds.), *Working capital: The power of labor's pensions* (pp. 93–127). Ithaca: Cornell University Press.

CalPERS. (2006). *Shareholder action.* Retrieved 3 October 2006 from the CalPERS Shareowner website: http://governance.calpers.org/alert/

Canada Senate Standing Committee on Banking, Trade, and Commerce. (1998). *The governance practices of institutional investors.* Ottawa: Author.

Canadian Labour Congress. (1990). *A new decade: Our future.* Ottawa: Author.

CanWest News Service. (2006). *Talisman faces appeal in Sudan suit.* Retrieved 26 September 2006 from the canada.com website: http://www.canada.com/topics/news/world/story.html?id=f3e71314-f816–4195–882c-a2aa16f170b2&k=33021

CAPSA/ACOR. (2004). *Proposed regulatory principles for a model pension law.* Retrieved 11 January 2007 from the CAPSA/ACOR website: http://

www.capsa-acor.org/capsa-newhome.nsf/257bb0033af16a0a85256c1a00
754637/c3d9a6e25544270a85256e200054c961?OpenDocument

Carmichael, I. (1996). *The development and control of occupational pension plans by workers in Canada*. Toronto: The Ontario Public Service Employees' Union Pension Trust.

Carmichael, I. (1998). *A survey of union pension trustees*. Toronto: Canadian Labour Market and Productivity Centre and the Ontario Public Service Employees' Union.

Carmichael, I. (2000). *Union pension funds, worker control, and social investment in Canada*. Toronto: University of Toronto.

Carmichael, I. (2005). *Pension power: Unions, pension funds, and social investment in Canada*. Toronto: University of Toronto Press.

Carmichael, I., & Quarter, J. (2003). Introduction. In I. Carmichael & J. Quarter (Eds.), *Money on the line: Workers' capital in Canada* (pp. 15–30). Ottawa: Canadian Centre for Policy Alternatives.

Carpentry Workers' Benefit and Pension Plans of British Columbia. (2006). *Pension plan*. Retrieved 3 October 2006 from http://www.cwbp.ca/pension_plan.shtml

Carroll, A.B. (1979). A three dimensional conceptual model of corporate social performance. *Academy of Management Review, 4*(4), 497–505.

Carroll, A.B. (1991). The pyramid of corporate social responsibility: Toward the moral management of organizational stakeholders. *Business Horizons, 34*(4), 39–48.

Carroll, A.B. (1999). Corporate social responsibility: Evolution of a definitional construct. *Business and Society, 38*(3), 268–95.

CAW. (2006). Revised Bill 206 submission. Retrieved 11 January 2007 from the CAW website: http://www.caw.ca/campaigns&issues/ongoingcampaigns/pdf/RevisedBill206Submission.pdf

Church, E. (2003, 22 January). Big corporate pension plans short billions, study predicts. *Globe and Mail*, p. B1.

Clark, G.L., & Hebb, T. (2004). Corporate engagement: The fifth stage of capitalism. *Relations industrielles / Industrial Relations, 59*(1), 142–70.

Clark, G.L., & Hebb, T. (2005). Why should they care? The role of institutional investors in the market for corporate global responsibility. *environment and planning a, 37*(11), 2015–31.

Clark, G.L., & Monk, A.H.B. (2006). *The 'crisis' in defined benefit corporate pension liabilities: Current solutions and future prospects*. Retrieved 14 November 2006 from the Oxford University Centre for the Environment website: http://www.ouce.ox.ac.uk/research/spaces/wpapers/wpg06-10.pdf

Clarkson, M. (1995). A stakeholder framework for analyzing and evaluating corporate social performance. *Academy of Management Review, 20*(1), 92–117.

Concert Properties. (2006). *Corporate profile*. Retrieved 6 October 2006 from the Concert website: http://www.concertproperties.com/corp_profile.cfm?propertytype=home

Conway, P. (2001). *How the Triple Bottom Line can firm up the development and measurement for reporting on desired outcomes*. Wellington: Public Sector Performance.

CPP Investment Board. (2006). *Responsible investing*. Retrieved 30 September 2006 from the CPP Investment Board website: http://www.cppib.ca/Corporate_Governance/responsible_investing.html

Daly, H., & Cobb Jr., J. (1994). *For the common good: Redirecting the economy toward community, the environment and a sustainable future* (2nd ed.). Boston: Beacon.

Davis, E.P. (1995). *Pension funds: Retirement income, security and capital markets; An international perspective*. London: Clarendon.

Deaton, R. (1989). *The political economy of pensions*. Vancouver: University of British Columbia Press.

Drucker, P.F. (1984). Converting social problems into business opportunities: The new meaning of corporate social responsibility. *California Management Review, 26*(2), 53–63.

Ekins, P. (Ed.). (1986). *The living economy: A new economics in the making*. London: Routledge and Kegan Paul.

Ekins, P., Hillman, M., & Hutchinson, R. (1992). *Wealth beyond measure: An atlas of the new economics*. London: Gaia Books.

Ellmen, E. (1989). *Profitable ethical investment*. Toronto: Lorimer.

Ellmen, E. (2006). *The evolution of public policy: The sustainable and socially responsible investment of Canada's pensions*. Pensions at Work Lecture Series. Retrieved 24 January 2007 from the Pensions at Work website: http://www.pensionsatwork.ca/english/pdfs/lectures/ellmen-notes.pdf

European Sustainable and Responsible Investment Forum. (2003). *Socially responsible investment among European institutional investor: 2003 report*. Paris: Eurosif.

Friedman, M. (1970, 13 September). Social responsibility of business is to increase its profits. *New York Times Magazine*, 32–3.

Gindin, S. (1997). Notes on labor at the end of the century. *Monthly Review, 49*(3), 140–58.

Government of Canada. (2006). *Annual report of the Canada Pension Plan 2002–2003*. Retrieved 23 September 2006 from the Human Resources and Social Development Canada website: http://www.hrsdc.gc.ca/en/isp/pub/cpp/report/2003/annrpt2003.pdf

Granovetter, M. (1985). Economic action and social structure: The problem of embeddedness. *American Journal of Sociology, 91*(3), 481–510.

Gray, R., Owen, D., & Adams, C. (1996). *Accounting and accountability: Changes and challenges in corporate social and environmental reporting.* London: Prentice Hall.

Harrington, D. (1987). *Modern portfolio theory: The capital asset pricing model and arbitrage pricing theory; A user's guide* (2nd ed.). Upper Saddle River, NJ: Prentice Hall.

Hebb, T. (2006). The economic inefficiency of secrecy: Pension fund investors' corporate transparency concerns. *Journal of Business Ethics, 63*(4), 385–405.

Hebb, T., & Mackenzie, D. (2001). Canadian labour-sponsored investment funds: A model for U.S. economically targeted investment. In A. Fung, T. Hebb, & J. Rogers (Eds.), *Working capital: The power of labor's pensions* (pp. 128–57). Ithaca: Cornell University Press.

Henderson, H. (1991). *Paradigms in progress: Life beyond economics.* San Francisco: Berrett-Koehler.

Hutchinson, M. (1996). *The promotion of active shareholdership for corporate social responsibility in Canada.* Unpublished research paper.

IBM. (2002). IBM earns first place in Business Ethics magazine's best corporate citizen ranking. Retrieved 24 January 2007 from IBM website: http://www-03.ibm.com/press/us/en/pressrelease/785.wss

International Labour Organization. (1998). *ILO declaration on fundamental principles and rights at work.* Retrieved 19 January 2007 from International Labour Organization website: http://www.ilo.org/public/english/standards/relm/ilc/ilc86/com-dtxt.htm

Kirby, M.J.L. (1998). *Pension fund governance in Canada: Notes for remarks to the International Pension Conference by the Honourable Michael J.L. Kirby.* Retrieved 11 January 2007 from the Parliament of Canada website: http://www.parl.gc.ca/36/1/parlbus/commbus/senate/com-e/bank-e/press-e/30sept98d-e.htm

Lévesque, B., & Ninacs, W. (2000). The social economy in Canada: The Quebec experience. In E. Shragge & J.-M. Fontan (Eds.), *Social economy: International debates and perspectives* (pp. 112–29). Montreal: Black Rose.

Louli, C. (2006). *Your money, your future.* Retrieved 15 January 2007 from the CUPE website: http://www.cupe.ca/www/news/your_money_your_futu

Lowry, R. (1991). *Good money: A guide to profitable social investing in the 90s.* New York: Norton.

Markowitz, H. (1952). Portfolio selection. *Journal of Finance, 7*(1), 77–91.

Martin, R. (2002). The virtue matrix. *Harvard Business Review, 8*(3), 69–75.

Mathews, M.R. (1997). Twenty-five years of social and environmental accounting research: Is there a silver jubilee to celebrate? *Accounting, Auditing & Accountability Journal, 10*(4), 481–531.

Mies, M. (1986). *Patriarchy and accumulation on a world scale: Women in the international division of labour.* London: Zed Books.

Milani, B. (2000). *Designing the green economy.* New York: Roman and Littlefield.

Milevsky, M.A., Aziz, A.R., Goss, A., Thomson, J., & Wheeler, D. (2004). *Cleaning a passive index: How to use portfolio optimization to satisfy CSR constraints.* Retrieved 22 January 2007 from http://ssrn.com/abstract=630622

Miller, M. (2002). 100 best corporate citizens: America's most responsible and profitable major companies. *Business Ethics,* March/April. Retrieved 6 October 2006 from http://www.business-ethics.com/2002_100_best_corporate_citizens.htm

Minns, R. (1996). The political economy of pensions. *New Political Economy, 1*(3), 375–91.

Minns, R. (2003). Collateral damage: The international consequences of pension funds. In I. Carmichael & J. Quarter (Eds.), *Money on the line: Workers' capital in Canada* (pp. 33–52). Ottawa: Canadian Centre for Policy Alternatives.

Monks, R. (2001). *The new global investors.* Oxford: Capstone.

Monks, R. (2005). Why is a corporation like a stray cat? Retrieved 21 November 2006 from http://www.ragm.com/inthenews/2005/BEfall2005_monks.pdf

Mook, L., Quarter, J., & Richmond, B.J. (2007). *What counts: Social accounting for nonprofits and cooperatives.* London: Sigel.

Mosher, A.B. (1952). Should retirement at age sixty-five be compulsory? *Canadian Unionist, 69,* 77–8.

Multi-Employer Property Trust. (2006). *Welcome to MEPT.* Retrieved 22 February 2007 from Multi-Employer Property Trust website: http://www.mept.com/

National Union of Public and General Employees. (2006). *Pension fund assets in Canada continue to grow.* Retrieved 17 February 2007 from National Union of Public and General Employees website: http://nupge.ca/issues/pen-n48-oct-06-06.htm

O'Grady, J. (1993). *Financial capital for economic renewal.* Paper presented at the Conference on Financial Capital for Economic Renewal, York University.

OECD. (2006). Overview of the financial wealth accumulated under funded pension arrangements. *Pension markets in focus.* Retrieved 14 January 2007 from the OECD website: http://www.oecd.org/dataoecd/21/28/37528620.pdf

OMERS. (2006). *Plan performance – 2005.* Retrieved 23 September 2006 from the OMERS website: http://www.omers.com/English/Asset-Returns.html

Ontario Teachers' Pension Plan. (2006). Fast facts. Retrieved 23 September 2006 from the Ontario Teachers' Plan website: http://www.otpp.com/web/website.nsf/web/fastfacts

Orlitsky, M., Schmidt, F., & Rynes, S. (2004). Corporate social and financial performance: A meta-analysis. *Organisation Studies, 24*(3), 403–41.

Polanyi, K. (1957). The economy as instituted process. In K. Polanyi, C. Arensberg, & H. Pearson (Eds.). *Trade and market in the early empires* (pp. 243–70). New York: Free Press.

Putnam, R. (1995). Bowling alone: America's declining social capital. *Journal of Democracy, 6*(1), 65–78.

Putnam, R. (1996). *The decline of civil society: How come? So what?* Ottawa: John L. Manion Lecture.

Putnam, R. (2000). *Bowling alone: The collapse and revival of American community.* New York: Simon & Schuster.

Quarter, J. (1992). *Canada's social economy: Co-operatives, nonprofits and other community organizations.* Toronto: Lorimer.

Quarter, J., Carmichael, I., Sousa, J., & Elgie, S. (2001). Social investment by union-based pension funds and labour-sponsored investment funds. *Industrial Relation / Relations industrielles, 56*(1), 92–114.

Rifkin, J., & Barber, R. (1980). *The North will rise again: Pensions, politics and power in the 1980s.* Boston: Beacon.

Roberts, B., & Cohen, M. (2002). Enhancing sustainable development by triple value adding to the core business of government. *Economic Development Quarterly, 16*(2), 127–37.

Roe, M. (1991). A political theory of the corporation. *Columbia Law Review, 91*(1), 10–67.

Roman, R., Hayibor, S., & Agle, B.R. (1999). The relationship between social and financial performance. *Business and Society, 38*(1), 109–25.

Sachs, W., Loske, R., & Linz, M. (1998). *Greening the north: A postindustrial blueprint for ecology and equity.* London: Zed Books.

Schumacher, E.F. (1973). *Small is beautiful.* New York: Harper and Row.

Shareholder Association for Research and Education. (2006). *About us.* Retrieved 3 October 2006 from Share website: http://www.share.ca/en/about

Sharpe, W.F. (1963). A simplified model for portfolio analysis. *Management Science, 9*(2), 277–93.

Shiller, R. (2000). *Irrational exuberance.* Princeton: Princeton University Press.

Shiva, V. (1989). *Staying alive: Women, ecology and development.* London: Zed Books.

Shragge, E., & Fontan, J.-M. (Eds.). (2000). *Social economy: International debates and perspectives.* Montreal: Black Rose.

Smith, M.P. (1996). Shareholder activism by institutional investors: Evidence from CalPERS. *Journal of Finance, 51*(1), 227–252.

Social Investment Forum. (2006). *2005 report on socially responsible investing trends in the United States: 10-year review.* Washington: Author.

Social Investment Organization. (2005). *Canadian social investment review 2004: A comprehensive survey of socially responsible investment in Canada.* Retrieved 19 January 2007 from SIO website: http://www.socialinvestment.ca/ SIReview04-original.pdf

Stanford, J. (1999). *Paper boom.* Ottawa: Canadian Centre for Policy Alternatives and James Lorimer.

Statistics Canada. (2003). *Canada's retirement income programs: A statistical overview (1990–2000).* Retrieved 26 February 2007 from Statistics Canada website: http://www.statcan.ca/english/freepub/74-507-XIE/0010074-507-XIE.pdf

Statistics Canada. (2006). *Pension savings of Canadians.* Retrieved 5 October 2006 from Statistics Canada website: http://www40.statcan.ca/101/cst01/labr78 .htm?sdi=assets%20rrsps

Stewart, G.B. (2003). Pension roulette: Have you bet too much on equities? *Harvard Business Review, 81*(6), 104–9.

Stromberg, G. (2005). *Perspectives on governance, risk, management and the pension promise.* Pensions at Work lecture series. Retrieved 26 February 2007 from Pensions at Work website: http://www.pensionsatwork.ca/english/pdfs/ lectures/StrombergLectureNotes.pdf

Sullivan, L. (1999). *The global Sullivan principles of social responsibility.* Retrieved 5 October 2006 from Global Sullivan Principles website: http://global sullivanprinciples.org/principles.htm

Talisman Energy. (2006). *Transparency.* Retrieved 26 September 2006 from Talisman Energy website: http://www.talisman-energy.com/cr_online/2005/ econ-transparency.html

Task Force on the Investment of Public Sector Pension Funds. (1987). *In whose interest?* Toronto: Queen's Printer.

ULLICO. (2005). *Annual report.* Retrieved 1 October 2006 from ULLICO website: http://www.ullico.com/b/PDFs/AnnualReport2005.pdf

Vaillancourt, Y., & Tremblay, L. (2002). *Social economy: Health and welfare in four Canadian provinces.* Halifax: Fernwood.

Waddock, S. (2000). The multiple bottom lines of corporate citizenship: Social investing, reputation, and responsibility audits. *Business and Society Review, 105*(3), 323–45.

Wahal, S. (1996). Pension fund activism and firm performance. *Journal of Financial and Quantitative Analysis, 31*(1), 1–23.

Wahal, S., & McConnell, J. (2000). Do institutional investors exacerbate managerial myopia? *Journal of Corporate Finance, 6*(3), 307–29.

Waring, M. (1996). *Three masquerades: Essays on equality, work and human rights.* Toronto: University of Toronto Press.

Waring, M. (1999). *Counting for nothing: What men value and what women are worth.* Toronto: University of Toronto Press.

Watson, R.D. (1995). The controversy over targeted investing. *Compensation and Benefits Management, 11*(1), 1–9.

Wheeler, D., & Sillanpää, M. (2000). *The stakeholder corporation.* Southport, U.K.: Pitman.

Zadek, S., Pruzan, P., & Evans, R. (Eds.). (1997). *Building corporate accountability.* London: Earthscan.

Zanglein, J. (2001). Overcoming barriers on the ETI highway. In A. Fung, T. Hebb, & J. Rogers (Eds.), *Working capital: The power of labor's pensions* (pp. 181–202). Ithaca: ILR Press/Cornell University Press.

2 Just Having It Is Not Enough: Labour's Voice on Pension Boards

JOHANNA WESTSTAR AND ANIL VERMA

Pension monies are the deferred compensation of employees, and with increased attention to good governance and corporate ethics and responsibility it makes sense to have employee representatives involved in decisions about the investment of those monies. The Certified General Accountants of Canada argue that a pension advisory committee comprising designates of plan members and the employer should be the minimum standard in pension governance (CGA-Canada, 2004). Interest in labour or plan-member representation also stems from other factors. For one, as a result of their size, pension funds can have a powerful impact on financial markets (Deaton, 1989; Drucker, 1976; Fleming, 1990). Pension funds also provide an opportunity for labour movements to push towards alternative investment policies (such as socially responsible and economically targeted investment) and participation in corporate governance (Ambachtsheer, 2005; Clark & Hebb, 2004; Fung, Hebb, & Rogers, 2001; Ghilarducci, 1992; Manley, Hebb, & Jackson, 2005; Salo, 2005). Greater union activism in pension funds may also be a means to union renewal. Wheeler (2004) suggests that increased use of worker capital to influence corporate strategy for more socially responsible outcomes may result in much-needed positive public relations for unions. Such a focus also broadens the labour agenda to larger social and economic arenas, providing unions with increased opportunity for visibility and coalition building. Increased involvement may also be a means to union renewal if union participation in pension-fund governance is demonstrated to lead to better outcomes for workers and for society.

Many trade unions have responded to these opportunities by increasing their involvement in pension-fund governance through the appointment of labour or member representatives to pension trustee boards or committees[1] (Carmichael, 1998; Carmichael & Quarter, 2003; CUPE, 1996, 2005; Fung et al., 2001; Ghilarducci, 1992; Quarter, 1995; Quarter, Carmichael, Sousa, & Elgie, 2001; Wheeler, 2004). In 1998 it was estimated that one third of all pension assets in Canada fell under some form of joint trusteeship (Falconer, 1999) and that 18 of the top 23 unions had won or were in the process of winning some form of joint trusteeship. Similar moves toward employee representation or joint trusteeship are occurring in other industrialized nations as well (for the United Kingdom, see Schuller & Hyman, 1983a, 1983b, 1984; Gribben & Faruk, 2004; Gribben & Olsen, 2002; and for the United States, see Wheeler, 2004).

But what use is a labour seat at the pension board table if the voices of labour trustees are not labour voices or if they are not heard by the others at the table? Numerous unions have won seats on the boards of trustees that govern their pension plans, and many more are attempting to obtain seats or increase their representation. However, many of these opportunities do not result in an effective voice for labour interests, as the result of a host of reasons, some of which have to do with factors external to and beyond the control of the union. But there are other reasons within a union's control, such as lack of training for the role and lack of guidance from the union that also limit the effectiveness of a labour voice in pension governance. Most unions have yet to articulate a comprehensive and proactive policy on their potential role in pension-fund governance. Since their goals in pension governance remain unclear, most unions do not appear to have a formal process to identify and develop their own talent in this area.

In this chapter, we present data from interviews and a unique survey of Canadian labour trustees on both public and private pension funds. Labour representation is modelled by a series of stages, with each stage adding new dimensions, decisions, and challenges for labour trustees, their unions, and the labour movement. We describe the daily experiences of labour trustees at each stage of their role and highlight the fact that, though many eventually become self-proclaimed integrated and participative board members, there is much that unions and the broader labour movement can do at each stage to increase the effectiveness of labour trustees on substantive labour issues. As such, this research has significant implications for union decision-making about resources necessary to develop trustees who will be effective *labour* voices at a table dominated by the bottom line.

Figure 2.1. Model of effective labour representation on pension boards.

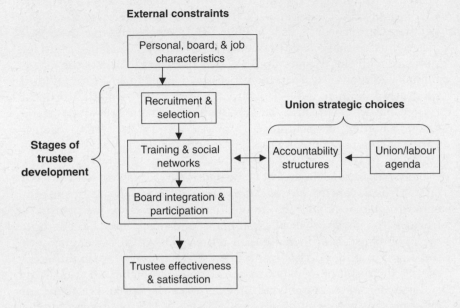

Model of Effective Labour Representation

Figure 2.1 presents our model of the stages of a labour trustee's development (recruitment and selection, training and social networks, and board integration and participation) and the external constraints (personal, board, and job characteristics) and union strategic choices (union agenda and accountability structures) that influence the role and the overall effectiveness of the labour trustee. Many aspects of this model mimic a human resource–management model of job attainment, where candidates are first recruited and selected on the basis of specific job-related criteria. In the second stage, successful candidates begin the job and undergo orientation and training to bring them to an acceptable level of job performance. During this period, the new hires also develop social networks with colleagues, supervisors, and external contacts and are assisted by the social networks they have previously developed. Following these steps, the new hires reach a certain mastery of the characteristics of the job and become integrated and participating members of the organization. Decisions and actions at each stage are influenced by the company's strategic plan and vision, and this link is reinforced by systems of accountability such as performance reviews and regular meetings. The personal characteristics that an individual brings to the job, the nature and description of the job itself, and the characteristics of the workplace also influence each of these stages. The final outcomes are job effectiveness and worker satisfaction.

This model is useful for the study of labour trustees because it highlights and isolates important levels that new trustees must move through to become effective labour voices. To fully infuse a union or labour agenda into the governance and decision making of a pension board requires that labour trustees be supported in each stage of their job. However, each stage adds new dimensions and challenges for labour trustees and their unions. Unions must first decide whether they wish to have a seat at the pension board, and if they do, they must make clear commitments to support their labour trustees, which include internal identification and development of suitable candidates, ongoing training, and the resources and support necessary to bring a clear union/labour agenda to the table. The next sections of this chapter detail the external constraints, methods of trustee development, and union strategy that labour trustees experience.

Methods and Data

For this research, we collected two types of data. First, we conducted semi-structured interviews with six labour trustees on pension funds and one labour representative on a pension-fund advisory committee. Four of these funds were based in Ontario, one in Quebec, and two under the federal jurisdiction. They were predominately public-sector funds. Most interviewees were white males, with one female and one racial minority represented. Tenure as a trustee ranged from several months to 10 years, all interviewees were over the age of 40 and had considerable seniority in their occupations and unions. These interviews provided substantial contextual background and were the framework from which we developed the model above and created a more detailed labour trustee survey (Weststar & Verma, 2006).

The second source of data is from this unique survey of labour representatives in Canada. The survey was administered through mail and on the Internet. As there is no published listing of labour trustees (i.e., total numbers, contact listings, or names of funds that have labour representation), locating the respondents was difficult. To spread awareness of the survey, we used word of mouth throughout the study and distributed flyers at pension conferences. We referenced the Directory of Pension Funds in Canada and searched the Internet for fund websites. Email and/or telephone contact was made with those trustees listed on fund websites. Where contact information was not listed, the fund itself was contacted. Some funds provided contact information, while most said they would pass the survey along to their labour trustees. On one occasion, the pension fund refused to contact their labour trustees on our behalf, and one labour trustee from that fund later indicated that she was not authorized to complete our survey. In many instances, we called union offices to request trustee contact information. On several occasions, the union staff did not know who their pension trustees were or who might know such information.[2] In the end, our efforts produced the names of 231 labour trustees and 117 usable surveys. This is a response rate of 51%; however, some of the 231 were never contacted directly and may not have received any notification of the survey. As well, it is likely that other trustees heard about the survey but did not complete it and so did not make our list. Our directory will be an asset to future research, but it is by no means a complete listing of trustees in Canada. The 117 responses represent 75 unique pension funds and 43 unique unions. Table 2.1 presents descriptive statistics about the funds and the personal characteristics of the labour trustees in our sample.

Survey and Interview Findings

Personal, Board, and Job Characteristics

Though all labour trustees are involved in pension-fund governance, their actual tasks vary widely, depending on the type and size of the plan, the governance structure, and the stakeholders involved. As indicated in Table 2.1, some plans comprise multiple employers and some comprise multiple unions. Some plans are jointly trusteed by the union and employer, while in others the union or the employer/government may be the sole sponsor. Funds also differ in the number of labour representatives on the board (see Figure 2.2). Boards can comprise a combination of employer representatives, government-appointed representatives, active union or non-union plan members (or their representatives), retirees (or their representatives), and/or other external trustees.

Table 2.1. Board and Trustee Characteristics.

	Sample characteristics	
Fund	Public sector	68%
	Average # of board members	10
	Region	
	Ontario	16%
	Quebec	23%
	Atlantic	14%
	Western	30%
	National	17%
	Structure	
	Single union	52%
	Single employer	31%
Trustee	Average age	52 yrs
	Female	24%
	Visible minority	5%
	Francophone	25%
	Education	
	≤ High school	19%
	Apprentice/skills certification	20%
	College/CEGEP	9%
	Undergraduate	21%
	Graduate	15%
	Postgraduate/professional	16%

The length of the term also varies, with survey responses ranging from one to ten years (mean = three years). The number of board meetings per year ranges from one to twelve (mean = five). However, some trustees report that their boards also operate subcommittees on which selected members of the full board sit. The most often reported subcommittee was the investment committee, although other advisory committees were also mentioned. Trustees who are part of these separate committees have additional meetings and preparation. Trustees report spending an average of 5.5 hours at each board meeting, four hours in preparation for each meeting, and 67 hours per year on other fund-related work. Preparation time typically consists of reading through a detailed binder of which one interviewee says, 'It takes a full day just to figure out what you understand and what you don't, let alone learn what you don't' (LTI04).[3] Meetings are generally structured around the

Figure 2.2. Board composition: Proportion of labour trustees.

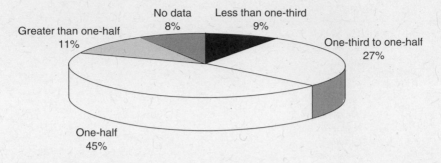

content of the binders, and trustees are often required to vote quickly on decisions that are based on the binder contents and may concern the allocation of millions of dollars (White, Hagglund, Duggan, & Ryan, 2005). Asking a question is allowed, acknowledges one trustee, but it is clear that questioning slows down the proceedings and in some cases causes annoyance (LTI04). When asked specifically about the time commitment, 74% agreed or strongly agreed that it was manageable, 14% were neutral, and 12% felt that it was not manageable. This range of responses could be an artefact of the wide differences in time commitment per board and per trustee.

Compensation schemes also vary by plan, though compensation is typically paid time for work missed due to meetings. Figure 2.3 outlines the common forms of compensation. These categories are not mutually exclusive, with the result that some trustees receive no compensation at all (approximately 25%), others receive paid time or a per diem, and others receive paid time plus a per diem. The key here is that regardless of the type of compensation, compensation is only for attending meetings and does not include preparation time for each meeting or the other trustee-related work that all trustees in the sample report throughout the year. Two trustees noted the inadequacy of time and compensation in the open comments section of the survey: 'I think it is very important that trustees are given time off with pay to travel, and prepare for the meetings. It should not cost an employee anything to sit as a trustee' (LTS129). 'Time needs to be made available for board representatives to participate fully because the time demands are increasing' (LTS138). As evidenced by the comments of a trustee on a university pension board, labour trustees have day jobs and other com-

Figure 2.3. Compensation received for attending board meetings.

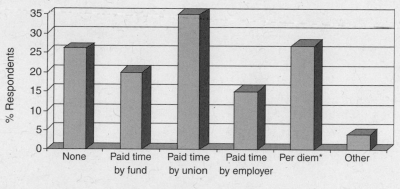

*Per diem also includes honoraria.
Note: Categories are not mutually exclusive.

mitments. Inadequate compensation for lost time and expenses further relegates pension work: 'I don't feel I'm able to do as good a job as I'd like to be doing for my union due to other pressing time commitments and teaching commitments – because of the lack of time to attend and participate fully' (LTS65).

Trustee Development: Recruitment and Selection

Figure 2.4 depicts the variety of means by which union members come to be labour trustees. Appointment mechanisms or appointing bodies are varied, primarily as a result of the different governance models in the Canadian pension-fund landscape (see Appendix 2.A). The categories below represent the prime mechanism or authority behind the appointment; however, some labour trustees are hired by the union from outside the union or are recommended by the union but are officially appointed by the government or the plan itself. A major point on the recruitment of candidates for the trustee position is that only 3% of the survey sample reported that they came forward with an independent application. According to interview reports, where unions play a substantial role in recommending candidates for appointment or where plan participants elect trustees, successful candidates tend to have been more active in the union. Some unions select or recommend union staff

Figure 2.4. Method of obtaining labour trustee position.

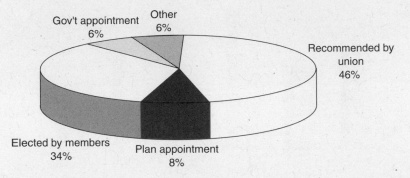

from applicable departments (i.e., pension and benefits departments or bargaining committees) because they are generally more knowledge-able about the issues than rank-and-file members and typically have a stronger and more grounded sense of the union agenda (LTI01). Simi-larly, union activists or elected union officials seem more likely to attain the position (LTI02). Indeed, the main factor linking the interviewees was that they were all labour activists and had held or were holding positions either as elected union officials or as union staff.

These comments are not meant to imply nepotism or to suggest that long-standing union activists are not suited for the job. Indeed, as will be more fully developed later in this chapter, candidates who have stronger ties to the union and a deeper sense of their labour voice may be more ideal candidates. It is important to note that most trustees come to their role with very little background knowledge or ability in pension matters, because they have not been specifically selected (except previous members of pension committees) for that skill set.

With respect to prior exposure to pension matters, 14% of the sur-vey respondents reported no prior exposure, 56% reported exposure through one or two sources, and 30% reported exposure through three or more sources. Figure 2.5 illustrates the main sources of previous pen-sion knowledge or awareness. On first glance it is promising that 86% of labour trustees had some awareness of pension issues before taking on their job at the board. However, half of those had experience from only one or two sources, and the sources reported most frequently were experience with their own pension and general labour education. This information taken together indicates that most trustees had general or policy-level awareness, but not specific preparation for the job of a

Figure 2.5. Proportion of respondents with previous exposure to pension issues.

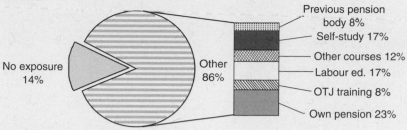

labour trustee. Trustees recognize this deficiency, and it hinders their early performance. Only 29% reported that they were prepared for their role as a labour trustee when they took up the position. Almost half reported that they were not prepared and 27% indicated that they were not sure – this in itself indicates less than complete preparation. One survey respondent noted in the open comments section, 'Regardless of background, very few are well prepared for the educational demands of being a Trustee' (LTS26).

TRUSTEE DEVELOPMENT: TRAINING AND NETWORKS

I think it would be helpful to have more training courses available, perhaps in manageable one-day chunks, and from a labour perspective. I'd also love to have some materials to use to help union members better understand the basics of pension plans. I suspect that even though we talk often, as a union, about bargaining issues and pension benefits the union is fighting for, many people don't really understand the basics of the plan. I've learned a lot on the job because our plan has had some funding issues that have made us deal a great deal with the federal regulator and that has taught us all a great deal about solvency and funding liabilities; we've replaced several fund managers and that has taught us a lot about what to watch for and how to track our investments. But it has all been a bit ad hoc and it would be great to have some resources to help the union trustees, at least, to better communicate the rights and responsibilities of average pension plan beneficiaries to our members. (LTS146)

This statement is an excellent summary of the daily experiences and needs of labour trustees. Information and insight are picked up on the job as the board puts out fires. Trustees do not have the time or the

Table 2.2. Courses Taken by Labour Trustees.

Topic/type		Count	% of total courses taken
Fiduciary responsibility		8	3
Investment & governance		41	14
Issues from labour perspective		18	6
Benefits & administration		7	2
Other	Certified course	90	31
	Basics course	68	23
	Advanced course	6	2
	Conferences	33	11
	Other	20	7
Total		291	100*

*Total does not add up to 100% as a result of rounding.

Table 2.3. Training Needs Reported by Labour Trustees.

Topic	Need more training (%)		
	(Strongly) agree	Neutral	(Strongly) disagree
Fiduciary responsibility	48	35	17
Pension law	80	17	3
Investment & governance	80	17	3
Issues from labour perspective	71	19	10
SRI/ETI	72	20	8
Actuarial valuation	68	21	11
Benefits & administration	64	28	8

resources to develop long-range or proactive material for their constituency or to meet their own learning needs. The labour trustees we interviewed repeatedly iterated that continuous training was necessary to master the pension domain. Tables 2.2 and 2.3 show that survey respondents felt similarly. The 117 trustees surveyed have participated in at least[4] 271 pension-related courses, workshops, or conferences since becoming trustees. The distribution of courses among trustees was fairly even, with 13–17% reporting each of zero, one, two, three, and four courses taken. About 20% of the sample managed to document five or more courses, despite the format of the survey, which was structured for four courses. Certified courses were typically offered by financial institutions and included the Advanced Trustee Management System (ATMS) modules offered by the International Foundation of Employee Benefit Plans (IF); the Canadian Securities Course offered by CSI; Pension Investment Management Services (PIMS) offered by Mercer's and the Schulich School of Business at York University; or the courses offered by Humber College's Centre for Employee Benefits. Courses classified as basic were most often introductory pension courses or pension fundamentals courses offered by unions. Some unions also provided advanced courses. For most trustees, conferences refer to the annual conference of the International Foundation of Employee Benefit Plans.

Despite the number of courses that trustees seem to already be attending, 70% agree that they need more training in at least one of the listed areas. Not surprisingly, trustees who have served on the board for three years or fewer report a higher need for training ($M = 0.78$, $SD = 0.42$) than trustees with more than three years of experience ($M = 0.58$, $SD = 0.50$). This difference was significant, $F(1,116) = 5.32$, $p < .05$); however, in the interview transcripts and survey responses of new and experienced trustees, phrases such as *continuous improvement, continuing education, mastery,* and *repetition is the key* are very common. One 10-year veteran sums it up: 'We require more training. It's a highly technical world' (LTS21).

Of the courses reported by trustees, the pension fund paid for 53%, while the union funded 37% of the courses, the employer paid for 8%, and the remaining 2% of courses were funded by trustees themselves or through other sources. These figures indicate that labour trustee education is not so much a question of access as availability. Most trustees reported that the courses they had taken and conferences they had attended were somewhat to very valuable in assisting them with their role. However, many trustees said that typical courses are not sufficient because they are introductory level, last only a few days, and are most often provided from a financial or business perspective. This means they rarely deviate from, let alone question, the traditional means of pension governance. As well, these courses cater primarily to pension trustees or board members in general and do not address some of the needs specific to labour trustees, such as reconciling their role or introducing alternative perspectives. In addition to these challenges, one survey respondent highlighted the difficulty in finding pension education that is beyond an introductory level, but not steeped in industry jargon:

Pension education is difficult. I have been to more education sessions and conferences that have been unsatisfactory than those that I have enjoyed. Also, the use of technical language that is over the heads of many trustees can be problematic at conferences especially. This is really true with investment issues and valuation terminology and concepts. We have been struggling with our investment manager and actuary to provide information in plain language and have not been successful although they acknowledge the problem. (LTS115)

In the words of another trustee, 'It is imperative union trustees get advanced education from a number of sources to be able to be well trained as a fiduciary. Unions need to invest substantially more resources into the education of reps on pension and benefit issues' (LTS13). Some unions and education providers are heeding this call for ongoing training specific to labour trustees on pension boards and beyond the introductory level (i.e., CUPE, SHARE, CLC, Manitoba Centre for Labour Capital, Pensions at Work, FTQ). The Fédération des travailleurs et travailleuses du Québec (FTQ), one of the central labour bodies for unions in Quebec, is a leader in developing and administering training programs for labour trustees (Hannah, 2003; LTI05). The large majority of the 18 courses 'from a labour perspective' were reported by trustees from Quebec.

Formal courses are an important means by which labour representatives can increase their knowledge, abilities, and self-efficacy, but trustees can also access knowledge and receive support through the development of networks with knowledgeable others. Interviewees reported that they spent little time with other representatives outside of board meetings and that there is a lack of independent sources of advice and support. They reiterate the importance of advisors and friends internal and external to the board, but the bonds of trust are difficult to form. One trustee said, 'You are not ever sure who you can rely on, depend on, who will mentor you – who can you ask without making yourself look bad' (LTI04). In this environment where trustees are continually guarding their perspective and their potential weaknesses, the trust and understanding necessary to build a strong network of support is difficult to establish. Trustees' effort to develop relationships with other board members or pension advisors, staff, and managers is also thwarted by the pervasive sense of not belonging, of being unwanted or unaccepted. Trustees reported experiences of not being introduced the first time they attend meetings, of being asked for their résumés by

Figure 2.6. Trustees' frequency of contact with others (outside of board meetings).

0   20   40   60   80   100

% Respondents

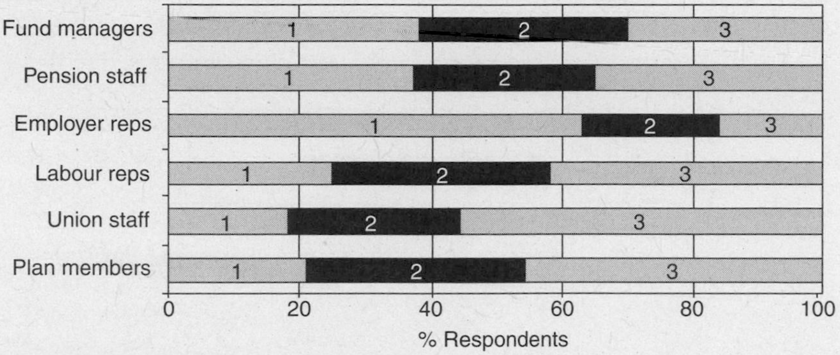

1 = rare or no contact. 2 = some contact. 3 = often or very often contact.

other board members, or feeling largely excluded from board decisions (LTI04; LTI05). As a result, the process of discovering potential allies or independent sources of advice seems slow and full of pitfalls.

To further assess the social networking opportunities available to trustees, survey respondents were asked how often they meet or have contact with pension staff, employer/government representatives, other labour representatives, and union staff outside of board meetings (see Figure 2.6). Among all listed groups, 29% of trustees never meet or rarely meet with anyone outside of board meetings, while 43% sometimes meet with other people or groups, and 27% meet often or very often with other people or groups. Survey respondents were also asked to rate the helpfulness of various people/groups in assisting them with their role as labour trustees and they value the help of pension staff, other labour representatives, and their own union staff the most (Figure 2.7).

These findings for labour representatives and union staff fit the reports from interviewees, as well as the frequency of data in Figure 2.6. However, 20% of labour trustees are rarely or never in contact with other labour trustees. One survey respondent indicated that he 'would like more mentoring and open dialogue among labour reps' and 'found it was hard to get in step with the other labour reps' when he first joined the board (LTS58). The other labour trustees referenced here are from the same union as this respondent. A respondent from Quebec sits on a board with one labour trustee from a different local and several

Figure 2.7. Helpfulness of others in assisting labour trustees with their role.

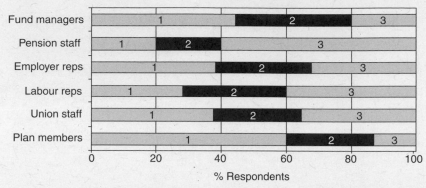

1 = not or minimally helpful. 2 = somewhat helpful. 3 = very to extremely helpful.

labour trustees from different unions. He reported that they are not in touch with each other and do not coordinate their efforts at the board table. It is interesting that labour representatives overwhelmingly rate pension-fund staff as the most helpful, even though they seem to have less contact with this group.

Trustee Development: Integration and Participation

An interviewee told us that the first step that a labour trustee must achieve is the 'technical proficiency of the financial lingo, how the financial industry operates, how pensions operate' (LTI01). This operational knowledge and resulting confidence (gained through training and networking) is necessary to gain acceptance at the board and to be an active and contributing member. All labour trustees that we interviewed had considerable experience on pension boards and with pension issues, and all felt that they were contributing and accepted members on the board. The survey allowed us to delve more deeply into the areas of contribution and acceptance with a broader range of labour trustees.

Respondents were asked to rate their level of contribution to the following pension-fund tasks or decision-making processes: (1) sharing or disseminating information, (2) interpreting the pension rules, (3) analysing investment policy, (4) monitoring fund performance, (5) applying or changing the rules/policies of the pension trust deed, and (6) selecting fund managers. Figure 2.8 displays the data. Overall, labour trustees

Figure 2.8. Level of labour trustee contribution to fund operation.

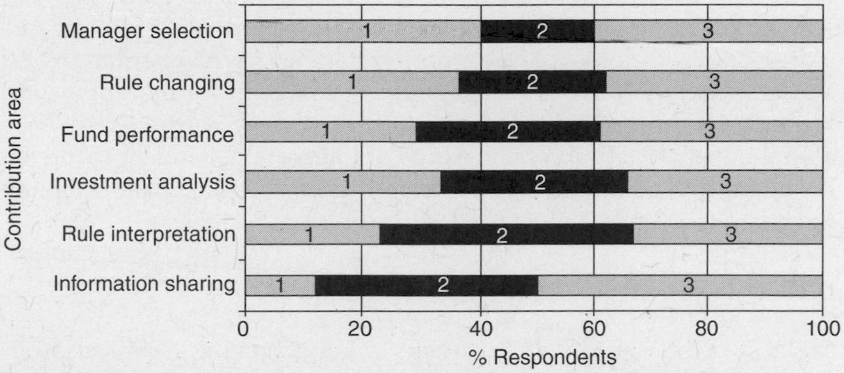

1 = low or no contribution. 2 = medium contribution. 3 = high to very high contribution.

feel that they make the largest contribution to information sharing. In changing the rules or rewriting/creating policies and being engaged in fund-manager selection, there seems to be a polarization among trustees. Some feel that they contribute very highly to these tasks, while a similar number feel that they make very little or no contribution in these areas. Contribution to investment analysis is the most evenly distributed, with just over one third of respondents reporting each of no contribution, medium contribution, and high or very high contribution. Using a composite of each task subgroup, 44% of trustees feel that they make a medium level of contribution to the board, while 31% rate their contribution value as high or very high, and 24% report making low or no contribution to the board. Trustees report that they contribute significantly more when they have had more experience on the board, $F(1,115) = 13.13$, $p < .001$. The mean contribution for trustees who have three or fewer years of experience on a pension board is 1.97 on a 1–5 scale where the mean contribution for trustees with more experience is 2.54.

In addition to the question above, trustees were asked a range of questions about their participation on the board and their level of integration on the board. Composite measures of these items are high; the mean of participation is 3.95 and the mean of integration is 3.81, both on a scale from low = 1 to high = 5. Table 2.4 presents a more detailed breakdown of the questions and shows that trustees generally feel that they are active and integrated board members. It should be noted that this scale may be influenced by social desirability such that respondents over-report their levels of participation and acceptance. Trustees who report being integrated are also likely to report being more participatory and contributory, have stronger networks with board members and pension staff outside of meetings, and have fewer training needs. The same is true for people who report being more participatory. They also are likely to report more feelings of integration, a longer tenure on the board, and more prior experience with pension issues before joining the board (see Table 2.5 for correlations of these variables).

Union Strategic Choices: Union/Labour Agenda and Accountability

The last section began with a quote about achieving technical proficiency. This trustee goes on to say that the next step is to develop critical thinking and alternative viewpoints on socially responsible investing (SRI), economically targeted investing (ETI), and strategic proxy voting of pension-fund shares. In his opinion, 'an educated trustee is not necessarily a critical trustee' (LTI01). As shown in Table 2.4, 85% of the survey respondents feel free to contribute ideas or thoughts from a labour perspective. However, an interview with an experienced trustee indicated that it might not always be so easy to maintain or bring forth these alternative viewpoints: '[Fiduciary responsibility] says you will act in the best interests of the pension plan and in saying that a lot of trustees will then lose their role as a union representative' (LTI03). This trustee goes on to describe the difficulty faced when introducing a labour perspective within the 'old boys club' of the board: 'Because there is this collegial atmosphere, there tends to be less challenging, and when you interject with a union perspective into that sort of milieu, if you seem too overt they can always fall back on the notion that you are not following your fiduciary responsibility' (LTI03).

However, the opposition toward alternative investment agendas is not completely one-sided. One survey respondent says that there is 'much opposition from all fronts, both from union and management,' and 'more proactive education and advocacy is required on economically targeted investments and ethical investments' (LTS32). Labour trustees who wish to bring progressive agendas to the table face the rhetoric of fiduciary duty and the traditional mindset of the management trustees and financial advisors, and they do so without purposeful support or clear messages from their unions. Thirty-five per cent of the survey respondents said that the guidelines they receive from their

Table 2.4. Trustees' Self-Perception of Participation and Integration.

Items	Participation (%)		Integration (%)	
	Agree	Disagree	Agree	Disagree
I often feel excluded from in-depth policy discussions.	13	74		
I often don't participate fully at meetings because I may not understand what is being discussed.	13	77		
I had an aptitude for pension issues prior to taking on this role.	56	21		
I feel free to contribute ideas or thoughts from a labour perspective.	86	3		
I avoid asking questions because this may reveal a lack of understanding.	5	87		
I now feel prepared to fulfil my role as a labour representative.	73	11		
I feel comfortable with other members of the pension body on which I serve.			80	7
I have adequate contact and information sharing with people inside and outside of the board.			65	15
My perspective is frequently not supported by non-labour representatives.			23	51
The meetings do not invite participation from all members.			11	82
Most substantive decisions are made within the meetings.			80	10
I feel free to ask for additional or clarifying information at meetings.			98	–
I feel accepted and integrated as a member.			87	4
There are not enough meetings.			30	40
I do not get enough information from the pension staff.			10	72
The meetings seem to rubber-stamp decisions that are made elsewhere.			15	70

Note. Numbers will not add up to 100, as the 'neutral' option was not included in this table.

Table 2.5. Correlates between Trustees' Self-Perceived
Integration and Participation.

	Integration	Participation
Integration	1.00	
Participation	0.47***	1.00
Prior exposure	0.05	0.19**
Meeting frequency	0.26***	0.30***
Months on board	0.18*	0.30***
Percentage union	0.09	0.02
Contribution to fund	0.41***	0.40***
Training needed	−0.33***	−0.39***

Significant at the .05 level; * at the .01 level.

Figure 2.9. Degree of trustees' accountability to their union.

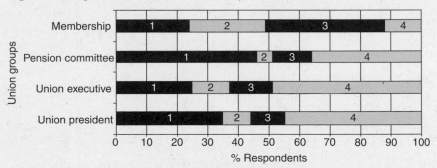

1 = never. 2 = annually. 3 = bi-annually. 3 = quarterly.

union about how to fulfil their role on the pension fund are either poor
or minimal, while 10% of the trustees do not receive guidelines at all. A
further 25% said that the guidelines were adequate and only 29% said
they were good or excellent.

On the reporting structures between the trustee and the union, 15%
of trustees surveyed do not report in any way to the union (or the membership) about their pension trustee position. Figure 2.9 shows the frequency with which trustees report to groups within the union.

Discussion: Labour's Options in Pension Board Governance

This study brings into focus a host of issues on labour's participation in

Figure 2.10. Charting labour's options in pension-plan governance.

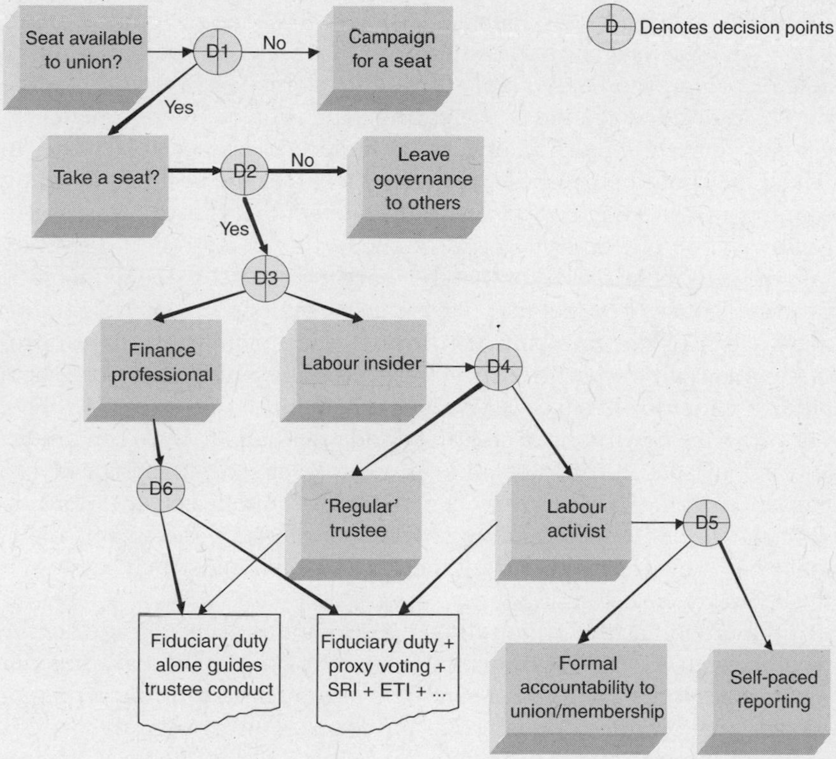

pension-fund governance. We started out wanting to examine factors such as selection and training of labour trustees. This line of investigation led us to basic questions about labour's role in pension-fund governance. Does labour want to participate in such matters? If yes, how is a union to go about it? Once labour representatives become trustees, what issues and methods will they pursue to maximize union interest? To put these issues in perspective, Figure 2.10 maps the decision points that unions need to address in considering their policy and strategy for pension-fund governance.

In the course of our research, we found that many unions do not have a seat on their pension boards, particularly in private-sector plans, and within that sector, in smaller plans. Thus, the first decision (D1) facing any union is whether a seat is available to the union on the pension board. If yes, the union can go to the next decision (D2): whether it wants to take the seat. If a seat is not available and if the union places a priority on getting a seat, then a decision can be made to campaign for a seat with the relevant authorities. In some cases where a seat is available or could become available through a campaign, a union like the CAW has decided against participating in pension-fund governance. In general, private-sector unions have hundreds of pension plans in which they could participate, but many feel that the cost of providing training and ongoing support to that number of labour trustees is prohibitive. The CAW takes the hard-line view that unions should not buy into the neo-liberal ideology that the market is central to the democratic process. Rather, they feel that private-sector unions should bargain for increased pensions and benefits through traditional arm's-length processes and fight the battle of social responsibility and workers' rights in other, broader forums (see CAW, 2006; Hannah, 2003; Standford, 1999). The opposite view is one of creativity and pragmatism, in which unions and labour should resort to all avenues to enact social change and to harness working capital. As well, in most cases public-sector unions do not have the luxury of bargaining over pension issues and so, outside of lobbying, they must be a part of the decision-making structure (i.e., on the board) to ensure change.

If the union has the option to take a seat and it decides to do so, the next decision (D3) is whether a finance professional or a labour insider would be selected to take the seat. The arguments for hiring a finance professional are that one is hiring an expert. However, many unions choose to appoint one of their own. Embedded within the decision process at this point is the challenge to ensure that labour trustees hit the ground running and don't use up the majority of their term just acquiring enough knowledge and confidence to stay afloat. The average term of a labour trustee is three years (though many are renewable) and the board meets at most 12 times a year. Given that labour trustees have daily jobs and responsibilities that compete for their time and resources, this is not an adequate learning time.

Traditionally, unions have favoured a method of selection in which their trustee for the pension board is nominated by the leadership. This process of identifying suitable candidates for pension board trusteeship is inherently political and is well integrated with the methods by which unions select people for other positions. The chosen individuals have the support of the union executive. They may have led in other duties. They may owe allegiance to certain union leaders and thus be appointed to the job. Our survey suggests that many individuals selected in this fashion have gone on to very successful careers (or stints) as effective labour trustees. In contrast to the 'nomination' approach, we followed the professional human resource management (HRM) model in designing our survey questions. As outlined earlier in our model in Figure 2.1, in the professional HRM approach, a job description is developed, then posted to attract a pool of qualified candidates. The 'best' candidate is then selected using tests and interviews. This candidate undergoes appropriate training to acquire skills necessary to be effective in the job. Our survey shows that the professional HRM approach is rare in labour circles. Given that unions are political organizations and that their nomination method produces reasonably good trustees, we find it unwarranted to recommend that the nomination process be replaced by a professional HRM procedure. However, our evidence suggests that there is room to integrate the best features of both approaches to improve upon current practice.

In a more integrated approach, unions can retain the basic steps of the nomination approach but add a few more steps suggested by the HRM method. For example, the union can make it known that it would be looking for people from time to time with certain skills to sit as a pension trustee. Courses on aspects of pension governance can be offered to those who express an interest. The advantage would be a bigger talent pool at the time of selecting a labour trustee. Developing a job description and skill requirements for the job would be also a step in this direction. Even though political considerations will continue to be important, adding these steps would give union leaders a better pool of candidates from which to choose. Likely it will also improve labour's clout on pension boards.

If the union chooses to recruit and select a union staffer or rank-and-file member, then the next decision (D4) is whether the union wants this person to become indoctrinated in a traditional pension role that emphasizes a narrow interpretation of the fiduciary role. In that case, the guidance given to this person by the union is to be a 'regular' trustee like all the others on the pension board. The alternative is to emphasize the *labour* part of a labour trustee and to support a more activist role. Both options require investment in training on pension fundamentals and the development of a mentor or support network among labour trustees. The latter option would require additional training in how to argue for alternative investment strategies and would benefit from a broader support network of other labour trustees, union members, and pension activists. Labour activist trustees also need a mandate from the union and ongoing consultation with the union executive to play the role effectively. Moving beyond the traditional perspective of the fiduciary role, activist labour trustees could broaden their scope to engage in proxy voting on issues of labour interest and develop investment policies that include socially responsible or economically targeted criteria. Such policies could take labour relations, employment standards, and environmental practices into consideration, place screens on enterprises that seek to privatize public services, and focus on investments that benefit communities through encouraged development of local business or promotion of affordable housing (Hannah, 2003; Manley et al., 2005; Thomson & Wheeler, 2004). The investment of pension funds could also be used strategically either against recalcitrant employers or toward employers with labour-friendly policies and behaviours. An example on the positive side is Concert Properties in British Columbia, a real-estate company that is owned by union and management pension plans (Concert Properties, 2006).[5]

This leads us to the next decision (D5), which is on the form of accountability to the union. It can be formal and structured or it can be informal. As outlined above, some trustees made regular reports to the executive and to the membership, while others had limited contact and received little or no guidance from the union. They reported largely at their own initiative, on issues they thought were of interest to their constituents, and sporadically rather than periodically. If a finance professional is hired to represent labour interests, the union will also have to decide (D6) if it wants the professional to engage primarily in their fiduciary role or whether it wants the representative to press for labour-leaning issues such as proxy voting, SRI, and ETI.

In conclusion, it is important to recognize that each of these decision points (and more broadly each stage of our model) has significant implications for the selection, training, role purpose, and ultimate effectiveness of labour trustees. On the basis of our research we recommend that unions develop policies for labour representation on pension boards and that these policies harmonize across the labour movement. Unions then need to commit to these policies and cultivate functional experts who will follow them through. This involves implementing more formal recruitment and selection (perhaps coupled with preparatory training programmes, mentoring, or other succession planning techniques) to ensure that trustees are as equipped as they can be for the role. It includes developing and accessing labour-centric training on pension issues beyond fundamental pensions training, so that labour trustees will have the arguments they need to push for responsible investment. It also necessitates that unions work at various levels to create social networks for knowledge sharing and support. These networks could be peer-based and include trustees within and across unions and within and across particular plans. Mentor networks could also be developed and include past trustees, union staff, pension activists, academics, and progressive members of the financial community who can provide independent advice. Such networks could operate regionally, nationally, and internationally and provide a wealth of information for labour trustees as well as a forum to debate and develop labour's policy and strategy for pension governance.

Some of these recommendations and decisions have consequences for a union's own governance (i.e., recruitment and selection, accountability structures, union-specific agendas on alternative investment), while others concern the labour movement at large (training, development of labour trustee networks, broader agendas for alternative investment, and the role labour should play in pension governance). Unions will find that unless these decisions are tackled proactively and strategically, achieving effective labour representation on pension boards will be a frustrating experience.

Appendix 2.A

Administrative Structures of Canadian Pension Plans

	Representative composition	Labour representative selection	Example
1	Sole union trusteeship plan administered by a financial institution	Elected by plan participants	Marine and Shipbuilders' Pension Plan; Carpentry Workers' Pension Plan of BC
2	Co-sponsored by union and government, joint trusteeship, rotating chair	Elected or selected by union/plan members	OPSEU Pension Trust
3	Equal representation, rotating chair	Elected or selected by union/plan members	HOOPP; CAAT

Appendix 2.A   (*Concluded*)

	Representative composition	Labour representative selection	Example
4	Equal representation, rotating chair	Union recommends representatives to government	Alberta Public Service Pension Plan
5	Equal representation for union and employer sponsors, independent chair	Sponsoring union selects its own representatives	Ontario Teachers' Plan under sponsorship of the Ontario Teachers' Federation
6	Equal representation, employer chair	Union recommends representatives to employer	Canadian Broadcasting Corporation
7	Legislated representation for union and employer not necessarily equal	Elected or selected by union/plan members	Pension Plans in Quebec
8	Advisory committee with equal representation, government/ employer sole trustee	Elected or selected by union/plan members	BC Municipal; BC Public Service; Canadian Pacific Rail
9	Advisory committee with equal representation, government sole trustee	Union recommends representatives to government	Nova Scotia Public Service
10	No joint trusteeship but equal representation, multi-union representation	Employee representatives appointed by government (often on recommendations by union)	Ontario Municipal Employees' Retirement System (OMERS); Local Authorities (AB)
11	Little or no union representation, unions aspire to more equal role		Ontario Hydro; Ontario Pension Board
12	No union representation		General Motors; Bell Communications Enterprises

Adapted from Carmichael, 1998, with additions from CUPE, 1996; Greenan, 2003; Ontario Teachers', 2004; OPSEU, 2004; LTI05; LTI07.

Appendix 2.B

Profile of Trustees Quoted in Chapter.

ID	Data source	Gender	Visible minority	Age bracket (years)	Board tenure (years)	Fund sector
LTI01	Interview	M	No	35–9	5.0	Public
LTI02	Interview	M	No	55–9	2.0	Public
LTI03	Interview	M	Yes	45–9	7.5	Public
LTI04	Interview	F	No	55–9	0.5	Public
LTI05	Interview	M	No	55–9	10.0	Private
LTS13	Survey	M	No	50–4	15.0	Public
LTS21	Survey	M	No	55–9	3.5	Public
LTS26	Survey	M	No	45–9	7.0	Private
LTS32	Survey	M	No	45–9	2.5	Public
LTS58	Survey	M	No	55–9	0.8	Public
LTS65	Survey	F	No	45–9	3.0	Public
LTS115	Survey	F	No	55–9	6.5	Public
LTS129	Survey	M	No	35–9	0.5	Public
LTS138	Survey	M	No	40–4	7.5	Public
LTS146	Survey	F	No	40–4	2.0	Private

Notes

1 Union representatives are also called member representatives, labour trustees, union trustees, and plan participant representatives, and they sit on pension boards, committees, and advisory committees. For brevity, we will use labour trustees and pension boards to denote all of these possibilities, unless otherwise stated.

2 When distributing the surveys in Quebec we were very appreciative of assistance from Denise Gagnon and Michel Lizee of the Fédération des travailleurs et travailleuses du Québec (FTQ).

3 See Appendix 2.B for a profile of all trustees quoted or referenced in this chapter. LTI = interview. LTS = survey.

4 There was sufficient space in the survey for respondents to provide detail about only four courses.

5 A longer discussion of socially responsible investing (SRI) and economically targeted investing (ETI) is beyond the scope of this chapter but can be found elsewhere in this book as well as in Ambachtsheer (2005); Clark and Hebb (2004); Fung et al. (2001); Ghilarducci (1992); Manley et al. (2005); Salo (2005).

References

Ambachtsheer, J. (2005). Socially responsible investing. *Benefits and Compensation International, 35*(1), 1–17.

Carmichael, I. (1998). *A survey of union pension trustees.* Toronto: Canadian Labor Market and Productivity Centre and Ontario Public Service Employees Union.

Carmichael, I., & Quarter, J. (Eds.). (2003). *Money on the line: Workers' capital in Canada.* Toronto: Canadian Centre for Policy Alternatives.

CAW. (2006). *CAW pension campaign.* Retrieved 1 June 2006 from Canadian Auto Workers Union website: http://www.caw.ca/campaigns&issues/ongoingcampaigns/pensions/index.asp

CGA-Canada. (2004). *Addressing the pensions dilemma in Canada.* Retrieved May 2005 from http://www.cga-online.org/servlet/portal/serve/Library/Advocacy+and+Research/CGA-Canada+Key+Areas+of+Interest/Pensions/ca_rep_pensions.pdf

Clark, G.L., & Hebb, T. (2004). Pension fund corporate engagement: The fifth stage of capitalism. *Relations Industrielles / Industrial relations, 59*(1), 142–71.

Concert Properties. (2006). *Concert Properties Limited.* Retrieved 1 June 2006 from Concert Properties website: www.concertproperties.com

CUPE. (1996). *Pension plan governance: A review of several models.* Retrieved 25 June 2005 from CUPE website: http://www.cupe.ca/pensions/pensiongovernance

CUPE. (2005). *Why we need joint trusteeship of our pension plans.* Retrieved 23 January 2006 from CUPE website: http://www.cupe.ca/pensions/Why_We_Need_Joint_Tr

Deaton, R.L. (1989). *The political economy of pensions: Power, politics and social change in Canada, Britain and the United States.* Vancouver: University of British Columbia Press.

Drucker, P. (1976). *The unseen revolution: How pension fund socialism came to America.* New York: Harper and Row.

Falconer, K. (1999). *Prudence, patience and jobs: Pension investment in a changing Canadian economy.* Ottawa: Canadian Labor Market and Productivity Centre.

Fleming, J. (1990). No more Mr. nice guys. *Report on Business Magazine, 7,* 13–16.

Fung, A., Hebb, T., & Rogers, J. (Eds.). (2001). *Working capital: The power of labor's pensions.* Ithaca: Cornell University Press.

Ghilarducci, T. (1992). *Labor's capital: The economics and politics of private pensions.* Boston: MIT Press.

Gribben, C., & Faruk, A. (2004). *Will UK pension funds become more responsible? A survey of trustees.* London: Just Pensions and UK Social Investment Forum.

Gribben, C., & Olsen, L. (2002). *Will UK pension funds become more responsible? A survey of member nominated trustees.* London: Just Pensions and UK Social Investment Forum.

Hannah, J.-A. (2003, 28 October). *Remarks to the IQPC Canada Conference: Pension Investment & Governance.* Paper presented at the IQPC Canada Conference, Toronto, Ontario.

Manley, K., Hebb, T., & Jackson, T. (2005, 3–5 June). *Pension fund investment in underserved capital markets: Implications for Canadian policy makers.* Paper presented at the Canadian Industrial Relations Association Annual Meeting, London, Ontario.

Quarter, J. (1995). *Crossing the line: Unionized employee ownership and investment funds.* Toronto: Lorimer.

Quarter, J., Carmichael, I., Sousa, J., & Elgie, S. (2001). Social investment by union-based pension funds and labour-sponsored investment funds in Canada. *Relations industrielles / Industrial Relations, 56*(1), 92–115.

Salo, J. (2005). *Shareholder activism, social and environmental standards: An analysis of recent trends from annual general meetings 2001–2004.* Paper presented at the 2nd Annual Pensions at Work Conference, Toronto, Ontario.

Schuller, T., & Hyman, J. (1983a). Information, participation and pensions: Strategy- and employee-related issues. *Personnel Review, 12*(3), 26–30.

Schuller, T., & Hyman, J. (1983b). Pensions: The voluntary growth of participation. *Industrial Relations Journal, 14*(1), 70–9.

Schuller, T., & Hyman, J. (1984). Forms of ownership and control: Decision-making within a financial institution. *Sociology, 18*(1), 51–70.

Standford, J. (1999). *Why real prosperity requires a new approach to Canada's economy.* Toronto: Lorimer and Canadian Centre for Policy Alternatives.

Thomson, J., & Wheeler, D. (2004). *Human capital based investment criteria for total shareholder returns: A Canadian and international perspective.* Retrieved October 2005 from Pensions at Work website: www.pensionsatwork.ca/english/pdfs/thomson_wheeler_human.pdf

Weststar, J., & Verma, A. (2006). *Effective labor representation on pension bodies.* Retrieved March 2006 from www.pensionsatwork.ca/english/pdfs/weststar_effective.pdf

Wheeler, H. (2004). Producers of the world unite! A return of reformist unionism? *Labor Studies Journal, 29*(3), 81–100.

White, P., Hagglund, L., Duggan, L., & Ryan, S. (2005, 14–15 October). Panel discussion: *Access to trustee education in Canada: Issues and problems.* 2nd Annual Pensions at Work Conference. Retrieved 23 November 2006 from Pensions at Work website: http://www.pensionsatwork.ca/english/conference_05.php

3 Fiduciary Duties, Investment Screening, and Economically Targeted Investing: A Flexible Approach for Changing Times

GIL YARON

> The investor, though a trustee of funds for others, is entitled to consider the welfare of the community, and refrain from allowing the use of the funds in a manner detrimental to society. (Scott & Fratcher, 1987, p. 500)

The legal boundaries of pension-plan investment practice continue to be the subject of much debate in Canada. This is particularly so in the context of applying non-financial criteria to investment decision-making where the absence of legislative or judicial guidance continues to leave uncertainties for pension trustees.

This chapter introduces the reader to the fiduciary duties of prudence and loyalty through a comparative legal analysis. It examines legal barriers to two socially responsible investment practices – investment screening and economically targeted investing (ETI) – and concludes that, subject to the terms of the trust, screening and ETI are legally permissible investment practices. The chapter argues that the traditional interpretation of the law has been unnecessarily rigid and narrow, especially in light of rapid changes in investment practice. These changes have been influenced by the establishment of modern portfolio theory as the framework for institutional portfolio management, the introduction of a plethora of new investment products and services, the growing awareness of the interrelationship of so-called externalities and market performance, and the rise of institutional investors as major players in capital markets.

Investment screening typically takes three forms – positive screens, negative screens, and the 'best-of-sector' approach (a technique to create screens) – and is defined in the introduction to this book. There are two primary motivations for the application of non-financial screens. First, an investor may be concerned that a non-financial factor, such as climate change, may adversely affect investment returns, as well as the health of capital markets and the economy as a whole, with direct ramifications for the individual pension plan. An Investor Summit on Climate Risk at the United Nations in November 2003 led to a commitment by eight large institutional investors to develop action plans to address risk associated with global warming (CaLPERS, 2004). Internationally, 143 institutional investors participating in the Carbon Disclosure Project have called on FT500 companies to disclose information on greenhouse gas emissions to assist investors in better assessing associated risk (Carbon Disclosure Project, 2006).

Second, plan beneficiaries may be concerned that investments are consistent with their values, the interests of their communities, the rights of workers, and the environment. Since the campaign against apartheid in the 1980s, pension funds and other institutional investors have employed negative screens to exclude investments that do not comply with a particular value set. More recently in Canada, there have been renewed calls for the Ontario Teachers' Pension Plan to divest itself of all holdings in tobacco (Vasil, 2004) and for the Canada Pension Plan to divest itself of both tobacco and military investments (Picard & Chase, 2004). The 'values' based approach to investment screening has been the focus of legal debate on investment screening and is accordingly the focus of this chapter.

In addition to investment screening, Canadian pension plans are exploring opportunities to target some of the $836.8 billion in trusteed retirement assets (as of the first quarter of 2006) towards projects that provide market returns while also addressing some of the pressing economic and social concerns facing communities (Statistics Canada, 2006). Economically targeted investments (ETIs) are investments 'designed to produce a competitive rate of return commensurate with risk as well as create collateral economic benefits for a targeted geographic area, group of people, or sector of the economy' (Carmichael, 2005, p. 67). Confusion often arises because of the overlap between ETI and alternative investments. While both include investments in non-traditional sectors of the economy, the primary difference is that ETIs seek to attain collateral benefits in addition to market-grade rates of return through investments in such ventures as mortgage trusts, affordable housing, commercial building, regional development, small business, emerging technology sectors, real estate, and local community investment (Calabrese, 2001; Carmichael, 2005; Falconer, 1999). Examples include invest-ments in real estate in Old Winnipeg by the $750-million Workers Compensation Board Investment Fund and the $2.1-billion Teachers' Retirement Allowances Fund as part of their private equity portfolio (Cash, 2004); the commitment of $300 million by the Ontario Municipal Employees Retirement System (OMERS) towards building 2,300 to 2,500 rental apartment units in the Toronto area (Maloney, 2002); and other significant private equity and venture capital commitments by pension funds across the country (Falconer, 2000).

Much of the pension industry continues to instruct plan administra-tors that the application of non-financial criteria to the selection of investments is illegal. A brief survey of pension lawyers in Canada reveals differences of opinion (Yaron, personal communication, June–August 2004). Comments made by Claude Lamoureux, president of the Ontario Teachers' Pension Plan, to the 2000 annual general meeting of plan members are typical:

> Our investment decisions are based on the law. Pension plans do not have the legal authority to restrict investments based on social, political or eth-ical criteria. This is the law ... if all the teachers of Ontario want us to fol-low a social investment policy and are willing to take the risk of lower returns, then first agree on what is acceptable and what is not acceptable as an investment ... Then convince the Ontario government – who is the other partner in the plan – to change the law. (Lamoureux, 2000, p. 12)

This common response raises two separate issues: first, in the use of non-financial criteria, whether the application of non-financial criteria by way of investment screens and economically targeted investing is compatible with the fiduciary obligations of pension trustees, and sec-ond, whether integrating non-financial criteria through a values-based approach is permissible.

There has been virtually no guidance from regulators or courts in Canada to clarify these issues. A 1993 survey on ETIs conducted by the Institute for Fiduciary Education (IFE) found that 37% of 119 public pen-sion funds in the United States identified conflicts with fiduciary duties as the principal barrier to economically targeted investing (Zanglein, 2001). Changes to policy in other countries have left Canada's regula-tory framework increasingly out of step with international norms, and left its pension trustees with inadequate guidance in an increasingly complex and ever-changing investment environment.

The Fiduciary Obligations of Pension Trustees

The duties of pension trustees may be documented in the trust agreement, pension statutes, regulations, and common law. Where the trust agreement sets out legal duties, these supersede legislation and common law. Subject to the terms of the trust, most jurisdictions provide some statutory provision covering one or more aspects of the fiduciary obligations of pension trustees. For pension plans, where legislation is silent, the common law of trusts applies, and this has been affirmed by Canadian courts (*Bathgate v. National Hockey League Pension Society*, 1994).

Virtually all consideration of these duties in the context of investment screening by foreign judiciary and international legal scholars occurred in relation to the South African anti-apartheid divestment campaigns; some were opposed to screens (Langbein & Posner, 1976, 1980), and some in favour (Dobris, 1986; Ravikoff & Curzan, 1980; Scott & Fratcher, 1987; Troyer, Boisture, & Slocombe, 1985). Judicial consideration of fiduciary duties and ETI has been limited to American courts prior to 1990. Unfortunately, neither issue has received direct consideration by Canadian courts (Longstreth, 1986).

The Duty of Prudence

The duty of prudence is generally understood to require pension trustees to exercise the care, skill, and diligence of a prudent person in dealing with the property of another. The standard of care was originally articulated in *Whiteley v. Learoyd* (1887). While a generally consistent statutory framework exists among Canadian jurisdictions, there is no consensus on the exact definition. Three jurisdictions (federal, BC, and Alberta) provide specific provisions articulating the duty in the management of pension investments. The remaining provinces (except for PEI, which has yet to bring into force its pension legislation) provide a generic standard of care in the administration of the pension plan. In the context of social investment, American legal commentators have given a flexible interpretation to the duty of prudence under the *Employee Retirement Income Security Act* (Hutchinson & Cole, 1980). In Canada, the Manitoba Law Reform Commission (MLRC), charged with reviewing the subject of ethical investing by trustees in 1993, has interpreted the application of the standard in similar terms.

The evolving nature of the duty is reflected in its history (Goodman, Kron, & Little, 2003; Manitoba Law Reform Commission, 1993). At common law, a trustee's obligation was originally to act as an ordinary prudent person would in conducting his or her own affairs (*Speight v. Gaunt*, 1882). This was later modified in *Whiteley v. Learoyd* (1887) to require the trustee to act as a prudent individual would in managing the assets of another. Until 1961, the common law duty of prudence for trustees was qualified by the 'legal list' of permissible investments. Trustees were prohibited from investing in commercial stock on the basis of the regulators' view 'that commercial and industrial stocks were essentially speculative in nature and therefore unsuitable as trustee investments' (Manitoba Law Reform Commission, 1993, 8n29). Subsequently, the legal list was gradually relaxed, in large part because pension funds sought more control over a growing array of investment options. New investment strategies such as indexation became more acceptable to institutional investors (Koppes & Reilly, 1995). In 2002, BC became the last jurisdiction in Canada to replace the legal list with a general duty of prudence; however, some jurisdictions continue to impose mandatory or voluntary criteria for assessing the prudence of any particular investment decision (Yaron, 2001). Most provinces continue to also place limits on investments by pension plans. Nine jurisdictions in Canada have adopted the federal regulations governing permissible investments, which set numerous parameters on the investments of registered pension plans, including limits on investments in individual companies.

The Duty of Loyalty

The duty of loyalty requires that pension trustees act honestly, in good faith, and in the best interests of beneficiaries, treating all beneficiaries with an even hand (*Balls v. Strutt*, 1841; *Bathgate v. National Hockey League Pension Society*, 1994; *Boe v. Alexander*, 1987; *Cowan v. Scargill*, 1984; *Gisborne v. Gisborne*, 1877). Only Saskatchewan and BC have codified the duty, and BC requires that plan investments and other financial decisions be made in the best financial interests of plan members, former members, and other plan beneficiaries. The obligation also contains a number of corollary duties (discussed below), including the obligation to make decisions based on the interests of plan members and beneficiaries and not based on personal or other conflicting interests. American courts have ruled that the *Employee Retirement Income Security Act* permits trustees to maintain dual loyalties to both plan members and beneficiaries; however, the priorities and interests of plan members must come first (*Herdrich v. Pegram*, 1998).

Compatibility of Screening and ETI with the Fiduciary Duties of Pension Trustees

This section addresses whether the legal duties of pension trustees permit them to consider investment screening and ETI as part of a pension plan's investment policy and strategy in the light of non-financial criteria (1) as part of a plan's financial risk analysis, or (2) based on general moral or ethical principles. First, the law does not prohibit pension trustees from considering non-financial criteria, which include not only social, environmental, and ethical factors, but also corporate governance practices, as possible risk factors in setting investment policy and evaluating investments. There is no legal basis for arguing against the application of non-financial criteria to risk analysis, aside from remote arguments that associated analytical costs outweigh risk-reduction benefits to the plan. Nevertheless, opposition remains. As one commentator (Carmichael, 2005) has observed,

> The prudent man ideology still retains its power with many trustees. Social or political investment strategies remain cast as moral views, or views lacking in an objectivity, that would otherwise be obtained through a purely financial strategy or process. (p. 36)

This is due in large part to the failure of current accounting practice to capture and quantify social and environmental costs. These costs are externalized, that is ultimately borne by the public, and not viewed as material in assessing the financial performance of investee companies. The problem is compounded when considering the long-term implications of such factors on the economy, which should be the focus of pension funds as long-term investors, but are often considered too remote in evaluating the financial benefit to the individual pension plan (Hawley & Williams, 2000). Some studies demonstrate the costs associated with certain harmful social and environmental practices (Cowe, 2004; CSR Europe & Deloitte and Eurotext, 2003; CSR Europe and Eurotext, 2002; Haurant, 2004; UNEP Finance Initiative, 2004). However, others are not so clear (Entine, 2003). Nevertheless, the possibility of such a relationship argues that non-financial criteria should at least inform the investment analysis employed by pension plans. Some non-financial criteria – corporate governance indicators – are widely used as part of prudent risk-based financial analysis by investors of all stripes, despite the equally inconclusive evidence linking such practices to corporate financial performance. On this basis, prudence requires that pension trustees consider non-financial indicia as part of portfolio risk analysis. Failure to consider non-financial indicators, such as climate change or corporate operations in zones of conflict, could constitute a breach of fiduciary duty where it is determined that trustees ought to have had a reasonable expectation that such factors could materially influence the long-term performance of plan investments (UNEP Finance Initiative, 2005).

The more contentious debate is whether the consideration of non-financial criteria, as part of a values-based approach to investment decision-making, is consistent with the duties of prudence and loyalty. Both statutes and case law will be considered.

Statutory Authorities

There is little legal interpretation of the prudence rule with respect to the application of non-financial criteria. Rather, the determination of which investment practices are considered prudent has been left almost entirely to the courts. However, in 1988, Ontario provided an example of permissive law. Repealed in 1997, the *South African Trust Investments Act* was enacted by a Liberal government, with the support of all political parties, to address the legal barrier to investment resulting from the fiduciary obligations imposed by trust law. The legislation allowed fiduciaries of trusts, charities, and pension funds, subject to approval by a majority of beneficiaries, the discretion to divest themselves of such investments, even where such action could impair investment performance.

Furthermore, in 1992, the Financial Services Commission of Ontario issued a bulletin affirming the legality of ethical investments (Financial Services Commission of Ontario, 1992). The question asked, 'Is it imprudent for a pension fund to take the position that it will make only ethical investments?' The brief response stated that ethical investing is permitted, but the statement of investment policy must state this position and set out the criteria, and members of the plan should be notified. The bulletin does not define *ethical investing*; however, the term is commonly understood to be synonymous with socially responsible investing. With Ontario's adoption of the federal investment guidelines in 2000, the position detailed in the bulletin was declared 'inactive.' Although inactive, the policy remains posted on the Financial Services Commission of

Ontario website, and its substance was recently affirmed by a representative of that body who stated that subject to the requirement that
investment returns not be impaired, and if plan members want it, plan
administrators would need to change investment policies and procedures (Vasil 2004). Another senior pension lawyer is also of the opinion
that 'the statement is a strong indication that the Commission does not
view ethical investing as imprudent in and of itself' (Gold, 2003). These
statements would seem to qualify views such as those articulated by the
Ontario Teachers' Pension Fund. While it is important to note that policy statements are not law, courts are inclined to find them highly persuasive in the absence of legislative or judicial authority.

On 19 April 2005, Manitoba became the first Canadian jurisdiction to
adopt legislation clarifying the duty of pension trustees on the use of
non-financial investment criteria. Section 28.1(2.2) of Bill 10 (*The Pension Benefits Amendment Act*) states,

> Unless a pension plan otherwise provides, an administrator who uses a
> non-financial criterion to formulate an investment policy or to make an
> investment decision does not thereby commit a breach of trust or contra-
> vene this Act if, in formulating the policy or making the decision, he or she
> has complied with subsections (2) and (2.1).

Subsection 28.1(2) articulates the general applicable standard of care,
and subsection 28.1(2.1) articulates the duty of prudence specifically
with respect to investments.

The United States and a number of other OECD countries have also
recognized the consideration of non-financial criteria by pension trustees. Numerous OECD countries, led by Britain in 2000, adopted regulations that require pension funds to disclose the extent to which social,
environmental, or ethical considerations are taken into account in
investment decision-making. This disclosure obligation is important
for several reasons. First, it implies that these governments view the
application of non-financial screens to the investment process to be
prima facie acceptable. If governments expect pension funds to make
disclosures about such practice, it is presumed that the practice itself is
considered legal by the respective government.

Second, and more important, Britain's adoption of the requirement
creates a tension with the ruling in *Cowan v. Scargill* (1984, 1985a,
1985b). That case stands for the proposition that the interests of plan
members are generally their financial interests and that the application

of non-financial criteria adversely affects investment returns. Application of non-financial criteria on moral grounds will be acceptable only in rare circumstances where all plan members share a common view. In contrast, Britain's adoption of the disclosure requirement suggests that the government recognizes the need for greater accountability of pension funds to the interests of their beneficiaries and that these interests may extend beyond the financial.

With specific reference to ETI, the US Department of Labor, which administers the *Employee Retirement Income Security Act*, issued a 1994 interpretative bulletin on the fiduciary standards of prudence and loyalty under the *Employee Retirement Income Security Act* permitting investment in ETI. While the interpretative bulletin makes specific reference to ETI, it also clearly states that the principles and standards outlined are intended to apply to all investment practices, including investment screening (Department of Labor, 2002). As with the Financial Services Commission of Ontario policy, the US Department of Labor's interpretative bulletin is merely persuasive and not binding on courts.

The *New Zealand Superannuation Act*, a national pension fund for all New Zealanders created pursuant *New Zealand Superannuation Act*, 2001, provides unique limits on acceptable pension investments. Section 58 of the act provides that the fund must be managed and administered to '[avoid] prejudice to New Zealand's reputation as a responsible member of the world community.' The fund's investment policy expands on what constitutes investment activity prejudicial to the country's reputation:

> It shall be a breach of the policy ... if a sovereign or corporate issuer of securities is widely regarded internationally as having participated in gross abuses of fundamental human rights; or serious infringements of labour and employment standards; or serious infringements of environmental standards; or promoting transnational organized crime or terrorism; or other conduct which is so reprehensible that it may prejudice New Zealand's reputation as a responsible member of the world community or its reputation as a responsible global investor in sovereign or corporate securities. (Guardians of New Zealand Superannuation, 2006, p. 25)

It may be argued that these statutory examples illustrate that the application of non-financial criteria to investment decision-making is prohibited where legislation does not authorize such activity. On the contrary, it seems that these legislative and policy provisions seek merely to provide clarification to the confused and conflicting state of common law.

Common Law

This section examines a series of cases as an indication of whether the consideration of non-financial criteria, as part of a values-based approach to investment decision-making, is consistent with the duties of prudence and loyalty.

Cowan v. Scargill (1984, 1985a, 1985b). For Canadian pension fiduciaries, *Cowan v. Scargill* (1984, 1985a, 1985b) remains the most often-cited decision on this point. In it, the employer trustees of the jointly trusteed Mineworkers' Pension Scheme brought an action against the scheme's union trustees. The employer trustees alleged that the defendant union trustees had breached their fiduciary duty by refusing to approve the scheme's investment policy unless it was amended to prohibit an increase in the percentage of current overseas investment, to require withdrawal from existing overseas investments at the most opportune time, and to prohibit investment in energies in direct competition with coal. Chief Justice Megarry held that the union trustees had breached their duty of loyalty by placing the interests of the union in promoting the British coal industry and its workers ahead of the interests of plan members and beneficiaries.

The decision made several points that are central to the discussion at hand:

- When the purpose of the trust is to provide financial benefits for the beneficiaries, as is usually the case, the best interests of the beneficiaries are normally their best financial interests (*Cowan v. Scargill*, 1985a, p. 287).
- Under a trust for the provision of financial benefits, the paramount duty of the trustees is to provide the greatest financial benefits for the present and future beneficiaries (*Cowan v. Scargill*, 1985a, p. 289).
- Investments made for social or political reasons that are equally beneficial to plan beneficiaries from a financial perspective are acceptable (*Cowan v. Scargill*, 1985a, p. 287).
- The word *benefit* is to be interpreted broadly. Where beneficiaries share strong views on particular issues, trustees, in rare circumstances, may make decisions for the benefit of beneficiaries other than their financial benefit (*Cowan v. Scargill*, 1985b, p. 288).

These statements by Megarry continue to be cited as authority for the view that the application of non-financial criteria by pension trustees in the investment process constitutes a breach of their fiduciary duties of prudence and loyalty. However, American and British courts have rendered other decisions, which challenge these findings. The decision itself must also be considered in light of a number of substantive and procedural weaknesses that undermine its authority (Farrar & Maxton, 1986; Pearce & Samuels, 1985).

First, it is a well-established principle in trust law that trustees must act within the purpose and terms authorized by the trust (*Balls v. Strutt*, 1841). In its findings, the court failed to acknowledge that the pension scheme in question was an extraordinary trust set up under a scheme for nationalization, the object of which was to develop the industry in the national interest and safeguard the welfare of employees (Farrar & Maxton, 1986). This purpose would appear to be consistent with the types of investment screens introduced by the union trustees.

Second, the court provided no authority in support of its position that trust law applies to pension schemes. Courts have subsequently affirmed views expressed by Megarry on applying trust principles to pension plans (*Bathgate v. National Hockey League Pension Society*, 1994; *Boe v. Alexander*, 1987), but Megarry did not consider some of the unique aspects of pension schemes in drawing his conclusion. Pensions are a form of deferred remuneration with employee contributions in many instances, whereas trusts are established by way of a gift. Furthermore, as one commentator notes, the application of law to private trusts can be prejudicial to plan members in that 'the strict operation of private trust principles can limit [employee] rights of participation and control' where employees make mandatory or voluntary contributions to the plan (Farrar & Maxton, 1986, pp. 33–4). These distinctions are important when considering the role that plan members and beneficiaries have in directing the investment policy of a plan.

Third, this case was argued by the defendant who, in addition to lacking the skills of a professional litigator, had his credibility called into question because of untrue statements he made about the content of a legal memorandum. Commentators have also said that the 'lack of balanced legal argument undermines the authority of the decision and has led Sir Robert Megarry V.C. to formulate principles which are unduly narrow and arguably incomplete' (Farrar & Maxton, 1986, p. 34).

Fourth, this judgement was based on a poor set of facts and ignored the highly charged political context at the time between the Thatcher government and the miners' union. The requirement by union trustees for an absolute prohibition on the named investments presented a significant barrier to the court. Megarry, both in his decision and subsequent commentary (Megarry, 1989), emphasized that the proposed amendments calling for exclusions of entire sectors of the economy provided no discretion to the trustees to amend the policy if it proved disadvantageous to plan members. This view contrasts sharply with the situation in *Board of Trustees v. City of Baltimore* (1989), where the municipal ordinances calling for divestment by the City's pension plans allowed the trustees to deviate from the requirements under certain circumstances.

Fifth, the Megarry decision is nearly 20 years old and was decided prior to the conflicting judgment in *Board of Trustees v. City of Baltimore* (1989). According to one commentator, Megarry's treatment of the three authorities referenced in his decision and discussed later in this paper was 'somewhat cavalier' (Nobles, 1984, p. 169). In his judgement, he distinguishes *Evans v. London Co-operative Society Ltd* (1976) on the grounds that it focused on the interpretation of a specific provision of a plan's investment policy while ignoring the decision's more general statements about the common law. The court also took a very narrow interpretation of *Blankenship v. Boyle* (1971), whereas critics argue a proper reading of the facts demonstrates 'that due consideration of the beneficiaries' interests cannot exclude the industry's ability to fund pensions' (Nobles, 1984, p. 170). Similarly, Megarry approved narrowly on its facts the actions of the trustees in *Withers v. Teachers' Retirement System of the City of New York* (1978/1979), which recognized the need to deviate from standards of prudence in certain instances.

Sixth, the changes to investment policy and practice over the past two decades, including the wide acceptance of portfolio theory (Markowitz, 1952), challenge many of assumptions underlying the court's reasoning. The removal of the legal list of permissible pension investments means that trustees now have much more latitude in the nature of investments they may consider. Pension funds are now invested in a variety of higher risk vehicles, including real estate and hedge funds, as part of a balanced risk portfolio, which would previously have been considered imprudent. The introduction of these classes of investments means that pension funds have the opportunity to achieve even greater diversification, thereby reducing the potential implications of either screening out part of the investment universe or investing a portion of the plan's portfolio in any one particular type of investment.

Therefore, *Cowan v. Scargill* (1984, 1985a, 1985b) should be limited to the facts in that case. Furthermore, any principles emanating from the decision should be considered and interpreted in light of the current understanding about investment screening and ETI.

Harries and Others v. Church Commissioners for England and Other (1993). This case involved the investment policy of a charitable trust. Yet its findings may be extended to the pension fund context to some degree. In this 1993 decision, representatives of the church, including a commissioner, sought a declaration requiring the Church Commissioners of England, a large charitable trust, to exercise its office to prevent the investing of assets in a manner incompatible with the object of promoting the Christian faith through the established Church of England. In denying the declaration, the court upheld the position in *Cowan v. Scargill* (1984, 1984a, 1984b) on the duties of trustees to maximize returns on investment. Aside from articulating this standard and its associated problems (see discussion below), the court identified four instances where trustees should consider non-financial criteria:

1. Where the trust deed requires consideration of non-financial criteria.
2. The rare circumstance where the practices of a company in which the trust invested might conflict with the objects of the charity. In such instances, trustees should not invest, even if it resulted in significant financial detriment to the charity, although the court notes that this outcome would be unlikely, given the range of available alternative investments. Examples cited include investment of cancer research charities in tobacco companies, temperance charities in brewery and distillery shares, and the Society of Friends in companies involved with production of armaments.
3. Where those who support or benefit from the charitable trust feel that a particular investment would conflict with the objects of the charity, so long as the trustees are satisfied that course would not involve a risk of significant financial detriment.
4. Where investments by a charity deter donations to the charity or make potential recipients of aid unwilling to be helped because of the source of the funds, trustees have the responsibility to balance the potential financial losses against the risk of financial detriment resulting from excluding the investments.

The court reviewed the commissioners' existing investment policy, with exclusions from investment in companies whose main business is armaments, gambling, alcohol, tobacco, newspapers, or companies that have more than a small amount of business in South Africa, and found, not surprisingly, that an ethical investment policy already existed. The policy also stipulated that commissioners ensure that environmental factors are properly taken into account when considering development opportunities. It is not clear whether the application of these non-financial criteria fall under the second or third instance described by Donald Nicholls in his decision. Most significantly, he stated he could see nothing in the church's ethical policy that was inconsistent with general fiduciary principles.

   Board of Trustees v. City of Baltimore (1989). The 1989 decision of the Maryland Court of Appeal in *Board of Trustees v. City of Baltimore* stands in sharp contrast to the findings in *Cowan v. Scargill* (1984, 1985a, 1985b). In this case, the trustees of three municipal pension funds sought a declaration declaring invalid a number of city ordinances that mandated the funds to divest their holdings in financial institutions that make loans to South Africa or Namibia or companies doing business in those countries. The ordinances permitted trustees to suspend divestiture for up to 90 days if the rate of return on the funds was substantially lower than the average of the annual earnings on the funds over the past five years, inconsistent with generally accepted investment standards for conservators of pension funds, or would otherwise cause financial losses to the funds. The main argument of the trustees was that the ordinances violated the contractual rights of plan beneficiaries by altering the common law duties of prudence and loyalty and were therefore unconstitutional. The Court of Appeal, upholding the trial court's decision, drew several conclusions in dismissing the claim.

   First, the court found that consideration of non-financial criteria in making investment decisions does not per se violate a trustee's duty of prudence and loyalty. Investment screens may be applied to a pension plan's portfolio, subject to the availability of alternative investments with comparable risk and returns. The court cited Austin Wakeman Scott, an American authority on trusts, whose view was based on an analogy to corporate directors making charitable contributions. Trustees, he said, may consider such matters as pollution, race discrimination, fair employment, and consumer responsibility (*Board of Trustees v. City of Baltimore*, 1989, p. 736).

   As a corollary, the court ruled that collateral benefits might be taken into consideration when making investment decisions, provided they do not compromise the interests of plan members and beneficiaries.

Citing Scott, the court found that pension trustees, as with corporate directors, are entitled to consider the welfare of the community, and refrain from allowing the use of funds in a manner detrimental to society (*Board of Trustees v. City of Baltimore*, 1989, p. 736).

Second, the court articulated a different standard of prudence from the British decisions in *Cowan v. Scargill* (1984, 1985a, 1985b) and *Harries and Others v. Church Commissioners for England and Other* (1993). According to the court, a trustee's duty is not necessarily to maximize the return on investments but rather to secure a just or reasonable return without undue risk (Dobris, 1986; Ravikoff & Curzan, 1980; Troyer et al., 1985). The court found that, notwithstanding the effect of the ordinances on the plan's portfolio, barring investment in 120 of the S&P500 companies representing approximately 40% of the index's market capitalization and resulting in a portfolio of relatively smaller companies with more share price volatility, they did not imprudently increase risk or decrease income. The court found that alternative investments were available and a shift to passive management could duplicate the performance of the benchmark index. Concerns about the impact of screening the funds' active managers were dismissed where the court found that no contractual right existed to a particular management style.

Third, the trustees argued that the ordinances would compromise the plan's portfolio by requiring investment managers to reject their first choice of investments. In response, the court found that it did not follow that the second choice was necessarily inferior to the first. The court noted that managers ordinarily invest in a limited universe of companies, and the restrictions would require the managers only to do additional research, which had the added possibility of benefiting the plan.

Fourth, the Court of Appeal held that minimal costs to the plan's total assets accrued in applying social considerations does not violate a trustee's duty of prudence. In that instance, the trial court determined the initial and ongoing costs of divestiture to be one sixteenth and one tenth of 1% respectively of the funds' total value.

Fifth, and an important difference from the facts in *Cowan v. Scargill* (1984, 1985a, 1985b), the court looked favourably upon the inclusion of the escape provision in the ordinance permitting the trustees to suspend divestiture. The judgement acknowledged the presence of numerous safeguards in the ordinances, including the suspension provision, which guaranteed that divestiture could not occur unless consistent with the trustees' duty of prudence. This suggests that such a provision is an indication of a prudent investment strategy.

Withers v. Teachers' Retirement System (1978). In an earlier 1978 American decision, the Teachers Retirement System (TRS) of the City of New York agreed to purchase City bonds for $860 million as a part of a financial plan to stave off the City's bankruptcy. According to the court, the trustees' primary concern was to prevent the depletion of the City's funding to the pension fund, which was its principal source of contributions. Evidence indicated that the plan had a funding deficit and that existing assets would be exhausted in meeting the benefits owed to retired beneficiaries to the exclusion of active members if the City went bankrupt. The court noted that in making the decision to purchase the City bonds, the trustees went to great lengths to satisfy themselves that the City could not obtain financing from other sources, and sought the fullest possible protection for their beneficiaries with respect to the investment. Since the survival of the fund as an entity was dependent on the solvency of the City, the court held that the trustees had not breached their duty by authorizing the investment. The court declared that there was no evidence of union involvement in the decision taken by the TRS, unlike *Blankenship v. Boyle* (1971), where union trustees held pension assets in a union-owned bank in liquid form for the benefit of the bank.

Critics have distinguished this case on the basis of its unique facts (Hutchinson & Cole, 1980; Langbein & Posner, 1976). They argue that the situation where the plan's survival was dependent on the solvency of the municipality was an extreme situation that cannot be compared with other contexts in which non-financial criteria are normally considered. However, the recent rash of corporate insolvencies in Canada and the decisions that pension plans have had to take in order to resuscitate their corporate plan sponsors suggests that the *Withers v. Teachers' Retirement System* (1978) scenario is not one of a kind. At a minimum, the case supports the proposition in *Board of Trustees v. City of Baltimore* (1989) that pension trustees may consider collateral issues when determining the long-term best interests of plan beneficiaries. This does not mean that pension trustees may make investments with unacceptable levels of risk in order to address collateral concerns, but rather that the American courts take a broad view of what constitutes prudence and the best interests of plan members when it comes to investing pension assets.

Martin v. City of Edinburgh District Council (1988). Resolutions adopted by members of the Labour Party of Edinburgh City Council authorized the withdrawal from 58 trusts of investments in companies operating in South Africa valued at more than £2.25 million. At issue was whether the council had given proper consideration to what was in the best interests of the beneficiaries and whether it had sought or obtained proper professional advice in considering the best interests of the beneficiaries.

First, the court held that council had breached its duty by failing to obtain any professional advice prior to authorizing the resolution to divest and for neglecting to put their minds to whether the divestments were in the best interests of plan members. Second, the court upheld the fiduciary principles in *Cowan v. Scargill* (1984, 1985a, 1985b) requiring that trustees not allow extraneous factors to fetter their investment decisions or permit complete delegation of authority for making investment decisions.

However, the court disagreed with Megarry on two grounds. First, the court rejected the requirement that trustees must invest in the most profitable investment, on the grounds that it effectively substituted the discretion of money managers for the discretion of trustees. Second, Murray took a practical approach in interpreting the conflict of interest standard for pension trustees in recognizing the reality that all pension trustees, whether employer or employee representatives, come to the table with personal values and interests that reflect the entity they represent. These perspectives should be recognized, not artificially ignored, in the process of determining what is in the best interests of plan participants.

Donovan v. Walton (1985). This case considered the duties of prudence and loyalty in the context of an ETI investment. The US Department of Labor alleged that the trustees of the Operating Engineers Local 675 Pension Trust Fund had breached their fiduciary duties by constructing and financing an administration building on property owned by the fund and leasing space to the union. Trustees representing labour and management jointly administered the fund. The trustees had decided to purchase land and construct an administration building 'based on deliberative research and analysis by both the trustees and independent consultants' (*Martin v. City of Edinburgh District Council*, 1988, p. 609). A committee was established by the trustees to review real property investments and identified a property, which would satisfy the need for portfolio diversification, prudent returns, and employment opportunities for members of the fund. The fund decided to self-finance the project because high interest rates at the time were unprecedented. The building's design and construction were open to competitive bidding and the project was continually assessed, with the successful contractor using union labour at an increased cost. One of the member unions, the International Union of Operating Engineers Local 675, was identified as the principal tenant. That union's business manager and CEO was also a trustee of the fund and chair of the committee advising on this real estate project.

The court found that the decision to purchase the real estate was not a breach of the trustees' fiduciary duties. Despite cost overruns, the court affirmed that the trustees' decision should be judged on the process followed in evaluating the investment, not the investment's actual performance. In this case, the trustees had retained numerous expert advisors, conducted thorough, ongoing research, and made necessary modifications based on new information and financial considerations as the project proceeded. All evidence suggested that the investment appeared to be prudent at the time of consideration by the trustees. The fund's decision to use its own assets to finance the project was under the circumstances also deemed prudent.

In related proceedings based on the same facts (*Brock v. Walton*, 1986), the US Department of Labor alleged that the fund's trustees had breached their fiduciary duties by offering mortgages below market rates of interest to plan members through a mortgage loan program. At issue was whether the requirement that trustees charge a reasonable rate of interest on loans meant that they must charge prevailing market rates. The Court of Appeal affirmed the district court's decision that a reasonable rate of interest may be below the prevailing market rate. This decision is important in the context of understanding the fiduciary obligation of pension trustees to obtain a reasonable rate of return for the pension plan. The court noted that rates could be so far below market rates to not be justified; however, such was not the case in this instance. Furthermore, this was not a case involving self-dealing or preferential loans.

Evans v. London Cooperative Society (1976). This 1976 decision involved a pension scheme established for the benefit of the defendant society's employees. The society was the plan sponsor and trustee, with the administration of the plan vested in a pension committee chaired by the president of the society. At issue was a rule (presumably part of the plan's trust agreement) that gave the trustees discretion to loan excess plan assets to the society at any rate above a prescribed minimum. On the advice of the plan's consultant and chair, the trustees had interpreted the rule to be mandatory and continued to make loans to the society on that basis at below market rates. While the court recognized that the plan had the discretion to establish a rule that allowed for loans at below market value, the court found the pension committee had breached its duty by failing to exercise its discretion when loaning assets to the society. The society was also found to have breached its fiduciary duty. The case is significant because it recognizes that trustees have the discretion to accept rates of return below market value, provided the trustees make the decision prudently.

Clearly, these cases conflict and are difficult to reconcile. While the courts maintain an objective tone in their reasons, many of the cases were set in highly charged social and political contexts. Despite the challenges for those seeking to rationalize the findings, some general observations can be made.

A review of both statutory and common law indicates that the law does not prohibit the use of investment screening and ETI as part of a pension plan's investment policy. Pension trustees may incorporate investment screening and ETI into a fund's investment strategy if it is articulated in the fund's investment policy, communicated to plan members, and does not impair the risk and return profile of the fund's portfolio. Furthermore, a close reading of cases in the United States and the United Kingdom indicates that, in principle, pension trustees may consider non-financial criteria for non-financial reasons when making investment decisions pursuant to the same conditions. However, uncertainty persists regarding the appropriate standards of prudence and loyalty and their corollary duties that pension trustees must consider when setting investment policy in these areas. This remains the primary barrier for pension trustees.

Legal Barriers to Investment Screening and ETI

While the law does not prohibit investment screening and ETI by pension plans, the issue is the appropriate circumstances under which pension trustees may elect to employ these practices. The following section considers three issues regarding the fiduciary duties of pension trustees in relation to screening and ETI: the maximum rate of return, the duty to achieve portfolio diversification, and the relationships among the best interests of plan members and beneficiaries, even-handed treatment, and non-financial interests.

The Maximum Rate of Return

The duty of loyalty requires that pension trustees act in the best interests of plan members and beneficiaries. British decisions, including

Cowan v. Scargill (1984, 1985a, 1985b) and *Harries and Others v. Church Commissioners for England and Other* (1993), have held the best interests of plan members and beneficiaries to be their financial interests – a position that has since been codified in British Columbia. The British courts noted above, along with some commentators, have read best financial interests to mean that pension trustees must obtain the maximum possible return on investments within accepted levels of risk (Edur, 1999; Langbein & Posner, 1980).

The alternative view holds that pension trustees must set policy to achieve a reasonable rate of return across the portfolio, consistent with a plan's funding requirements and risk tolerance. This alternative standard is affirmed by other Canadian jurisdictions, legal scholars (Fung, Hebb, & Rogers, 2001; Ravikoff & Curzan, 1980; Willis, 1992), the Restatement (Third) of Trusts (American Law Institute, 1992), several law reform commissions reviewing the standard in the context of trust legislation (Alberta Law Reform Institute, 2000; Manitoba Law Reform Commission, 1993), and American common law (*Foltz v. U.S. News & World Report Inc.*, 1989; *Withers v. Teachers' Retirement System*, 1978).

The conflicts between law and practice may be due to an imperfect understanding of investment practices, and blind restatements of the law that do not fully appreciate the manner in which pension investments are managed. In any event, the maximization doctrine cannot be said to be the accepted standard at common law. The standard may exist as a remnant of a period when the prudential value of investments was determined on an individual basis. In that context, the notion of maximizing returns makes sense. However, that approach to pension investment has been abandoned in both law and practice in favour of a portfolio-based approach. The more likely origin of the maximization standard is the British courts' adoption of the mathematical language of modern portfolio theory. First introduced by Harry Markowitz in his seminal 1952 paper 'Portfolio Selection,' modern portfolio theory looks at investment performance in a mathematical context based on averages and probabilities to generate the maximum return possible within that risk parameter. This does not mean that it will generate the maximum possible return from actual available investments. A portfolio's performance depends on myriad factors, including the specific investments selected and how those assets are allocated. Consequently, each portfolio will perform differently.

As an average of individual investment returns, the portfolio approach cannot maximize returns. It can merely optimize them. For pension plans that follow a portfolio-based approach, it is recognized that not all investments will perform to maximize returns at the same time. Each will respond differently over time. Therefore, a pension plan will seek to include investments with varying expected rates of return and risk as part of its diversification strategy, thereby achieving an optimal average rate of return over a prescribed period.

This interpretation of portfolio theory undermines the pronouncements made in *Cowan v. Scargill* (1984, 1985a, 1985b) and other British decisions applying the maximization doctrine. In *Cowan v. Scargill*, Megarry asserts that where alternative investments are made that are equally financially beneficial to beneficiaries, trustees will not be criticized. Conversely, investments that are less financially beneficial may leave trustees open to criticism. This perspective is problematic in the context of portfolio theory because a portfolio-based approach is based on the assumption that not all investments will perform well all the time and that a portfolio must include a diversity of investments with different risk-and-return characteristics in order to achieve the target rate of return in the plan's investment policy.

In this context, screened investments and ETI are not only acceptable but may make sense as a means of achieving optimal diversification within a balanced portfolio. For example, the General Board of Pension and Health Benefits of the United Methodist Church (US$10 billion) in the United States found that investments in affordable housing helped offset the poor performance of equities. Similarly, the California Public Employees' Retirement System reports that its highest returns came from its mission-related Single Family Housing Program – with more than 20% annually, and social returns, leading to the building of 32,000 homes in 200 California communities (Thomsen & Wheat, 2003). Such investments may also perform poorly. It is therefore the role of the pension trustee to monitor such investments to ensure that their inclusion benefits the pension plan over the long term.

The practice of maximizing returns may also be at odds with the long-term investment orientation of pension plans. Pension plans are by definition long-term investors concerned with ensuring that contributions and investment returns are sufficient to meet the pension promise by matching assets and liabilities, not with beating the market. The preoccupation of money managers on short-term performance should not divert the trustee's focus on meeting the long-term funding requirements for the pension plan. The facts in several cases demonstrate that a long-term orientation to plan investment is not always necessarily consistent with maximizing returns in the short-term. In *Blankenship v. Boyle* (1971), the court stated,

> While the beneficiaries have suffered as a result of the Fund's loss of investment income, they have benefited to some extent from the Union's activities over the past twenty years. In the longer view of matters, the Union's strength protects the interests of the beneficiaries, past and prospective. (p. 112)

In *Withers v. Teachers' Retirement System* (1978), where funds were invested in city bonds, it was held that

> their obligation, plainly, was to manage the fund so as to enable it to meet its obligations not only to current retirees, but also to those scheduled to retire in the future, whose pension and annuity rights would have been similarly earned over their years of active service and to whom the fund therefore had a legal responsibility. (p. 1257)

Finally, there is a fundamental problem with applying a standard that considers outcomes when the common law clearly articulates that pension trustees are to be evaluated on the basis of process, not performance (Manitoba Law Reform Commission, 1993). At most, it can be argued that trustees have a duty to make investment choices that they believe will result in maximum overall returns across the entire portfolio given the possible available investments, the plan's risk tolerance, and any other relevant considerations.

To summarize, Canadian pension trustees do not have a fiduciary obligation to maximize returns in the short term, but rather to set investment policy with a reasonable expectation that the portfolio will achieve a reasonable rate of return over the long term that satisfies the individual pension plan's funding requirements while minimizing risk through a portfolio-based investment approach.

Replacing the maximization doctrine with a reasonable return standard has significant implications for pension plans that seek to incorporate investment screening and ETI into their investment policies. In that context, screened investments and ETI – which by definition are intended to provide a market-grade return – may form part of a balanced portfolio. This is consistent with the US Department of Labor's bulletin on ETI, which authorizes such investments, provided that they aim to provide 'a risk-adjusted, market-grade return that is equal or superior to a comparable investment of comparable risk and otherwise supports a plan's fiduciary imperatives' (Department of Labor, 2002, 29CFR 2509.94.1).

The Duty to Achieve Portfolio Diversification

In the context of portfolio theory, pension trustees have a fiduciary duty to ensure that the plan's investment portfolio is diversified as a recognized means of mitigating market risk. Through a strategy of diversification, pension plans seek to minimize market risk by holding a range of asset classes and investments within each class that have differing risk/return characteristics. Canadian law imposes no standard for diversification, although federal investment regulations implicitly recognize the importance of portfolio diversification by imposing limits on specific classes and types of investments. In the United States, s. 1104 (a) (1) (C) of the *Employee Retirement Income Security Act* requires the fiduciary to 'diversify the investments of the plan so as to minimize the risk of large losses, unless under the circumstances it was clearly prudent not to do so.' Specific percentages are not specified.

Critics of socially responsible investment argue that applying non-financial screens violates the duty to diversify the plan's portfolio because it reduces the universe of possible investments and increases the risk to the plan's portfolio (Langbein & Posner, 1976). With respect to ETI, the argument is that allocating assets to such investments means fewer assets are available to be invested in other asset classes with lower risk profiles.

At issue is what level of diversification is required by pension plans, and what impact screening and ETI have on portfolio diversification. Again, judicial statements emanating from the *Cowan v. Scargill* (1984, 1985a, 1985b) decision imply a maximization standard. Megarry stated, 'It is the duty of trustees ... to take advantage of the full range of investments authorized by the terms of the trust, instead of resolving to narrow that range' (1984, p. 289). He later observed that he found it 'impossible to see how it will assist trustees to do the best they can for their beneficiaries by prohibiting a wide range of investments that are authorized by the terms of the trust' (1985b, p. 766). However, a reading of the entire body of jurisprudence on point provides a more nuanced understanding of the issue.

It is well established that the level of diversification required is plan specific and fact dependent. Furthermore, portfolio diversification is determined and influenced by myriad factors, some or all of which have the potential to affect the level of diversity. First, investment styles are highly selective; for example, an active manager selects a subset of equities based on the manager's particular investment philosophy. Some pension plans have also adopted 'immunization strategies,' which invest all plan assets in bonds on the basis that long-term bonds most closely match the liabilities of a pension plan. Despite the pronouncements by some courts, the law recognizes that an investment strategy involves the selection of certain investments to the exclusion of others. According to the Restatement of Trusts (American Law Institute, 1992),

> Liberated portfolio concepts also allow for the introduction of active management strategies. These efforts may involve searching for advantageous segments of a market, or for individual bargains within the highly efficient markets as well as the less efficient ones. (p. 227)

The court in *Board of Trustees v. City of Baltimore* (1989) observed correctly that investment managers normally carry a small range of investments in their portfolios based on various criteria used as a means of differentiating themselves from the rest of the market and beating the standard benchmark for their asset class. The range of investments within a pension plan's portfolio will therefore vary, depending on the mix of managers selected. The application of investment screens may also have the benefit of identifying additional investment opportunities that were previously not in the universe of a plan's portfolio. As the Manitoba Law Reform Commission (1993) observed in its consideration of ethical investment by trustees, 'A policy of diversification might just as easily encourage investment of a percentage of assets in socially or ethically desirable investments whose characteristics differ from the other securities in a portfolio' (p. 35).

Furthermore, most small- and medium-size pension plans limit diversification by not investing in non-traditional asset classes, such as hedge funds. Trustees have an obligation to understand the nature of investments in the plan's portfolio as well as associated risks, and to monitor such investments. Often trustees in smaller plans do not have the requisite skill and expertise to fulfil this responsibility. Consequently, the majority of pension funds continue to limit diversification by investing solely in traditional asset classes (i.e., stocks, bonds), despite the availability of a wide range of alternative investment vehicles (Statistics Canada, 2002; Watson Wyatt, 2004). Similar arguments extend to the consideration of foreign investments by pension plans, especially in light of the federal government's anticipated removal of the cap.

On the basis of the above considerations and without legislative or judicial guidance in Canada, most leading pension lawyers consider that pension trustees have a fiduciary obligation to maintain adequate or optimal diversification. That is, they must ensure that the portfolio is sufficiently diversified to meet the plan's particular risk profile. This standard provides pension plans with discretion to consider invest-ment screens and ETI, provided that the overall desired risk/return profile is maintained.

Best Interests, Even-Handed Treatment, and Non-Financial Interests

The duty of loyalty requires that pension trustees act in the best inter-ests of plan members and beneficiaries. Most Canadian jurisdictions have codified this duty in statute. British Columbia's legislation is unique in this regard, explicitly referring to the best financial interests of plan members and beneficiaries.

Critics of socially responsible investment raise three common argu-ments when considering the best interests of plan participants in rela-tion to investment screening and ETI. First, they argue that the best interests of plan beneficiaries are limited to their financial interests. Is this the case, or does the law recognize a broader understanding that incorporates other possible interests? Second, they submit that any other interests shared by plan members and beneficiaries require una-nimity. How is a legal determination of the best interests of plan mem-bers and beneficiaries assessed? Does the law require unanimity, or is some other standard applied? And third, they contend that pension trustees are required to consider the interests of plan members and ben-eficiaries exclusively. This section considers each of these arguments.

Absent a provision in the trust agreement, the duty of trustees to act in the best interests of plan members has commonly been interpreted to mean their financial interests. Clearly, the financial interests of plan members are the paramount concern of plan trustees. Plan members and beneficiaries look to their pension plan to provide them with finan-cial security in their retirement. Accordingly, trustees must be con-cerned with ensuring that the plan provides the returns needed to adequately fund the plan and provide the pension promised. However, a larger policy consideration argues for a more expansive reading of best interests, that pension funds depend on a strong economy and healthy society in order to sustain returns (Barber & Ghilarducco, 1993). Theoretically, funded defined benefit plans apply current contributions towards payment of future liabilities. Consequently, current plan members and their beneficiaries have a long-term interest in the performance of the pension plan's investments. While this relates directly to their financial interests, it requires a broader consideration of the macroeconomic context in which those investments are made.

The facts in cases such as *Withers v. Teachers' Retirement System of the City of New York* (1978) and *Donovan v. Walton* (1985) provide examples of how broader considerations can influence the perspective of trustees on the best interests of plan participants. Similarly, the Dutch ABP pension scheme, with assets exceeding €170 billion and 2.4 million active participants, states that its investment strategy focuses on sustainable economic growth as being in the best interest of beneficiaries and long-term investments.

These considerations are still entirely defensible when discussing the best financial interests of plan members. The legal question arises where trustees consider the application of non-financial investment criteria absent of a financial rationale. In what instance and to what extent may trustees assume that the best interests of plan members are other than their financial interests?

In his judgement, Megarry suggested that the interests of plan members might not be limited to their financial interests. He noted the word *benefit* is to be given a very wide meaning, and there are circumstances in which 'arrangements which work to the financial disadvantage of a beneficiary may yet be for his benefit' (*Cowan v. Scargill*, 1984, p. 761). The court provided the example of divestment of South African securities, based on doubts about that nation's political stability and the long-term financial soundness of its economy. However, the court rejected other possible interests without providing reasons, including pay levels in South Africa, work accidents, pollution control, employment conditions for minorities, military contracting, and consumer protection. In relation to the facts of the case, the court stated that the interests of the British coal industry to the beneficiaries of the miner's pension plan were too 'speculative and remote' (p. 767). Without attempting to compare the issue of worker rights in Britain and South African apartheid, the political context in both situations involved governments that had policies that suppressed a segment of society (unions in the case of Britain; blacks in the case of South Africa) and had the potential to affect the political and economic stability of each respective nation. In that respect, it is difficult to reconcile the court's position that the health of Britain's coal industry was any more remote or insignificant to the beneficiaries of the miners' pension plan than the interests of blacks were to North American investors.

Moreover, Megarry stated that there would be very rare instances, in which case the burden would rest heavy on the one making the assertion, where strong views and common interests shared by plan members and beneficiaries might justify excluding specific investments such as alcohol or tobacco. Accordingly, we turn to discuss what standard pension trustees may apply to determine when the court will consider views to be strongly shared among plan members and beneficiaries.

The duty of loyalty requires that trustees treat all beneficiaries with an even hand. Critics of investment screening argue that trustees may not apply screening criteria because plan participants do not share the same values and interests, aside from a collective interest in receiving promised plan benefits, and applying values-based screens would favour the interests of some over others. Furthermore, they contend that even if unanimity existed among plan members, it would be difficult to determine because of the problems in ascertaining the interests of all current plan members, as well as current and future beneficiaries. Without this information, trustees fear their decision to apply non-financial screens could be seen to be motivated by personal interest or the interests of only some plan members.

The first criticism implies all plan members and beneficiaries must be in agreement on their interests. In theory, if one person believes that investing in tobacco is acceptable, then the argument is that trustees may not divest the portfolio of tobacco stock. Setting aside for the moment the point that trustees may not take direction from plan members, it is clear that unanimity is not the test for determining the best interests of plan members and beneficiaries. If it were, trustees would be incapable of setting investment policy (or making many other decisions about plan funding and benefits). Virtually any investment decision would constitute a breach of the trustee's duty of loyalty, since there will always be some level of disagreement about any investment-related decision (Lane, 1986).

The duty of loyalty demands that pension trustees act impartially, treating all plan members and beneficiaries with an even hand. This requires that pension trustees treat plan members and beneficiaries equitably, giving due consideration to the interests of all parties, not that their respective interests be given equal weight. The responsibility of trustees to provide equitable, not equal, consideration to the interests of plan members and beneficiaries accords with the position that their unanimous agreement is not required.

The second argument implies that policy concerning investment screening requires consideration of the views of plan members and beneficiaries. While surveys consistently demonstrate that the majority of pensioners do not want their retirement savings invested in ways that are harmful to others or the environment, the duty of loyalty prevents pension trustees from taking direction from plan members (Sparkes, 2000; Vector Research, 2001). As fiduciaries, trustees are charged with making decisions in the best interests of plan members based on a full understanding of all the relevant information – information that plan members may or may not have considered in formulating their views. The courts' approach is generally to consider whether the trustee, based on the facts, had a reasonable belief that he or she was acting in the beneficiaries' best interests. In *Cowan v. Scargill* (1984, 1985a, 1985b), Megarry ignored evidence of plan member support for the investment prohibitions (Nobles, 1984). Trustees may take the views of plan members and beneficiaries into consideration, but the decision is theirs alone.

It is commonly argued that pension trustees must act solely in the best interests of plan members and beneficiaries. At issue is whether pension fiduciaries may also consider the interests of plan members and beneficiaries as employees and members of the larger community, and whether the rule allows other interests to be satisfied incidental to those of plan members and beneficiaries. It is well established at law that the paramount duty of pension trustees, unless otherwise stated in the trust agreement, is to the members and beneficiaries of the plan. Some argue on the basis of American statutory law (*Employee Retirement Income Security Act*) that trustees must act exclusively in the interests of plan members and beneficiaries as members and beneficiaries of the plan – the exclusive purpose rule. Canadian legislation and common law, however, do not articulate such a requirement. In interpreting the statutory fiduciary obligations of pension trustees under the *Employee Retirement Income Security Act*, the US Department of Labor has stated that fiduciaries may consider collateral benefits in making investment decisions if these interests are subordinate to those of the plan beneficiaries. The selected investment must provide an investment return commensurate to alternative investments having similar risks (R.J. Doyle, personal communication, 1998).

The interpretation of the exclusive purpose rule has been further qualified by American courts. In *Board of Trustees v. City of Baltimore* (1989), the court stated that a trustee does not necessarily violate the duty of loyalty by considering the social consequences of investment decisions if the costs of doing so are minimal. This view was shared by the court in *Donovan v. Walton* (1985) where the benefits received by the union occupying space in the pension fund's building were viewed by the court as inseparable from the benefits derived the Fund and its participants. Even without these benefits to the Fund, the Employee Retirement Income Security Act simply does not prohibit a party other than a plan's participants and beneficiaries from benefiting in some measure from a prudent transaction with the plan. Furthermore, by adopting the 'exclusive purpose' standard, Congress did not intend to make illegal the fact of life that most often a transaction benefits both parties involved. What courts frequently find objectionable is an imprudent plan transaction in which the trustee has a personal stake.

The latitude granted to trustees in both cases appears to be strongly influenced by the absence of any conflict of interest. In contrast, conflicts of interest played a significant role in *Blankenship v. Boyle* (1971) the American case that stands in opposition to this line of cases. In that instance, the trustees of the jointly administered plan were found to have breached their duty of loyalty to plan members and beneficiaries, in part, by investing in various utility stocks at the recommendation of the union trustee for the benefit of the Union and the signatory operators. The court surmised in that instance that the trustees had made the investments as part of a union campaign to force the utilities to purchase union-mined coal. A bank in which the union held a majority ownership stake held the fund's assets. The union trustee on the pension plan was also a director of the bank. The pension plan had no formal investment policy and the trustees met irregularly with many decisions being taken without the presence of all trustees. Throughout its history, the pension plan elected to maintain a significant portion of its assets in the bank rather than investing them, which assisted the union in carrying out its activities. The court did temper the relief granted based on consideration of the collateral benefits that the union had provided to plan beneficiaries during the life of the pension plan. Clearly, it is a conflict of interest for a trustee to apply screens or select particular investments based on personal objectives or those of any entity with which the trustee is associated (e.g. plan sponsor, company or union). Aside from breaching a trustee's common law duty of loy-

alty, most Canadian jurisdictions have also incorporated statutory prohibitions into their pension legislation. Trustees must therefore ensure
that their actions do not and are not perceived to be in conflict with
those of plan members and beneficiaries.

Conflicts of interest underlay findings of breach of fiduciary duty in
both British decisions on point. However, British courts have not
adopted the exclusive purpose rule. In *Cowan v. Scargill* (1984, 1985a,
1985b), Megarry noted that the word *benefit* is to be interpreted broadly
when considering the obligation of trustees to act for the benefit of plan
members and beneficiaries to the extent of being against their financial
interest. He was clearly referring to the implications of considering the
interests of plan members as members of the community where such
considerations resulted in lower returns. On that basis, he rejected the
potential additional benefits as too remote and insubstantial.

In *Evans v. London Co-operative Society Ltd* (1976), while the trustees
were found in breach of trust for failing to exercise discretion in loaning
plan assets to the parent society at a competitive rate of return, the
court's comments also affirm that the interests of plan members as
employees could be taken into consideration. If members' employment
security was endangered, trustees could give the society preferential
terms for a loan.

The conclusion drawn from these decisions is that trustees must put
the financial interests of plan members and beneficiaries first. In addition, the majority of existing jurisprudence is also in agreement that pension trustees may take into consideration the interests of plan members
and beneficiaries as employees and community members, as well as the
interests of third parties where there are minimal or no adverse financial
consequences for the pension plan. Collateral benefits may be considered where the expected rate of return and associated risk is commensurate with that of alternative available investments. The thin line of
cases is split on whether trustees may consider other interests in making
investment decisions where there is a greater risk of poorer investment
returns. Relying on *Cowan v. Scargill* (1984, 1985a, 1985b), such practice
is acceptable where the trust agreement allows or where there is a substantial and proximate connection between the decision and strongly
held views of plan members and beneficiaries. In such instances, the
decision should be documented in the plan's Statement of Investment
Policy and Procedures and communicated to plan members.

Summarizing the discussion in this section, the weight of authority
and subsequent industry practice supports the view that investment

screening and ETI do not violate the fiduciary duties of prudence and loyalty per se. Yet pension trustees continue to face a range of legal barriers – both real and imaginary – when applying non-financial investment screens to plan investments and investing in ETI. The analysis provided in this section indicates that trustees may adopt these practices, provided that anticipated returns across the entire portfolio are not compromised, there are adequate returns within accepted levels of risk, adequate portfolio diversity is maintained, the practice is permitted under the plan's trust agreement and investment policy, and the practice is communicated to plan members. Furthermore, while the cases are conflicting, there is legal authority supporting the view that the best interests of plan members extends beyond their financial interests and that trustees are not limited to considering the interests of plan members and beneficiaries when making investment-related decisions. The investment decisions of pension trustees will ultimately be judged on the basis of the process applied in arriving at the decision, not the ultimate performance of the investment. As one court has stated, 'The fiduciary duty of care requires prudence, not prescience' (*DeBruyne v. Equitable Life Assur. Soc. of the U.S.*, 1990, p. 465).

Conclusion

It is clear from a review of the law that pension plans may consider non-financial criteria for financial or non-financial reasons and that neither unanimity nor additional legislative authorization is required. Specifically, the application of non-financial criteria by way of investment screens and economically targeted investing is compatible with the fiduciary obligations of pension trustees. While Canadian courts have not provided a clear pronouncement on the issue, the weight of current policy and practice indicates that trustee fiduciary duties include, and arguably require, consideration of non-financial factors, both where it can be demonstrated to be in the financial interests of plan members and where there is support for such considerations being in the long-term interests of plan members. Because pension funds are long term, it is prudent to consider the potential risks and opportunities that political, social, environmental, and ethical practices have and will have on financial markets and the fund's investments.

A modern reading of pension trustee fiduciary duties, supported by the majority of existing jurisprudence from the United States and Britain, suggests that when making investment policy, the law permits pension trustees to take values-based, non-financial criteria into consideration, including screening investments and ETI, provided a prudent process is followed that includes authorization from the plan's investment policy and communication to plan members. In all cases, pension trustees must exercise prudence through the consideration of expert advice and ongoing monitoring of investments while placing the interests of plan members and beneficiaries first and abstaining from any conflicts of interest. Unless the trust provides otherwise, investment decisions must be made with a view towards obtaining adequate returns and portfolio diversity in accordance with the plan's risk tolerance. The best interests of plan members and beneficiaries must remain paramount at all times, but other interests may be considered, provided they do not infringe on the interests of plan participants. The position of trustees in overseeing all aspects of plan administration requires that they make investment-related decisions based on a determination of the best interests of plan members and beneficiaries.

These conclusions reflect an understanding that the fiduciary duties of prudence and loyalty are evolving principles to be given a flexible interpretation in light of the specific circumstances of each pension plan. This flexible and evolving nature allows them to respond to constantly changing macroeconomic conditions and the specific investment environment of the individual pension plan. Viewed in this light, non-financial criteria are simply one more input into the investment decision matrix that seeks to address developments in international norms around human rights, the environment, and behavioural standards for multinational corporations.

An evolution in thinking is also required to transcend the traditional narrow reading of fiduciary law that is increasingly out of step with common institutional investment practices. It remains for Canadian regulators to provide interpretation and guidance on fiduciary standards of prudence and loyalty to keep in step with current fiduciary practice.

Note

This chapter expands on the author's initial research on the issue of the fiduciary duties of trustees and socially responsible investing. See Yaron, 2001.

References

Alberta Law Reform Institute. (2000). *Trustee investment powers*. Retrieved 30 December 2006 from Alberta Law Reform Institute website: http://www.law.ualberta.ca/alri/docs/Fr80.pdf

American Law Institute. (1992). *Restatement (third) of trusts*. St Paul: West.

Balls v. Strutt, 66 E.R. 984 (1841).

Barber, R., & Ghilarducci, T. (1993). Pension funds, capital markets and the economic future. In G. Dymski, G. Epstein, & R. Pollin (Eds.), *Transforming the U.S. financial system* (pp. 287–319). New York: Sharpe.

Bathgate v. National Hockey League Pension Society, 16 O.R. (3d) 761 (C.A. 1994).

Blankenship v. Boyle, 329 F. Supp. 1089 (1971).

Board of Trustees v. City of Baltimore, 562 A. 2d 720 (Md. 1989).

Boe v. Alexander, 41 D.L.R. 4th 520 (C.A. 1987).

Brock v. Walton, 794 F. 2d 589 (11th Cir. 1986).

Calabrese, M. (2001). Building on success: Labor-friendly investment vehicles and the power of private equity. In A. Fung, T. Hebb, & J. Rogers (Eds.), *Working capital: The power of labor's pensions*. Ithaca: Cornell University Press.

CalPERS. (2004). *Environmental investment focus of CalPERS Board Workshop*. Retrieved 24 December 2006 from CalPERS website: Calhttp://www.calpers.ca.gov/index.jsp?bc=/about/press/pr-2004/dec/environmental-investment.xml

Carbon Disclosure Project. (2006). *About us*. Retrieved 24 December 2006 from http://www.cdproject.net/aboutus.asp

Carmichael, I. (2005). *Pension power: Unions, pension funds, and social investment in Canada*. Toronto: University of Toronto Press.

Cash, M. (2004, 22 July). Crocus to direct fund for downtown. *Winnipeg Free Press*.

Cowan v. Scargill, 2 All E.R 750 (1984).

Cowan v. Scargill, 1 Ch. D. 270 (1985a).

Cowan v. Scargill, 1 Ch. D. supra note 45 270 (1985b).

Cowe, R. (2004). *Risk returns and responsibility report*. London: Association of British Insurers.

CSR Europe, & Deloitte and Eurotext. (2003). *Investing in responsible business*. Authors.

CSR Europe and Eurotext. (2002). *The European survey on socially responsible investment and the financial community*. Retrieved 15 May 2005 from www.bitc.org.uk/resources/research/research_publications/csr_europe_sri.html

DeBruyne v. Equitable Life Assur. Soc. of the U.S., 920 F. 2d 457 (C.A. 7th Cir. 1990).

Department of Labor. (2002). *Interpretive bulletin relating to the fiduciary standard under ERISA in considering economically targeted investments*. 29 CFR 2509.94-1. Retrieved 2005 from http://www.dol.gov/dol/allcfr/Title_29/Part_2509/29CFR2509.94-1.htm

Dobris, J.C. (1986). Arguments in favor of fiduciary divestment of 'South African' securities. *Nebraska Law Review, 65*(2), 209–23.

Donovan v. Walton, 609 F.Supp. 1221 (D.C. Fla. 1985).

Edur, O. (1999). Lead us not ... Will taking the moral high ground produce heavenly returns? *Benefits Canada, 23*(1), 29–32.

Entine, J. (2003). *Capitalism's Trojan horse: How the 'social investment' movement undermines stakeholder relations and emboldens the anti-free market activities of NGOs*. Washington, DC: American Enterprise Institute.

Evans v. London Co-operative Society Ltd, C.L.Y. 2059 (Ch.D. 1976).

Falconer, K. (1999). *Prudence patience and jobs*. Ottawa: Canadian Labour Market and Productivity Centre.

Falconer, K. (2000). Venturing forth. *Benefits Canada, 24*(11), 109.

Farrar, J.H., & Maxton, J. K. (1986). Social investment and pension scheme trusts. *Law Quarterly Review, 102*(32).

Financial Services Commission of Ontario. (1992). *Ethical Investments*. Retrieved 17 May 2005 from http://www.fsco.gov.on.ca/English/pensions/policies/inactive/I400–350.pdf

Foltz v. U.S. News & World Report Inc., 865 F. 2d 364 (D.C.Cir. 1989).

Fung, A., Hebb, T., & Rogers, J. (Eds.). (2001). *Working capital: The power of labor's pensions*. New York: Cornell University Press.

Gisborne v. Gisborne, 2 App. Cas. 300 (H.L. 1877).

Gold, M. (2003). *Socially responsible investment: The legal perspective*. Unpublished manuscript.

Goodman, S.B., Kron, J., & Little, T. (2003). *The environmental fiduciary: The case for incorporating environmental factors into investment management policies*. Oakland, CA: Rose Foundation.

Guardians of New Zealand Superannuation. (2006). *Statement of investment policies, standards and procedures*. Retrieved 15 March 2007 from http://www.nzsuperfund.com/files/SIPSP2006.pdf

Harries and Others v. Church Commissioners for England and Other, 2 All E.R. 300 (Ch.D. 1993).

Haurant, S. (2004). Ethical investment 'gains momentum' [Electronic version]. *Guardian Unlimited*. Retrieved 2 June 2006 from Guardian Unlimited website: http://business.guardian.co.uk/story/0,,1229883,00.html

Hawley, J.P., & Williams, A.T. (2000). *The rise of fiduciary capitalism*. Philadelphia: University of Pennsylvania Press.

Herdrich v. Pegram, 154 F 3d 362 (7th Cir. 1998).

Hutchinson, J.D., & Cole, C.G. (1980). Legal standards governing investment of pension assets for social and political goals. *University of Pennsylvania Law Review, 128*(6), 1340–88.

Koppes, R.H., & Reilly, M.L. (1995). An ounce of prevention: Meeting the fiduciary duty to monitor an index fund through relationship investing. *Journal of Corporate Law, 20*(3), 413.

Lamoureux, C. (2000). *Presentation by the Ontario Teachers' Pension Plan Board.* Paper presented at 8th Annual Meeting of Stakeholders, 7 April, Toronto. Retrieved 3 December 2006 from Ontario Teachers' Pension Plan Board website: http://www.otpp.com/web/website.nsf/web/AnnualMtgSpeech2000/$FILE/AnnualMtgSpeech2000.pdf

Lane, P. (1986). Ethical investment: Towards the best interest of everyone. *Advocate, 45*, 171–182.

Langbein, J.H., & Posner, R.A. (1976). Market funds and trust-investment law. *American Bar Foundation Research Journal, 1*(1), 1–34.

Langbein, J.H., & Posner, R.A. (1980). Social investing and the law of trusts. *Michigan Law Review, 79*(1), 72–112.

Longstreth, B. (1986). *Modern investment management theory and the prudent man rule.* New York: Oxford University Press.

Maloney, P. (2002, 31 May). Big kickstart for rental housing. *Toronto Star*, p. B01.

Manitoba Law Reform Commission. (1993). *Ethical investment by trustees.* Winnipeg: Author.

Markowitz, H. (1952). Portfolio selection. *Journal of Finance, 7*(1), 77–91.

Martin v. City of Edinburgh District Council, S.L.T. 329 (O.H. 1988).

Megarry, R. (1989). Investing pension funds: The mineworkers case. In T.G. Youdan (Ed.), *Equity, fiduciaries and trusts* (p. 149). Toronto: Carswell.

Nobles, R. (1984). Conflicts of interest in trustees' management of pension funds. *Industrial Law Journal, 14*, 1–17.

Pearce, P., & Samuels, A. (1985). Trustees and beneficiaries and investment policies. *Conv, 52.*

Picard, A., & Chase, S. (2004, 18 August). End CPP investment in tobacco, doctors demand. *Globe & Mail*, p. A5.

Ravikoff, R.B., & Curzan, M.P. (1980). Social responsibility in investment policy and the prudent man rule. *California Law Review, 68*(3), 518–47.

Scott, A.W., & Fratcher, W.F. (1987). *The law of trusts* (4th ed., Vol. 3). Boston: Little Brown.

Sparkes, R. (2000). SRI comes of age. *Pension investor* (June).

Speight v. Gaunt, 22 Ch. D. 739 (C.A. 1882).

Statistics Canada. (2002). *Quarterly estimates of trusteed pension funds.* Retrieved

24 September 2007 from http://www.statcan.ca/english/freepub/74-001-XIB/0010274-001-XIB.pdf

Statistics Canada. (2006). Employer pension plans (trusteed pension funds) [Electronic version]. *The Daily.* Retrieved 2 January 2007 from http://www.statcan.ca/Daily/English/060922/d060922a.htm

Thomsen, M., & Wheat, D. (2003, Spring). The new fiduciary duty. *Business Ethics, 17,* 12.

Troyer, T.A., Boisture, W.B., & Slocombe, W.B. (1985). Divestment of South Africa investments: The legal implications for foundations, other charitable institutions, and pension funds. *Georgetown Law Journal, 74,* 127.

UNEP Finance Initiative. (2004). *The materiality of social environmental and corporate governance issues to equity pricing.* Geneva: UNEP.

UNEP Finance Initiative. (2005). *A legal framework for the integration of social, environmental, and governance issues into institutional investment.* Retrieved 1 October 2005 from http://www.unepfi.org/fileadmin/documents/freshfields_legal_resp_20051123.pdf

Vasil, A. (2004, 19–25 February). What teach is smoking: Greenpeace questions ethics of teachers' pension strike in big tobacco. *NOW Magazine,* p. 25.

Vector Research. (2001). *Public opinion poll.* Toronto: Canadian Democracy and Corporate Accountability Commission.

Watson Wyatt. (2004). *Pension fund investment: The Canadian climate.* Retrieved 24 September 2007 from http://www.watsonwyatt.com/canada-english/pubs/memoranda/showarticle.asp?ArticleID=12532&articledate=3/30/2004&Component=Memorandum&pdfURL=pdf/wm18-1.pdf

Whiteley v. Learoyd, 12 Ch. 727 (H.L. 1887).

Willis, R.T. (1992). Prudent investor rule gives trustees new guidelines. *Estate Planning, 19*(6), 338–46.

Withers v. Teachers' Retirement System, 447 F.Supp. 1248 (N.Y.D.C. 1978).

Yaron, G. (2001). The responsible pension trustee: Reinterpreting the principles of prudence and loyalty in the context of socially responsible institutional investing. *Estates, Trusts and Pensions Journal, 20*(4), 305.

Zanglein, J.E. (2001). Overcoming institutional barriers on the economically targeted investment superhighway. In A. Fung, T. Hebb, & J. Rogers (Eds.), *Working capital: The power of labor's pensions.* Ithaca: Cornell University Press.

4 Human Capital–Based Investment Criteria for Total Shareholder Returns

JANE THOMSON COMEAULT AND DAVID WHEELER

Many empirical studies have explored the relationship between the social and economic performance of firms. A comprehensive review of these studies has found that when treated as an independent variable, corporate social performance is positively correlated to financial performance in 53% of cases (Margolis & Walsh, 2001). In recent years, these studies have been supplemented by evidence from specialist stock market indices, all of which indicate equal or superior stock market returns from selected socially responsible investment (SRI) strategies (DiBartolomeo & Kurtz, 1999; Heaps, 2004; Mutual Fund Review, 2002).

Observing the increasing value of 'intangible' resources, strategic management theorists have developed a 'resource-based view' of the firm that posits internal capabilities (or resources) as sources of competitive advantage (Barney, 1991; Grant, 1996). Valuation methods of these intangibles are still highly variable or non-existent. Human capital is one key intangible resource that is not adequately evaluated by most investors, as a result in part of lack of measurement or corporate disclosure of organizational information. This presents an opportunity for further analysis (beyond traditional financial analysis) of human capital management within a firm.

This chapter will first review the concept of corporate social responsibility and its relationship to socially responsible investment, shareholder value, and the potential for investment of pension funds by the trade union movement. Second, it will examine the relationship between human capital performance and financial performance. Third, it will describe a study undertaken to identify human capital investment criteria for establishing positive screened pension-fund investment portfolios and increasing rates of return. Finally, a further study

(Milevsky, Aziz, Goss, Comeault, & Wheeler, 2006), undertaken as part of Pensions at Work, is discussed and illustrates how these criteria may be applied to a passive index for establishing their contribution to long-term financial value. Both studies extend research on corporate social performance and the resource-based view of the firm.

Socially Responsible Investment

SRI in general has enjoyed significant growth in the past decade (Eurosif, 2003; Social Investment Forum, 2003; Social Investment Organization, 2003). The main drivers of this growth have been an increased appreciation of novel risks, stakeholder interests, demands for transparency, and confidence in the performance and availability of SRI products. Supporting evidence for the empirical link between social and financial performance of firms (Margolis & Walsh, 2001) has been somewhat reinforced by the performance of specialist stock market indices. These include the Domini Social Index (DSI, U.S.), the Jantzi Social Index (JSI, Canada), and the Dow Jones Group Sustainability Index (DJSI, International). Neither the empirical studies on corporate social performance nor the specialist SRI indices demonstrate causality between superior social or environmental performance and economic performance.

One theory explaining the phenomenon relates to the numerous drivers of performance, and thus it is possible that positive correlations between economic performance and corporate social performance reflect a third variable, such as superior management capabilities to navigate complexity in the global business environment (Wheeler, Colbert, & Freeman, 2003). Others lend support to this notion (Feltmate, Schofield, & Yachnin, 2001; Innovest, 2003), describing corporate social performance as a proxy measure for identifying companies with superior quality of management. This is a criterion that mainstream analysts are constantly trying to assess; in SRI it is simply reframed from the perspective of sustainability.

It is also possible that the performance of SRI funds can be attributed to the extensive research involved. For example, more time is spent analysing predictive (leading) indicators of future economic performance than on simply assessing current or retrospective indicators of performance: governance, human capital investments, social capital investments, sustainable product investments, and so on. Whether causal or not, the empirical evidence provides a tentative basis for a 'business case' for investing in stocks of companies with superior social and environmental performance.

Pension Assets

The past 50 years have seen enormous expansion and change in financial markets (Kaufman, 2000), especially in the growth of institutional investments (OECD, 2004). It is estimated that US$11 trillion, or around one third of the global equities market, comprises workers' capital held in pension funds worldwide (Robinson, 2002, citing Watson Wyatt Global Investment Review 2002).

There are more than 13,800 registered pension plans in Canada (Statistics Canada, 2002). Figure 4.1 shows pension funds as a subset of institutional investments in Canada increasing over 800% from US$42.5 billion in 1980 to US$343 billion in 2000 (OECD, 2004). More recent estimates assess total assets held by employer-sponsored pensions at approximately CAD$836.8 billion (Statistics Canada, 2006), plus approximately $17.5 billion (Canadian Pension Plan Investment Board, 2003), and $16 billion (MacDonald, 2003) held by the CPP Investment Board (CPPIB) and the Quebec Pension Plan (QPP) respectively. Pension funds represent the second largest pool of investment capital in Canada (Statistics Canada, 2002), owning about 20% of the stock of big-name publicly traded companies in Canada. Although much of this represents the deferred wages of Canadian workers, little is invested with regard for the special interests of labour (Heaps, 2004).

Unions internationally are considering how to enable their members, especially representatives who sit on trustee boards, to become more financially literate and more effective in their influence on investment decisions concerning their deferred income (Barber, 2003; Robinson, 2002; Trade Unions Congress, 2003; Yaron, 2003). Typically, labour and trade unions govern themselves according to social values representative of their membership. Some of these values are aligned with sustainability strategies such as employee wellness, safety, community investment, and environmental responsibility; thus it is possible to envisage the emergence of investment criteria that may be correlated with union values as well as economic performance of stocks (Kasemir & Suëss, 2002).

Further, it might be argued that it is contradictory for unions to advocate for healthier workplaces, human rights, and employee benefits from their employers, while investing their pension contributions

Figure 4.1. Financial assets of Canadian institutional investors, 1980–2001.

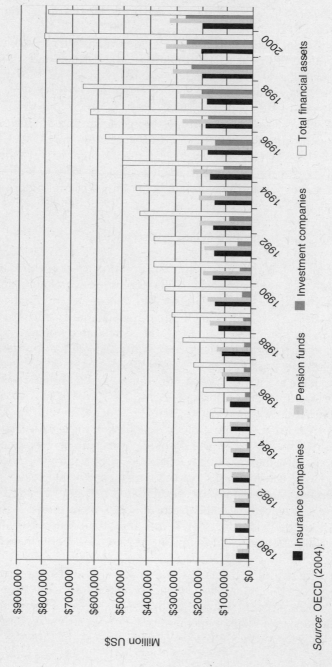

Million US$

Insurance companies Pension funds Investment companies Total financial assets

Source: OECD (2004).

in firms with poor performance on these factors (Canadian Labour Congress, 2003; Trade Unions Congress, 2003). In February 2003, with this in mind, UNISON (the largest trade union in the U.K.) awarded a £100 million SRI pension-fund mandate to Morley Fund Management (Mathias, 2003). This is a trend we are likely to see more of in the coming years, especially as workers exercise more active joint trusteeship on pension boards (Eurosif, 2003; Trade Unions Congress, 2003) and the business case for SRI becomes better appreciated. However, there remains the question of fiduciary duty and the misunderstandings that still attach to SRI. Discussion of strategic management and the generation of competitive advantage are necessary in order to build a case for human capital as a source of value creation for shareholders as well as other stakeholders.

Human Capital and Financial Performance

The focus of this research is human capital–related performance of the company as a subset of sustainability factors. Several empirical studies have explored the linkage between human capital and financial performance using a range of methodologies. Margolis and Walsh (2001) cover 23 such studies related to 'human resource management'; Stiles and Kulvisaechana (2003) cover 11 studies specific to human resource practices and organizational performance. The vast majority of these studies have found positive correlations between human capital performance and financial performance.

In particular, Watson Wyatt (2002) conducted a study in 2001 identifying 49 human capital practices believed to increase shareholder value. A firm that improved 43 of 49 of its human resource practices realized a 47% increase in market value. Human capital practices were argued to be leading indicators of financial performance based on comparisons of 50 companies that participated in this and a previous study in 1999. Statistically significant correlations were found between 1999 human capital indicator scores and 2001 financial performance (.41) versus 2001 human capital indicator scores and 1999 financial performance (.19).

In further studies, human capital practices were found to account for up to 43% of the difference between a company's market-to-book value and its competitors (Deloitte & Touche, 2002), and organizations linking human resource management practices to strategy were reporting higher performance outcomes (Hueslid, 1995, in Stiles & Kulvisaechana, 2003). Waddock and Graves (1997) argue that perceived quality of management can be explained by the quality of performance with respect to specific primary stakeholders: owners, employees, customers, and (marginally) communities. Their study of Fortune 500 companies found that 'the relationship between quality of management ... and employee relations is strongly and consistently positive' (p. 22).

Stiles and Kulvisaechana (2003, p. 3) completed an exhaustive literature review to assess the linkage between human capital and organizational performance and concluded, 'On the evidence of this review, the link between human capital and organizational performance is convincing.' Notably, they assert that the largest impediment to this assessment is the challenge of measuring human capital (which is not unlike the broader challenge of measuring corporate social performance for SRI specialists).

Finally, organizational knowledge is displacing financial capital as the driver of competitive performance (Chartered Institute of Personnel and Development, 2001; Stewart, 1997). The effects of a more knowledge-based economy coupled with the demographics of an aging workforce make retention and recruitment an increasing concern for employers. As a result, organizations compete to be an 'employer of choice' in order to attract talent. In fact, 89% of Canadian CEOs identified attracting and retaining high-calibre employees as a priority for 2004 (KPMG/Ipsos-Reid, 2004). This trend does not go unnoticed in the market; a survey of U.K. pension-fund trustees indicates that 81% perceive that 'good employment practices' have a positive impact in the longer term (Gribben & Faruk, 2004).

Corporate Strategy and the Resource-Based View of the Corporation

A company's strategy is essentially management's game plan for positioning the firm in its chosen market in order to create sustained competitive advantage, which is the edge of a company over its rivals in market share over the long term (Porter, 1985; Thompson & Strickland, 1998). There are many approaches to strategic management (Mintzberg, Ahlstrand, & Lampel, 1998); however, this discussion centres on the resource-based view of the firm.

The resource-based view of the firm was first introduced by Penrose in 1959, but not popularized until the 1990s. Prior to this period, strategic management theories analysed mostly external factors, taking an 'outside-in' view, focusing on competitive threats and market opportunities (Porter, 1985). In 1991, Barney turned the resource-based view into a full-fledged theory by reframing strategic analysis as an 'inside-out' view, arguing that a firm's resources can become a source of competitive advantage if they are bundled together in unique and dynamic ways. At the same time, Grant (1991) was expanding on the theory. He observed that in a volatile external environment, involving shifting market conditions such as consumer preference and evolving technologies, organizations have to look to internal capabilities for a stable sense of direction; otherwise, they would be in a constant state of changing direction and definition at the whim of market shifts.

Barney (1995) defines a firm's resources and capabilities to include 'all of the financial, physical, human and organizational assets used by a firm to develop, manufacture, and deliver products or services to its customers' (p. 50). A firm's resources and capabilities can also be divided into tangible and intangible resources or assets. Resources and capabilities may contribute to the success of the organization but still not be strategically important. Barney (1991, 1995) stipulates four criteria necessary for competitive advantage: value, rareness, imitability, and non-substitutability.

Intangible Resources and Human and Social Capital

It has been observed by many that sources of value creation and competitive advantage are changing from tangible to intangible resources (e.g., Collins & Porras, 1994; Interbrand, 2003; Kotter & Heskett, 1992; O'Reilly III & Pfeffer, 2000; Wheeler, 2004b; Wheeler et al., 2003). Human, intellectual, and social capital are key intangible resources contributing to competitive advantage and value creation.

Human capital comprises the knowledge, experience, and skills of the people within the organization, as well as their ability to collectively innovate and use judgement to make decisions; the firm cannot *own* human capital. In contrast, intellectual capital includes patents, trademarks, licences, and brands, which are all owned by a company. Social capital encompasses a firm's reputation and relationships, often articulated through brand loyalty, trust, and goodwill. It involves shared language, networks, and mutual understanding and is created through positive interactions between a company and its stakeholders (Nahapiet & Ghoshal, 1998). Unlike other forms of capital, 'social capital is owned jointly by the parties in a relationship, and no one player has, or is capable of having, exclusive ownership rights' (Nahapiet & Ghoshal, 1998,

p. 244). In other words, human capital resides in people and social capital in the relationships between them. An organization must develop the capabilities to build and leverage social capital in order to achieve its objectives. In this way, social capital is a resource but not necessarily one that can be managed or controlled in a direct way by the firm. Nevertheless, it can facilitate the sharing of knowledge, thus reducing transaction costs, increasing learning and innovation (Nahapiet & Ghoshal, 1998), and hence, the potential for competitive advantage.

Human and social capital resources are mobilized through organizational routines or processes. Grant (1991) distinguishes between the terms: 'The capabilities of a firm are what it can do as a result of teams of resources working together' (p. 120). 'Creating capabilities is not simply a matter of assembling a team of resources: capabilities involve complex patterns of coordination between people and between people and other resources' (p. 122). Johnson and Scholes (1999, p. 513) define organizational routines as 'organization specific "ways we do things around here" that tend to persist over time and guide people's behaviour.'

Intangible resources including human capital, intellectual capital, and social capital can be a source of competitive advantage when capabilities built around them are exploited across the value chain, and they have rare, inimitable, and non-substitutable qualities (shown in Figure 4.2). Given the complex, global, and uncertain economic environment that businesses must navigate (Hart & Milstein, 2003; Wheeler, 2004a; World Resources Institute, United Nations Environment Program, & World Business Council for Sustainable Development, 2002), a focus on value creation, defined by stakeholders and organization, will secure sustainable (or long-term) competitive advantage. Wheeler et al. (2003) created a framework for classifying organizational culture in the creation and distribution of value. The framework integrates business concepts including stakeholder theory, corporate social responsibility, and sustainability (shown in Figure 4.3). This framework recognizes that different stakeholders have different conceptions of value, and maximum value is created when a firm can reconcile value as defined by the organization as well as its stakeholders (Wheeler, 2004b).

Essentially, what distinguishes a Level 1 organization from a Level 3 organization is the depth of understanding of the nature of value creation. Level 3 organizations recognize that trade-offs between organization and stakeholder do not have to be made, and win-wins are possible, and indeed desirable (Wheeler, 2004a). While organizations are likely to simultaneously operate in any levels of the pyramid, the

Figure 4.2. Intangible resources to competitive advantage.

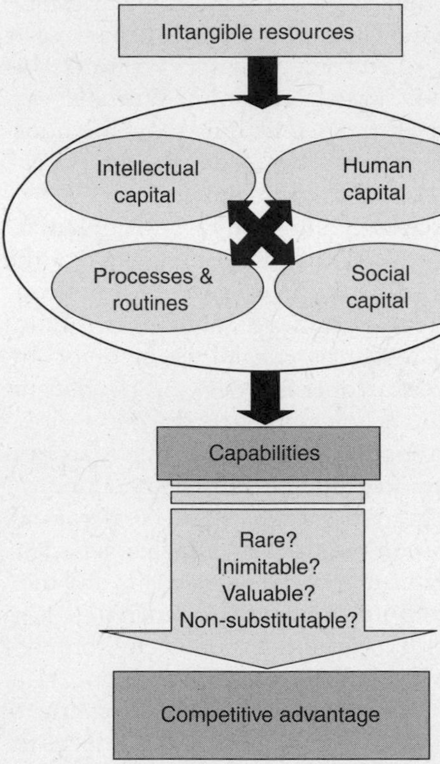

goal is to create the most value through pursuit of business objectives with maximum benefit to the most stakeholders.

Establishing Investment Criteria

The objective of this research was to establish a candidate set of investment criteria that could be applied to a basket of financially screened investments to further refine an investment portfolio and thus create maximum value by (a) increasing total shareholder returns over time, and (b) supporting human capital development in companies by allocating more money to firms that perform better in this regard.

One challenge of this task was to identify criteria for a wide range of companies that would be sufficiently interesting to a variety of stakeholders, including investors and labour unions. A qualitative tri-

Figure 4.3. Framework for classifying organizational cultures in the creation and distribution of economic, social, and ecological value.

Do maximum good
(i.e., *create maximum value*)

Sustainable organization culture
Maximizes the creation of value simultaneously
in economic, social, and ecological terms

Level
3

Relationship management culture
Value is created but is typically traded off,
usually after the demands of investors
are satisfied

Level
2

Compliance culture
Preserves value consistent with laws
and norms and seeks to avoid the
unaceptable destruction of value
(economic, social, or ecological)

Level
1

Do minimum harm
(i.e., *avoid destroying value*)

Source: Wheeler, Colbert, & Freeman, 2002 (after Schein, 1985)

angulation (Patton, 2002) methodology was undertaken to meet these challenges, and maximum value creation (Wheeler et al., 2003) was applied to narrow the pool of candidate criteria to a reasonable number (14 in total). The methods for establishing candidate investment criteria were taken from three major categories: (a) academic and applied literature, (b) relevant criteria in use by analysts, and (c) direct interviews.

A review of Canadian and international social screens or CSP-related standards was conducted. Numerous SRI indices, research firms, and investment managers use social screens to a certain degree. These were reviewed, specifically looking at metrics relating to human capital development. Sources included Michael Jantzi Research Associates (MJRA), KLD Research & Analytics, Innovest IVA, FTSE4Good, Real Assets, Global Reporting Initiative (Global Reporting Initiative, 2002), Sustainable Asset Management (SAM), Dow Jones Group Sustainability Indices (DJSI), Ethibel, GrowthWorks Working Opportunities Fund, and AMP Henderson (AMP Henderson, 2000).

International guidelines or codes were considered on two levels.

First, signatories to these codes or guidelines would be a candidate for human capital–based investment criteria, indicating a firm's commitment to human rights and ethical issues. Second, the contents of the codes and guidelines could be used as indicators; for example, the OECD Guidelines for Multinational Enterprises (OECD, 2000) or ILO Guidelines.

Thirty-seven interviews were conducted between December 2003 and March 2004. In order to establish human-capital investment criteria that might also be aligned with labour union policy objectives, 62% were leaders with major unions, and many also served as pension-fund trustees on one or more boards.

The remaining interviews (14) were conducted with pension-fund administrators, investment managers, SRI specialists, consultants, and representatives of NGOs engaged in pension-fund investment. Each brought a distinct perspective and potential access to other sources of information. In general, the interview participants had many years of experience in their area of expertise.

Most of the interviews (76%) were completed by mid-February 2004. At this point recurring themes (Patton, 2002) occurred in the interviews and very little (or no) new information was being uncovered. In parallel, themes for measuring human capital emerged from the literature review and criteria in use by SRI analysts. Candidate indicators were identified under each theme by coding citations in interviews and desk research for frequency of recurrence.

Narrowing the Candidate Investment Criteria

The challenge of establishing indicators lies in separating a core set from over 45 potential indicators. In order to reduce the number of human capital indicators, the conditions set were measurability, comparability, accessibility, materiality, significance, and maximum value creation (Mansley, 2002).

1. *Measurability.* Is there something perceptible to measure? If so, what is the unit of measurement?
2. *Comparability.* This factor is crucial for investors and analysts when distinguishing between companies (Southwood, 2003). For example, a commonly occurring indicator from the interviews was 'undisrupted work' or labour disputes in recent past. However, this would be limited to unionized companies. Differences in sector, firm size,

and geographic location of operations were considered to some extent with every indicator.

3. *Accessibility.* To avoid exhaustive specialist surveys, ideally the information is available in the public domain. The threshold chosen was a five-minute telephone conversation with a firm's human resources department as well as a phone call to one or more of the representative unions at the firm (where unionization is present), to access desired information not otherwise found within the public domain. The accessibility of some indicators was tested through talking with SRI specialists, union representatives, health and safety boards, and human resource managers.

4. *Materiality.* Does this condition indicate important risks and opportunities available to the firm? Are the indicators relevant to all companies?

5. *Significance*, in a statistical sense. This factor could be hypothesized only at the time of the study but was grounded in the literature review, SRI criteria, and interviews. A combination of leading and lagging indicators was selected to obtain a sense of what a company espouses versus its record of action. Another consideration was the sensitivity of the indicators to the market and how well they reflect 'real time' in signalling meaningful aspects of the company's business.

6. *Value creation.* The final distillation is the potential for simultaneously maximizing value creation in a financial, social, and ecological sense (Wheeler et al., 2003).

The candidate criteria were evaluated for where each would reside in the framework. Normative or Level 1 indicators were rejected in favour of more instrumental (Level 2), or ideally, positive (Level 3) indicators for maximum value creation. Level 3 indicators achieve the greatest 'win-wins' with investors, workers, and other stakeholders and are therefore more likely to have higher levels of inter-stakeholder synergy. Some indicators were discarded if they were too heavily skewed to one stakeholder's perspective. Complementary or crosscutting indicators of human capital, social capital, and organizational routines were favoured for their potential maximum value creation.[1] Each candidate indicator was evaluated for its ability to add value to a company's resources and capabilities. With those conditions in mind, the list of over 45 candidate criteria was narrowed to 14 indicators, with associated metrics.[2]

1. Board composition: diversity in expertise, gender/race, geography, sector, demography
2. Health and safety record: fatalities and lost time
3. Health and safety culture: degree of focus on health and safety reflected by company communications, values, reporting practices, representation by senior managers and Board
4. Reputation: company representation in independent rankings of 'good companies'
5. Community investment: amount of pre-tax dollars donated as percentage of profit
6. Employee attitude survey: presence of a survey and extent of disclosure of results
7. Employee retention: annual turnover as percentage of total
8. Work–life balance: availability of on-site child care, flexible work arrangements, wellness programs, parental leave benefits
9. Performance-based compensation: presence of an employee-share-ownership program or profit sharing
10. Pension plan: presence of employer sponsored pension plan
11. Training: hours or dollars spent per employee, per annum
12. Policies: presence of policies on environment, health and safety, diversity/non-discrimination, human rights, code of conduct for suppliers, benefits, or human resources
13. Convictions or fines: number of convictions or fines a company is charged with, including labour issues, environment, health and safety, or ethical issues
14. Freedom of association: percentage of workforce unionized

Discussion

A few points of clarification must be made regarding what the proposed human capital–based investment criteria identified here *do not* represent. They should not be presumed to be an exhaustive list of human capital value-creation indicators for a firm and its stakeholders. Moreover, these 14 criteria (or a subset of them) should not be viewed as the ultimate answer for approaches to human capital management. No *single* criterion is likely to predict performance. Rather, a bundle of human capital indicators should be examined to better assess a firm's ability to realize competitive advantage (Stiles & Kulvisaechana, 2003). Further, these human capital investment criteria should not be viewed as a cause of increased shareholder returns.

This research explores human capital management (including social capital vis-à-vis stakeholder relations and the organizational resources and capabilities of the firm) as a potential performance enhancement and risk-reduction strategy that might guide investment. Human capital criteria represent a form of social screen, and it is commonly argued that the application of a screen to investment increases a portfolio's risk exposure by narrowing the universe of investments. For example, a recent study by Geczy, Stambaugh, and Levin (2003) used sophisticated financial modelling (Capital Asset Pricing Model [CAPM]) and found SRI to place between a slight cost and a loss of 30 basis points on investment portfolios.

This study generated a lively response from Innovest (2004), who pointed out that Geczy et al. compared funds with different risk/return profiles. Innovest countered with its own study (Innovest, 2004), which provides evidence for a positive correlation between corporate social performance and financial performance. The counter-argument is that any criteria applied to investment narrow the universe unless one invests in every company that is publicly traded or uses a random approach to selecting stocks. The human capital screen suggested in this research does narrow the universe of potential investments, but assumes that human capital criteria represent practices of importance to a company's success as a business and therefore are important to consider.

Nevertheless, research has yet to provide incontrovertible evidence that screened funds outperform or underperform their unscreened counterparts. As noted above, a number of literature reviews conclude that the balance tips frequently, if marginally, in favour of SRI increasing total shareholder returns (Cowe, 2004; Low & Cohen Kalafut, 2004; Margolis & Walsh, 2001; Stiles & Kulvisaechana, 2003).

Another argument against the application of social screens is fiduciary duty. As discussed by Yaron (2001) and also his chapter in this book, pension-fund fiduciaries have a legal responsibility to act according to the 'principle of prudence' and the 'principle of loyalty,' which, among other things, include achieving a reasonable rate of return and maintaining an adequate diversity of investments (Yaron, 2001). In Canada, there is no consensus on whether SRI within institutional investing satisfies fiduciary duty and no legality suggesting that it does not (Yaron, 2001). Consequently, trustees may become cautious when considering SRI, since the general perception is that the investor must sacrifice returns and/or narrow the universe when applying SRI. However, as discussed earlier, this does not necessarily follow. Indeed, if it did, there would be no purpose in pursuing careers in investment portfolio management, and mutual funds would be based purely on indexed products.

Perceptions of SRI may be overcome by reframing it as a value-add approach rather than an ethical approach. Ambachtsheer (2003) argues that the lexicon of SRI will not revolutionize institutional investing. However, investors must be aware of how companies are managing their intangible assets, and SRI does exactly that. Despite the absence of demonstrated causality between corporate social performance and financial performance, it is becoming more and more difficult to ignore a company's intangible assets in the analysis of potential investments. This point is emphasized in chapter 5 by Clark and Salo, who point out the importance of intangible assets in 'new paradigm' firms. In fact, as Yaron argues in chapter 3, fiduciaries may be seen to be neglecting their responsibilities if they do not consider social and environmental risks (Baue, 2004).

Human Capital as a Strategic Resource

The human resource management function of a firm is often seen as a cost to be minimized rather than a resource to be optimized (Ulrich, 1998). Therefore, there is an opportunity for human resource functions to be more strategic in managing or catalysing the human capital–base of a firm. As argued previously, people hold the means to bring together valuable resources and capabilities to create sources of competitive advantage. Doing so requires leadership to align the human resource function with corporate strategy, as well as resources, capabilities, and routines.

The historically non-strategic nature of human resource management is manifested in a lack of measurement and tracking of human capital metrics, and this deficiency has been observed by many (Deloitte & Touche, 2003; Kingsmill et al., 2003; Southwood, 2003). Further, little of human resource management is publicly disclosed. This may be because a firm (a) doesn't measure it, (b) chooses not to disclose it for fear of losing competitive advantage, or (c) does not disclose it because it doesn't see it as 'material' or interesting to stakeholders (namely shareholders). Greater disclosure is required for investors to adequately evaluate firms' social performance. It is likely that as more people recognize the value of human capital as a source of value creation, measurement and evaluation of human capital indicators will follow. In this light, the absence of an indicator can be seen as an indicator in itself. Firms that measure and report on human capital metrics are more likely to value it, and thus perform better compared to their less transparent peers.

A number of reporting initiatives are working incrementally towards increased disclosure of human capital, and other social, environmental, and ethical issues (for example, Global Reporting Initiative, 2002; Kingsmill et al., 2003). However, legislation would yield a step change. Canada could observe and learn from the U.K. legislated requirement for pension funds to include information in their Statement of Investment Principles on the degree to which (if any) social, environmental, and/or ethical issues are considered in investment analysis. Further, the U.K. Department of Trade and Industry (DTI) has completed a review of Company Law, and preliminary indications are that companies will be advised to include information on human capital management in their Operating and Financial Review as human capital management is becoming increasingly recognized to be material (Department of Trade and Industry, 2004).

It became apparent during the review of the human resource literature that little research has been done on blue-collar workers. Much of the literature on human resource practices and talent is relevant for well-educated, highly skilled workers, and the results may not apply to blue-collar workers.

Differentiation from Existing SRI Criteria

There is a plethora of SRI criteria, proposed and in practice, so why create more? This chapter proposes a focused set of human capital investment criteria that build on strategic management theory as well as the aforementioned proposed and applied criteria.

The quality of information and research by SRI specialists has been gently criticized for its inconsistency, lack of verification, and immateriality (Beloe, Scherer, & Knoepfel, 2004). The human capital indicators in this chapter attempt to overcome that challenge using the six guidelines of measurability, comparability, accessibility, materiality, significance, and value creation.

Having determined the 14 human capital criteria, a further study (Milevsky et al., 2006) was undertaken as part of the Pensions at Work project to illustrate how these criteria could be applied to a passive index to establish their contribution to long-term financial value. The human capital criteria were used as a negative screen to eliminate stocks of companies that failed to meet the standard.

The difference between negatively and positively screened funds is discussed in the first chapter of this book, but bears repeating at this point. Negative screens (often used in the construction of ethical funds) apply normatively chosen exclusionary criteria such as an absence of tobacco or military hardware stocks as precondition(s) for the investment portfolio. Investments are then selected from the remaining universe of potential investments. In contrast, positive screens are applied by specialist investment managers to a pool of conventionally chosen companies (based on financial metrics), which are then selected according to a proprietary mix of corporate social, environmental, governance, and other performance criteria. For example, positive screens may evaluate companies based on issues related to corporate governance, employee and supply chain diversity, stakeholder engagement, the natural environment, human rights, and corporate ethics policies. In each case, an attempt is made to avoid sources of risk and maximize sources of future value. This method is sometimes referred to as 'best in class' investing (Mansley, 2000).

The research by Milevsky, Aziz, Goss, Comeault, and Wheeler (2006) illustrates how portfolio optimization can be used to locate statistical portfolio substitutes for investments and companies that fail a human capital screen. A 'cleansing' for the Canadian S&P/TSX 60 index was used, based on the human capital criteria as outlined in this chapter. Companies with the lowest CSR scores were removed in increments of two from the original portfolio and then scenario optimization was used to replicate the original index with the 'cleansed' portfolios. The optimization was constrained so that the portfolio was rebalanced only by selling the offending securities and reallocating funds into the remaining securities. To test the performance of the revised index, a distribution of 76 two-week returns was used, ending in 5 July 2005. The effectiveness of each replicating portfolio was tested by calculating their first four moments of daily return data, and they were compared to the original portfolio.

While the mathematics behind constrained portfolio optimization was developed by Markowitz more than 50 years ago, the authors found that the economic penalty for eliminating a small group of undesirable stocks – whether justified or not – was economically insignificant when the remaining investments were properly realigned. The results run counter to the argument from many investment managers who say that restricting the investment universe will either decrease return or increase risk (both undesirable outcomes for institutional investors).

Conclusion and Future Research

The resources and capabilities form the basis for a firm's strategy and potential for competitive advantage. Firms are increasingly valued on the basis of intangible resources; however, the valuation methods are highly variable, with potential for market inefficiencies as a result. Human capital is a key intangible resource that is not adequately evaluated by most investors, due in part to lack of measurement and disclosure of such organizational attributes. Although this deficiency poses many challenges, it also presents an opportunity to those who are willing to undertake further analysis (over and above traditional financial analysis) of human capital management within a firm. Indeed, as noted above, the 14 indicators identified here were applied as a screen to an investment portfolio in order to demonstrate that there may be no diminution of risk-adjusted rates of returns in a passive index, even where the level of stock substitution is quite significant.

Thus, it appears that there are no regulatory or practical barriers to driving win-win outcomes between labour union interests in promoting good human resource practice in the workplace and the interests of investors in maximizing rates of return over the long term. Paradoxically, labour trustees may make more progress on their objectives of promoting good labour practices in the workplace if they align themselves more directly with the interests of investors (which of course include their own members) rather than seeing SRI as an opportunity to force more normative agendas against the interests of the firm or (in some cases) the practice of free enterprise more generally. We have seen no reliable, disinterested evidence that high percentages of labour union members wish to sacrifice long-term performance of their pension plans in favour of their trustees adopting moral positions. Ultimately, labour union members want to see their pension promise upheld, and it appears that using human capital screens, as suggested in this chapter, should not hinder fund performance.

Our work demonstrates that a middle path option, where metrics relevant to labour unions, their members, *and ordinary investors* are applied to investment portfolios, may hold much promise for transcending the traditional – yet divisive – capital *versus* activist debates that have characterized the SRI story.

Notes

1　An example of a 'maximum value creating indicator' is on-site child care. A representative from an Ontario manufacturing firm spoke of the advantages the organization enjoyed by having an on-site child-care centre. If a meeting runs slightly late, or parents need an extra 20 minutes to finish for the day, they can complete the task without worry: the child is happily playing at the care centre, and the organization enjoys a more productive and happier workforce.
2　Further details on each indicator are available as an Appendix to a full text article at http://www.pensionsatwork.ca/english/pdfs/thomson_wheeler_human.pdf.

References

Ambachtsheer, K. (2003). Is SRI bunk? *The Ambachtsheer Letter: Research and Commentary on Pension Governance, Finance and Investments*. Letter 252. February.

AMP Henderson. (2000). *Socially responsible investment paper: Equal opportunities*. Sydney: AMP Henderson Global Investors.

Barber, B. (2003). *UKSIF 2003 annual lecture*. Retrieved 6 October 2003 from http://www.uksif.org/cmsfiles/277826/UKSIF_Annual_Lecture_and_AGM_2003.pdf

Barney, J. (1991). Firm resources and sustainable competitive advantage. *Journal of Management, 17*(1), 99–120.

Barney, J. (1995). Looking inside for competitive advantage. *Academy of Management Executive, 9*(4), 49–61.

Baue, W. (2004). *Moving from the business case for SRI and CSR to the fiduciary case*. Retrieved 19 February 2004 from Social Funds website: http://www.socialfunds.com/news//article.cgi/1346.html

Beloe, S., Scherer, J., & Knoepfel, I. (2004). *Values for money: Reviewing the quality of SRI research*. London: SustainAbility.

Canadian Labour Congress. (2003). *A workplace that works*. Ottawa: Author.

Canadian Pension Plan Investment Board. (2003). *2003 Annual Report*. Retrieved 10 February 2007 from CPP Investment Board website: http://www.cppib.ca/files/PDF/Annual_reports/ar_2003_MDA.pdf

Chartered Institute of Personnel and Development. (2001). *The case for good people management: A summary of the research*. Retrieved 12 January 2007 from Chartered Institute of Personnel and Development website: http://www.cipd.co.uk/subjects/corpstrtgy/general/case4gdpm.htm?IsSrchRes=1

Collins, J., & Porras, J. (1994). *Built to last: Successful habits of visionary companies*. New York: Harper Business.

Cowe, R. (2004). *Risk returns and responsibility*. London: Association of British Insurers.

Deloitte & Touche. (2002). *Human capital study: Creating shareholder value through people*. Toronto: Deloitte & Touch.

Deloitte & Touche. (2003). *2003/2004 state of the human resources function in Canada*. Toronto: Deloitte & Touche.

Department of Trade and Industry. (2004). Company law: Draft regulations on the operating and financial review and directors' report. Retrieved 12 January 2007 from CBI website: http://www.cbi.org.uk/ndbs/positiondoc.nsf/1f08ec61711f29768025672a0055f7a8/35DFBCB81E2845CC80256F56003C CEC5/$file/ofrregs0504.pdf

DiBartolomeo, D., & Kurtz, L. (1999). Managing risk exposures of socially screened portfolios. Working paper. Northfield University. Retrieved 5 September 2007 from http://www.northinfo.com/files.asp

Eurosif. (2003). *Socially responsible investment among European institutional investors 2003 report*. Retrieved 9 September 2007 from Eurosif website: http://www.eurosif.org/publications/sri_studies

Feltmate, B., Schofield, B., & Yachnin, R. (2001). *Sustainable development, value creation and the capital markets*. Ottawa: Conference Board of Canada.

Geczy, C., Stambaugh, R., & Levin, D. (2003). *Investing in socially responsible mutual funds*. Philadelphia: Wharton School, University of Pennsylvania.

Global Reporting Initiative. (2002). *Sustainability reporting guidelines*. Boston: Author.

Grant, R. (1991). The resource-based theory of competitive advantage: Implications for strategy formulation. *California Management Review, 17*, 114–135.

Grant, R. (1996). Toward a knowledge-based theory of the firm [Special issue]. *Strategic Management Journal, 17*(Winter), 109–22.

Gribben, C., & Faruk, A. (2004). *Will UK pension funds become more responsible? A survey of trustees*. London: UK Social Investment Forum Just Pension programme.

Hart, S., & Milstein, M. (2003). Creating sustainable value. *Academy of Management Executive, 17*(2), 11–18.

Heaps, T. (2004). Responsible investing guide. *Corporate Knights, 2*(3), 19–30.

Hueslid, M. (1995). The impact of human resource management: An agenda for the 1990's. *International Journal of Human Resource Management, 1*(1), 17–42.

Innovest. (2003). *New alpha source for asset managers: Environmentally enhanced investment portfolios.* New York: Author.

Innovest. (2004). *Innovest releases new study: Rebuts Wharton's.* New York: Author.

Interbrand. (2003, 4 August). The top 100 brands. *Business Week,* 72–78.

Johnson, G., & Scholes, K. (1999). *Exploring corporate strategy* (5th ed.). London: Prentice Hall.

Kasemir, B., & Suëss, A. (2002). *Sustainability information and pension fund investment.* Cambridge: Environment and Natural Resources Program, Kennedy School of Government, Harvard University.

Kaufman, H. (2000). *On money and markets: A Wall Street memoir.* New York: McGraw-Hill.

Kingsmill, D., Alexander, H., Bellinger, P., Bishop, D., Dawson, S., Goodwin, F., et al. (2003). *Accounting for people: Report of the task force on human capital management.* London: U.K. Government.

Kotter, J., & Heskett, J. (1992). *Corporate culture and performance.* New York: Free Press.

KPMG/Ipsos-Reid. (2004, 19 January). Ninth annual survey of Canada's most respected corporations: 2003 survey results. *Globe and Mail,* p. B1.

Low, J., & Cohen Kalafut, P. (2004). *Clear advantage: Building shareholder value.* Washington, DC: Global Environmental Management Initiative.

MacDonald, J. (2003). The top 100 pension funds. *Benefits Canada, 27*(4), 40–52.

Mansley, M. (2000). *Socially responsible investment: A guide for pension funds and institutional investors.* Sudbury, U.K.: Monitor.

Mansley, M. (2002). *Health and safety indicators for institutional investors: A report to the health and safety executive.* London: Claros Consulting.

Margolis, J.D., & Walsh, J.P. (2001). *People and profits? The search for a link between a company's social and financial performance.* Mahwah, NJ: Erlbaum.

Mathias, A. (2003). Morley wins UK's largest SRI mandate. *Environmental Finance,* 23 October, 11.

Milevsky, M., Aziz, A., Goss, A., Comeault, J., & Wheeler, D. (2006). Cleaning a passive index. *Journal of Portfolio Management, 32*(3), 110–18.

Mintzberg, H., Ahlstrand, B., & Lampel, J. (1998). *Strategy safari: A guided tour through the wilds of strategic management.* New York: Free Press.

Mutual Fund Review. (2002, Spring). SRI: A brave new world? *Mutual Fund Review,* Spring, 6–15.

Nahapiet, J., & Ghoshal, S. (1998). Social capital, intellectual capital and the organizational advantage. *Academy of Management Review, 23*(2), 242–66.

O'Reilly, C.A., III, & Pfeffer, J. (2000). *Hidden value: How great companies achieve extraordinary results with ordinary people*. Boston: Harvard Business School Press.

OECD. (2000). *The OECD guidelines for multinational enterprises*. Paris: Author.

OECD. (2004). *OECD statistical databases: Financial assets of institutional investors in $U.S. millions*. Paris: Author.

Patton, M. (2002). *Qualitative research and evaluation methods* (3rd ed.). Thousand Oaks, CA: Sage.

Porter, M. (1985). *Competitive advantage*. New York: Free Press.

Robinson, J. (2002). *Workers' capital and corporate social responsibility*. Global Unions Group Discussion Paper. Retrieved 7 September 2007 from International Labour Organization website: http://www.ilo.org/public/english/dialogue/actrav/publ/130/11.pdf

Social Investment Forum. (2003). *2003 report on socially responsible investing trends in the United States*. Washington, DC: Author.

Social Investment Organization. (2003). *Canadian social investment review 2002: A comprehensive survey of socially responsible investment in Canada*. Toronto: Author.

Southwood, P. (2003). *Reporting on employment practices: PIRC report to the West Midlands Pension Fund*. London: Pension Investments Review Committee.

Statistics Canada. (2002). Quarterly estimates of trusteed pension funds. *30*(1).

Statistics Canada. (2006). Employer pension plans (trusteed pension funds): Third quarter 2005. *The Daily*, 23 March 2005. Retrieved 5 October 2005 from Statistics Canada website: http://www.statcan.ca/Daily/English/060323/d060323d.htm

Stewart, T. (1997, 17 March). Brain power: Who own it ... how they profit from it. *Fortune, 135*, 104–9.

Stiles, P., & Kulvisaechana, S. (2003). *Human capital and performance: A literature review*. Retrieved 10 February 2007 from Accounting for People website: http://www.accountingforpeople.gov.uk/downloads/judge_literature_review.pdf

Thompson, A., & Strickland, A. (1998). *Crafting and implementing strategy: Text and readings* (10th ed.). Boston: Irwin/McGraw-Hill.

Trade Unions Congress. (2003). *Working capital: Institutional investment strategy*. London: Author.

Ulrich, D. (1998). A new mandate for human resources. *Harvard Business Review, 76*(1), 124–34.

Waddock, S., & Graves, S. (1997). Finding the link between stakeholder relations and quality of management. *Journal of Investing, 6*(4), 20–5.

Watson Wyatt. (2002). *Human capital index: Human capital as a lead indicator of shareholder value*. Washington, DC: Author.

Wheeler, D. (2004a). *The resource-based view of strategic management: Organizational capabilities and competences* (Lecture notes). Toronto: Schulich School of Business.

Wheeler, D. (2004b). The successful navigation of uncertainty: Sustainability and the organisation. In R. Burke & C. Cooper (Eds.), *Leading in Turbulent Times* (pp. 182–207). Oxford: Blackwell.

Wheeler, D., Colbert, B., & Freeman, R. E. (2003). Focusing on value: Reconciling corporate social responsibility, sustainability and a stakeholder approach in a network world. *Journal of General Management, 28*(3), 1–28.

World Resources Institute, United Nations Environment Program, & World Business Council for Sustainable Development. (2002). *Tomorrow's markets: Global trends and their implications for business*. Washington, DC: Author.

Yaron, G. (2001). The responsible pension trustee. *Estates, Trusts & Pensions Journal, 20*(4), 305–88.

5 Corporate Governance and Environmental Risk Management: A Quantitative Analysis of 'New Paradigm' Firms

GORDON L. CLARK AND JAMES SALO

The risk-management practices of modern corporations differ significantly in both quality and quantity. These differences are growing in today's marketplace, because the risks facing corporations today are more significant and less understood than ever before. The development in the importance of a firm's intangible assets is a major source of this increasingly complex risk (DeLoach, 2000). Unlike tangible assets, which are physical, like machinery, buildings, and land, intangible assets do not have a physical existence and are therefore significantly more difficult to value by financial analysts. Examples of intangible assets include goodwill, strong brand image, and positive employee morale. Intangible assets cause significant financial risk because they can make firms more vulnerable to outside actors who can affect the firm's financial performance.[1] In response to the growing financial risk, the leaders of some firms dedicate significant resources to proactive risk-mitigation, to lower the threat to intangible assets, while the leaders of other firms choose to overlook or underestimate the importance of intangibles and, instead, focus strictly on managing risks to the firm's tangible assets. In this chapter, these two divergent management styles are developed and a unique indicator is created to place firms into groups characterized by the relative importance of intangibles as an element of their corporate value. Evidence is then presented that suggests that intangible assets may play a role in determining the risk-management practices of modern corporations.

Intangible assets are becoming an essential element for the modern corporation's sustained financial success in today's competitive global marketplace. In order to continue to create attractive profit margins, managers are investing greater amounts of resources into the development and orchestration of these difficult-to-replicate assets as a means of differentiating themselves from the competition (Teece, 2000).

This is why intangible assets, as a proportion of corporate value, have grown from 17% in 1978 to 69% by the end of 1998 (Blair & Kochan, 2000) and are now a key element determining the market value of traditional businesses (Boulton, Libert, & Samek, 2000). In one survey, CEOs claimed that the importance of corporate reputation had grown rapidly over the previous five years and that they expected its importance to continue to grow (Haapaniemi, 2000).

The development and management of a successful global brand image and positive corporate reputation is one dominant method managers use to increase their firm's intangible assets.[2] However, with the development of a significant brand image, corporations create greater firm vulnerability by allowing public scrutiny and increased expectations for both positive financial and 'social' corporate behaviour (Holt, Quelch, & Taylor, 2004). The public sees globally recognized brands and the firms that develop them as powerful institutions that are capable of doing great good and also causing significant harm. If a corporation does not meet the expectations of its stakeholder groups, it risks reputation damage, which can have negative impacts on the financial well-being of the firm.[3] Over 90% of financial analysts agree that a company that fails to manage its reputation will suffer financially (Hill & Knowlton, 2006).

This research examines how the financial structure of firms, particularly the level of investment in intangible assets, affects corporate risk-management practices. It is predicted that firms with a greater dependence on intangibles are more likely to manage environmental and corporate governance risks than firms with a dominant tangible asset financial structure. A secondary objective of this research is to determine if there are major differences between intangible investments by specific home nation as opposed to by industry. We suggest that a firm's industry has greater importance than a firm's home nation in its relation to the level of importance of, and increases in investment in, intangible assets over time. Thus, specific industries are more likely to be at risk of threats to intangibles than industries or firms in particular home nations, and these industries are more keen to manage risks to intangible assets. The hypothesis of this chapter is that firms that have a relatively high dependence on intangible assets, compared to their peers, will manage risks better than firms that depend primarily on tangible assets. In addition, it is expected that firms from tangible heavy industries like industrial manufacturing and utilities will manage risk less proactively than intangible-rich industries like media, banking/ investment, and consumer goods and services.

Corporate governance and environmental performance ratings are used as indicators of management's responsiveness to threats to their intangible assets, particularly threats to corporate reputation and brand image. Corporate governance and environmental performance are justified as indicators of risk for this research, as both are increasingly linked to corporate financial performance,[4] have particularly significant implications for a firm's brand image and corporate reputation,[5] and are becoming central strategic management issues for corporate leadership.[6] In 2003, 24% of CEOs surveyed by Hill and Knowlton stated that the handling of social and environmental issues was a central concern for the protection of corporate reputation. Another sign of managers' growing interest in preventing threats to reputation and brand image is the recent emergence of an information market for performance ratings in a number of these 'non-financial' areas[7] and the rise of brand or reputation consulting firms that manage annual general meetings to protect corporate reputation.[8] Overall, poor corporate governance and environmental performance have become de facto negative 'signals' to the financial market, alerting investors and consumers to questionable corporate behaviour.

In the next section, the modern corporation's rise to power and the evolution of the struggle for corporate control are briefly recounted. The reasons for divergence in management styles between the more traditional 'classical' model and the emerging 'new paradigm' model of the firm are then explained. The subsequent section details the development of the research sample, describes the proprietary data used, and explains the creation of a unique quantitative indicator used to calibrate the significance of intangible assets for each firm. Next, the quantitative methods are described and the results are examined for each of the two main research objectives. The chapter concludes with an evaluative commentary on whether intangible assets, or more broadly, a firm's financial structure, help to determine the extent to which management tries to mitigate potential risks to brand image and corporate reputation and details the implications of this relationship.

Management of the Firm

Over the last 150 years, the modern corporation has become the world's dominant economic institution. The rise to power of the corporation as a business model results from its capacity to combine the capital and the economic power of unlimited numbers of individual people as investors. As early as the sixteenth century, these 'joint stock companies' emerged to bypass the practical limitations of personal partnership firms that depended on owners knowing each other and trusting each other when pooling their money (Bakan, 2004). Joint stock corporations allow firms to have a greater number of owners since they do not require personal relationships, and as a result, they have far greater access to capital and more ability to accumulate it.

Since their creation, joint stock corporations have been troubled by the separation between ownership and management. Unlike personal partnerships, where the firms are commonly owned and managed by the partners, investors in joint stock firms may never have direct contact or communication with the corporation they 'own.' Managers are hired by the owners to run the firm, often without proper accountability, as a result of the diluted ownership of the firm by hundreds of thousands of shareholders, and the owners surrender control of firm-level decision-making to professional managers who administer the firm on their behalf (Berle & Means, 1933). As a result, managers become the dominant actor in decision-making, and the owners' role is reduced to that of capital providers awaiting the pay-off of managers' decisions.

This separation of ownership and control complicates oversight and creates greater potential for corruption (Bakan, 2004). Ultimately, the shift of control from owners to managers allows for economically inefficient agency costs resulting from managers serving their own interests over those of the company's shareholders (Fama, 1965).[9] The increasing distribution of ownership through the mid-twentieth century led to a 'cult of corrupt corporate managers' (Hebb, 2006) – people who were all too willing to serve their own interests ahead of those of the firm's shareholders. This trend was at its apex in Anglo-American capital markets in the 1980s (Hebb, 2006). A number of academic studies revealed that there was a significant loss of economic value resulting from these principal/agent problems in U.S. corporations (Jensen & Meckling, 1976). With the rise of shareholder awareness of these agency problems and a general public distrust of corporations' ultimate objectives, a significant power struggle developed between owners and managers for control of the corporation.[10] It has been argued that these agency problems were caused by a lack of clarity about the purpose of the corporation (Jensen, 2000).

Until the early 1990s, Milton Friedman's dictum that 'the business of business is business' was sufficient to legitimize the 'role of the corporation in society.' This view protected managers' autonomy from the backlash of public perception that corporations were soulless, uncaring, impersonal, and amoral (Clark et al., 2006). This established logic effectively gave management permission to sideline shareholders' and public stakeholders' concern about corporations' long-term responsiveness and contributions to social welfare. Recently, the protective barrier surrounding this adage has been severely weakened. Mechanisms for corporate control that were promoted in the 1980s have now been replaced by shareholder value as the central goal of the modern corporation (Hebb, 2006). The importance of corporate social citizenship has grown as the values of society have changed.

A major influence in the current reorientation is the rise of institutional investors as a dominant market force. Institutional investors have profoundly altered the balance of power between owners and managers by re-centralizing the power of uncountable investors into a functional body that controls enough shares to demand that their concerns be heard by firm management (Clark, 2000; Davis & Steil, 2001; Hawley & Williams, 2000; Monks, 2001).[11] Coalitions of owners, in the form of institutional investors, have been formed and now challenge corporations on issues including governance structures and corporate strategies on climate change.[12] For example, in 2006, 47 corporate governance and 38 environmental resolutions were filed by the Interfaith Center on Corporate Responsibility (ICCR), a largely U.S.-based coalition of faith-based institutional investors (Interfaith Center on Corporate Responsibility, 2006).

With the rise to power of institutional investors and the shift of corporate control back to owners from managers, firms are becoming more accountable. Managers can no longer engage in unilateral corporate decision-making. Institutional investors are now influencing corporate decision-making and helping to push corporations to act in the best interest of shareholder value.[13] Corporate engagement is being used by groups from outside the firm to force management to raise standards across a range of issues including accountability, transparency, and social and environmental standards. Institutional investors have used corporate engagement to enhance shareholder value against entrenched self-interested managers (Clark & Hebb, 2004).

Both private/quiet and loud/public mechanisms of corporate engagement are now commonly used by shareholders to influence corporate practices.[14] While the preferred method of corporate engagement is direct private dialogue, out of the public view (Bogle, 2005), institutional investors are also using approaches that are more contentious. These approaches include mounting dissident shareholder resolution campaigns to raise concerns publicly at annual general meetings (AGMs) or utilizing other negative media attention against the corporation (Clark & Hebb, 2004).[15] This can lead to heightened scrutiny on a variety of social, environmental, and corporate governance issues (Clark et al., 2006). Overall, a number of recent changes in the market have led to an increased accountability of firm management and a broadening of the types of issues that managers must tackle to include social, environmental, and corporate governance standards.

Firm Management: The Classical and the New Paradigm

This chapter argues that the management of firms has begun to diverge into two separate frameworks: the 'classical model' and the emergent 'new paradigm model.' Conceptualizing these two differing models is essential to this research because they are the extreme forms of two styles of corporate management, which the quantitative findings of this chapter suggest manage risk differently. This section defines these two models by their historical context, asset structure, and resulting market positions. This is followed by a discussion of how these differences affect risk management behaviour.

The classical model was the traditional form of management that the 20th-century corporation followed. Classical model firms have a large amount of physical and tangible assets to be used in the production of revenue, commonly in the form of plants, factories, equipment, and organizational protocols, which they have inherited through mergers and acquisitions or accumulated over a significant period of time. That is to say, classical model firms tend to be older than new paradigm firms and have a financial composition that is made up primarily of tangible assets. They depend on the plants and equipment they own to drive the financial performance of the firm, as well as to act as financial barriers against the entry of potential competition.[16] Classical model firms tend to focus on selling specific products, not services, and as a result tend to have a limited ability to respond to changes in the market.

In contrast, the new paradigm firms are relatively young. They have been formed in the past 25 years through technological and organizational innovations (Zingales, 2000), or they are firms that have shifted away from a classical model as a result of pioneering strategic management practices.[17] The financial structure of these new paradigm firms differs significantly from classical model firms as they have two types of assets: tangible (e.g., manufacturing plants, equipment) and intangible (e.g., intellectual property, brand image). The managers of new paradigm firms continuously discount their firm's tangible assets in favour of developing their intangible assets (Roberts, 2004). Intangible assets include corporate knowledge, competence, intellectual property, brands, corporate reputation, and customer relationships (Teece, 2002). To these new paradigm firms, the scale of their tangible assets is less important than their organizational flexibility. Many of these firms take advantage of extensive international networks of suppliers and have a global market for their wares. They manage these supplier networks through contractual commitments that allow them to benefit from competition between potential suppliers for specified time-term contracts. New paradigm firms use their capacity for innovation and market leadership as a competitive advantage, as it allows them to evolve quickly and complement changing market tastes and preferences.

The rise of these new paradigm firms stems from the growth in the value and the significance of intangible assets. This growth is a result of the change in corporate competition and wealth creation that has come about through the decreased cost of information flow, the liberalization of product and labour markets, and the deregulation of financial flows (Teece, 2000). As corporations are becoming more reliant on the continuous innovation of products, processes, and organizational designs for their financial survival and growth (Lev, 2001), greater numbers are likely to evolve into a new paradigm model of management. In addition, the increasing power of investors (particularly institutional investors), insurers, and global competitors has changed the market, promoting new paradigm firms. Many issues that were previously considered social have started to become key strategic management issues for corporations, thus pushing management towards a new paradigm style of risk mitigation.

In its extreme form, the management of classical model firms is an entrenched style and is disconnected from the rest of the world in a number of ways. The managers of these firms are responsive only to information that originates within the firm, or information that is developed by the firm's leadership. Managers of these firms have a confrontational attitude towards suggestions from external groups including shareholders, regulators, and insurers, because these managers are accustomed to weak corporate governance structures and practices that afforded them almost sole control of the corporation. These managers try to keep as much information as possible private within the firm, avoiding transparency in order to limit the amount of information that could be leveraged against them. Therefore, the information is unavailable to investors, and, in general, to the global marketplace. This causes an information asymmetry between firms' managers and the market. In many cases, important performance information is not collected or analysed.

The ability of managers to remain entrenched in limiting the disclosure of information is diminishing. There has recently been a significant increase in disclosure requirements and in the creation of a number of voluntary initiatives that call upon all firms to disclose greater amounts of information. This loss of information control by the firm allows for greater pressure and influence from groups outside of the firm. This means that firms are becoming more sensitive to the pressures and demands of shareholders, stakeholders, the media, and the public in general. Overall, this increased sensitivity to outside pressures is leading to a more equal balance of power between corporate managers and investor-shareholders. This development allows for better governmental oversight, more accountability, and lower risk, and ultimately leads to greater shareholder value. These trends are prompting more firms to transition to a new paradigm model.

The managers of new paradigm firms are likely to be more responsive to these outside pressures because of the potential loss in value of their intangible asset holdings. New paradigm managers understand that protecting intangibles like corporate reputation and brand image against risk is essential in order to have stable and sustainable financial performance in today's marketplace. The divestment in corporations that were supporting apartheid in South Africa in the early 1980s was perhaps the first major signal to large corporations that there was significant financial risk associated with being unresponsive to the interests of this new type of consumer, particularly institutional investors. New paradigm firms, therefore, are likely to be responsive to input from groups external to the firm, to participate in collaborations and voluntary initiatives, and to utilize non-financial performance ratings to inform their decision-making and lower their risk profile. These new paradigm firms do this proactively in order to minimize risk to their intangible assets and in order to gain trust from their stakeholders.

A hypothesis has been constructed in this chapter that there are two progressively divergent risk-management models used by firm managers. In the remainder of this chapter, a method of testing this hypothesis is developed and implications and conclusions are drawn from the study results. In order to conduct this analysis, a quantitative indicator for classifying firms by the importance of their intangible assets is developed by utilizing financial data from three proprietary databases. The unique corporate performance data that allow the testing of the research question are introduced in the next section. This is followed by a description of the quantitative methods used for determining how well the firms in these classes are managing risks to their intangible assets.

It is expected that firms with a high dependence on intangible assets will manage risks better than firms that depend primarily on tangible assets. It is also expected that classical model firms will be from tangible-heavy industries like industrial manufacturing and utilities, whereas intangible-rich new paradigm firms will be from industries like media, banking/investment, and consumer goods and service companies. It is expected that there will be considerable differences in the significance of intangibles and therefore a difference in the risk-management practices between industries.

Calibration of Intangible Assets

In order meet the objectives of this chapter, a criterion must be established for quantitatively distinguishing firms with relatively high amounts of intangibles from those firms with relatively low amounts of intangibles (firms that primarily hold tangible assets). This classification allows evaluation of differences in how firms manage potential risks to corporate reputation or brand image. The strategy applied to answer the chapter's research questions is an empirical analysis of quantitative data from three proprietary databases: the Credit Suisse First Boston (CSFB) Holt database on corporate financial performance, which provides data on intangible assets and financial structure; the Innovest database on corporate environmental performance; and the Deminor database on corporate governance performance. These last two databases provide quantitative ratings of corporate strategic risk-management practices.

Past research in corporate performance has not had a useful and comprehensive quantitative indicator of intangible assets. To separate firms into high intangible and low intangible groups, these studies have, instead, used very rough indicators like a firm's industry, its ratio of research and development (R&D), or its advertising expenses to total assets (for example, see Doukas & Padmanabhan, 2002). Our research benefits from the use of an advanced and standardized firm-specific indicator of intangible assets, which is calculated using financial data from the CSFB Holt database on corporate financial performance. The CSFB Holt database is one of the most comprehensive financial performance databases available. CSFB Holt's primary clients are institutional investors and money managers who pay subscriptions to access its information. Of importance for this research is the fact that CSFB Holt has compiled and standardized corporate financial information for 17,000 firms globally (Credit Suisse First Boston – Holt, 2006). This information can be used to compare corporations against each other, regardless of home nation or industry.[18]

Innovest Strategic Value Advisors provided the corporate environmental performance data that are used in this research. Innovest assesses the environmental performance of approximately 90% of firms included in the world's primary stock market indices, which include the S&P 500, the FTSE 350, the FTSE EuropeTop, the Nikkei, and MSCI world indices. Innovest's ratings are independently determined and, unlike in many rating agencies, investors rather than firms pay for the ratings. Innovest's rating system is broken down into four main categories and then divided into 15 subcategories that, when combined, provide the overall rating of the firm. Each of the Innovest rating scores and sub-scores for firms is directly comparable, regardless of its industry and national jurisdiction. The four major categories are *profit opportunities, risk improvement, management performance*, and *environmental strategy*. The category of *profit opportunities* measures corporations' current and potential competitiveness in environmental opportunities. *Risk improvement* estimates firms' environmental risks and liabilities and evaluates how well they are being managed. *Management performance* evaluates the quality of essential environmental management practices including audit, disclosure, and impact assessment. *Environmental strategy* appraises a corporation's stated policies on the integration of environmental performance into the firm's business strategy, planning, and corporate culture.

Innovest's key strength is that its data collection is based on intensive interviews with senior executives and comprehensive evaluation of public and private firm-specific information. This gives Innovest the advantage of using information that would not be available to its clients unless they were directly and intensively engaged with specific firms. It promotes its data collection method and standardized ratings as an important 'information market' that adds value to the investment process by introducing new information and decision criteria not available to other rating agencies. Innovest has created a unique market niche that justifies the firm's premium charge for the information it gathers.

Deminor Rating, a corporate governance–rating agency, provided the third proprietary database.[19] Deminor rates corporate governance standards and practices and sells the standardized rating information to institutional investors. Since 2000, Deminor has rated firms listed in the FTSE Eurotop 300 Index on approximately 300 different governance criteria. Deminor ratings are based exclusively on publicly available information, with the major sources being corporate websites, news articles, and stock exchange announcements. For this research, the data are limited to the scores of the four major categories and the overall corporate governance score. These four categories, representing major pillars of corporate governance, are *rights and duties of shareholders, range of takeover defences, disclosure on corporate governance*, and *board structure and functioning. Rights and duties of shareholders* estimates if shareholders can exert sufficient pressure on firm corporate decision-making. *Range of takeover defences* evaluates a firm's hostile takeover prevention amendments that shelter the management from threat of replacement. *Disclosure on corporate governance* rates the availability and quality of information about a firm's corporate governance and financial practices that are publicly available to shareholders. *Board structure and functioning analyses* the firm's board composition, including diversity and experience of members, and the election practices, as well as remuneration and board functioning.

To allow for empirical analysis, the ratings and values from the three databases were organized and compiled into a single database.[20] The data were prepared first by creating two research samples: first, all firms that were rated by the corporate governance database and CSFB Holt; and second, all the firms that were rated by the environmental performance database and by CSFB Holt. These two samples included 164 and 274 firms respectively. Next, a unique indicator was created to classify firms according to the importance of intangible assets compared to tangible assets. A ratio using CSFB Holt's value for *goodwill* divided by the value for *plant assets* was chosen as the intangible importance indicator. *Goodwill*, as defined by the CSFB Holt database, is the amount that the firm's purchase price exceeds its net tangible assets.

Plant assets are defined as the monetary value, after depreciation, of all of the firm's tangible fixed assets used in the production of revenue.

Analysis

The objective of the following quantitative analysis is to empirically test whether there are differences in corporations' risk-management behaviour, depending on their relative investment in intangible assets, as a part of their overall financial structure. A second key objective of this research is to empirically test whether a firm's industry or home nation is related to its relative investment in intangibles. The remainder of this analysis section explains the quantitative analyses used to meet these two research objectives and then reports the empirical findings.

Asset Structure and Risk-Management Behaviour

In order to determine whether investment in intangible assets is related to firm risk-management practices, three types of analyses were utilized. First, a bivariate analysis was used to test for direct correlations between risk management, indicated by corporate governance and environmental performance ratings, and the significance of intangible assets within the firm's asset structure.[21] For this analysis, a Spearman's rank correlation coefficient was used to indicate the statistical significance between the variables. Second, a non-parametric median testing method was used to compare the sample firms,[22] which were classified into groups representing high, average, and low relative significance of intangible assets in order to look for risk-management score differences in 2004 (see Table 5.1).[23] This second analysis used the *goodwill / plant assets* intangible-importance indicator to divide the firms into three groups of roughly equal number. In order to assess if firms with greater investment in intangible assets have been responding to risks more than their peers, the non-parametric median scores were further utilized to examine the three intangible asset classes for differences in the change in risk-management performance scores between 2000 and 2004 (see Table 5.2). Third, beta and sigma measures of convergence were calculated between 2000 and 2004 for our samples, in order to assess whether convergence in the importance of intangible assets occurred during our study period (see Table 5.3).[24]

The results of the bivariate cross-analysis showed no signs of a direct relationship between the intangible significance indicator (goodwill %

Table 5.1. Median Values by Level of Intangibles.

	High	Medium	Low	Overall
Corporate governance performance – Deminor (n = 164)				
Rights & duties of shareholders	7.50**	6.50*	7.00	7.00
Range of takeover defences	4.50**	1.00	1.00	3.50
Disclosure on corporate governance	7.50	7.50**	7.50	7.50
Board structure & functioning	6.50	5.50*	6.50	6.00
Environmental disclosure sub-score	**10.00**	**10.00**	**10.00**	**10.00**
Overall corporate governance	**25.25***	**22.00**	**22.50**	**23.00**
Environmental performance – Innovest (n = 274)				
Audit	5.00	6.25**	4.63**	3.00
Certification	4.00	4.00	3.75	5.00
Corporate governance	5.00	5.67*	4.83**	4.00
Training & development	5.00*	6.00	5.00	5.00
Accounting & reporting	4.00	5.00	5.00	5.00
Management systems	5.00	7.00**	5.00**	5.00
Opportunity	6.10	6.00	6.20	5.25
Strategy	5.45	6.80	5.55	6.00
Historic liabilities	6.00	5.00	6.00	5.60
Industry specific risk	5.25	4.83**	6.00**	6.00
Leading & sustainability risk indicators	5.48	5.58	5.54	5.00
Operating risk	5.40	5.48	5.50	5.50
Performance	5.50	5.50	6.00	5.50
Products & materials	5.00	5.50	5.00	5.00
Strategic competence	5.00	6.00**	5.00	5.00
Overall environmental	**3.00**	**3.50**	**3.00**	**3.00**

Calculations are based on data provided by CFSB Holt, Innovest, and Deminor Rating.
Note: Significance at 10% (*), 5% (**), and 1% (***).

of plant value) and any of the corporate governance or environmental performance ratings, suggesting that there is no relationship between the importance of intangibles to a corporation and its risk management. On the other hand, the non-parametric median test, summarized below, found results that suggest a positive relationship between intangible assets and higher corporate risk-management practices.

The high intangible group scored significantly higher than the medium intangible group for the corporate governance performance indicator *rights & duties of shareholders*, and was 0.50 higher than the overall sample median. In addition, this same group scored signifi-

Table 5.2. Change in Intangible/Tangible Values by Level of Intangibles.

	High	Medium	Low	Overall
Corporate governance performance – Deminor (n = 164)				
Rights & duties of shareholders	4.00*	3.50	4.00	4.00
Range of takeover defences	1.75	0.00**	2.00	1.00
Disclosure on corporate governance	4.00	4.00	4.00	4.00
Board structure & functioning	3.00	3.50*	3.00	3.00
Environmental disclosure sub-score	**5.00**	**5.00**	**5.00***	**5.00**
Overall corporate governance	**12.75**	**12.00**	**13.00**	**12.50**
Environmental performance – Innovest (n = 274)				
Audit	0.00	0.00	0.00**	0.00
Certification	0.00	(–)0.90*	–0.67	–0.53
Corporate governance	0.00	(–)0.27*	–0.10	–0.07
Training & development	–0.45	0.00	0.00	0.00
Accounting & reporting	–0.03	0.05	0.30	0.30
Management systems	0.00	–0.13	–0.10	0.00
Opportunity	0.35	0.00	0.00	0.10
Strategy	0.05	0.30	0.20	0.10
Historic liabilities	0.10	0.00	0.00	0.00
Industry specific risk	0.00	0.00	0.03	0.15
Leading & sustainability risk indicators	0.00**	0.20	0.20	0.23
Operating risk	0.15	0.20	0.02	0.05
Performance	0.30	0.00	0.10*	0.00
Products & materials	0.00	–0.02	–0.12	0.00
Strategic competence	0.00	0.00	0.00	0.00
Overall environmental	**0.02**	**0.00**	**0.00**	**0.00**

Calculations are based on data provided by CFSB Holt, Innovest, and Deminor Rating.
Note: Significance at 10% (*), 5% (**), and 1% (***).

cantly higher than the rest of the sample (4.50**, compared to an overall sample median of 3.50) for *range of takeover defences*. It is also interesting to note that the high intangibles group had a statistically significant greater overall corporate governance score when compared to the overall median (25.25** for high, compared to an overall sample median of 23.00).

These findings were supported by the non-parametric analysis of environmental performance, where there were four statistically significant findings. The medium intangible firms' median performance scores were statistically higher than low intangible firms in measures of *audit, environmental corporate governance*, and *management systems*. The

Table 5.3. Convergence of Ratings.

	Spearman's Rho	SD 2000	% of M	SD 2004	% of M	Absolute change in SD	Relative change in SD
Corporate governance performance – Deminor (n = 164)							
Rights & duties of shareholders	(−)0.421**	1.17	40.25	1.22	18.09	0.05	−22.16
Range of takeover defences	0.018	1.51	65.16	3.43	79.91	1.92	14.75
Disclosure on corporate governance	(−)0.730***	1.38	44.02	0.96	13.25	−0.42	−30.76
Board structure & functioning	(−)0.604***	1.42	50.77	1.22	20.22	0.20	−30.56
Environmental disclosure sub-score	**(−)0.708*****	**3.06**	**76.50**	**2.45**	**23.10**	**−0.61**	**−47.98**
Overall corporate governance	**(−)0.099**	**3.06**	**35.42**	**5.62**	**28.52**	**1.69**	**−12.32**
Intangibles/plant (164)	0.191*	4774.41	1013.40	189.80	23.10	−4597.19	−823.60
Environmental performance – Innovest (n = 274)							
Audit	(−)0.449**	2.64	50.58	3.07	0.63	0.43	−49.95
Certification	(−)0.223**	2.94	65.50	2.90	0.98	−0.04	−64.52
Corporate governance	(−)0.500**	2.18	44.33	2.46	0.54	0.28	−43.79
Training & development	(−)0.297**	2.69	50.56	2.91	0.57	0.22	−49.99
Accounting & reporting	(−)0.448**	2.63	53.52	2.86	0.60	0.23	−52.92
Management systems	(−)0.440**	2.44	45.54	2.88	0.58	0.44	−44.97
Opportunity	(−)0.288**	1.56	25.95	1.53	0.25	−0.03	−25.70
Strategy	(−)0.490***	2.37	41.05	2.46	0.41	0.09	−40.64
Historic liabilities	(−)0.321**	2.57	45.54	2.48	0.41	−0.09	−45.13
Industry specific risk	(−)0.442**	2.25	43.12	97.51	−9.76	95.26	−52.88
Leading & sustainability risk indicators	(−)0.519**	1.91	35.45	1.92	0.34	0.01	−35.10
Operating risk	(−)0.479**	2.08	38.16	1.93	0.33	−0.15	−37.83
Performance	(−)0.509**	2.43	45.31	2.79	0.54	0.36	−44.77
Products & materials	(−)0.358***	2.50	49.43	2.68	0.60	0.18	−48.83
Strategic competence	(−)0.432**	2.37	43.78	2.82	0.53	0.45	−43.25
Overall environmental	**(−)0.357*****	**1.87**	**57.41**	**1.75**	**0.49**	**−0.11**	**−56.93**
Intangibles/plant (274)	−0.067	333.84	225.20	331.69	2.57	−2.14	−222.62

Calculations are based on data provided by CFSB Holt, Innovest, and Deminor Rating.
Note: Significance at 10% (*), 5% (**), and 1% (***).

fourth statistically significant score had low firms scoring higher than medium firms for industry-specific risks.[25] A possible explanation for this result is that particular industries have greater environmental risks than others (see Salo, 2005a), and also that particular industries have a greater reliance on intangible assets than others, but that these two groups do not necessarily overlap.[26] Medium intangible firms also scored higher than the rest of the sample in *strategic competence* (6.00***, compared to an overall sample median of 5.00).

The empirical examination of the change in risk-management performance between 2000 and 2004 yielded no additional evidence of a relationship between level of intangible assets and risk-management performance. However, it should be noted that the relative significance of intangibles grew overall in both samples (between 2000 and 2004, increased by 17.57 in the sample of 164 and by 5.3 in the sample of 274), perhaps suggesting that managers are recognizing the importance of intangibles and are investing more heavily in them (see Table 5.5).

The examination utilizing beta and sigma indicators of convergence did not provide any evidence of convergence in the importance of intangible assets for the entire sample of firms. In the sample of 164, the Spearman's rho beta indicator (.191**) suggested a slight divergence in the amount of intangibles (see the Spearman rho and Intangibles/plant [164] cell in Table 5.3). Conversely, the values of the sigma indicators, which were both highly negative, suggest convergence was occurring (see absolute and relative change in standard deviation and the cells that intersect with *intangibles/plant* [164] and *intangibles/plant* [274] in Table 5.3). In summary, there is no significant evidence that goodwill % of plant value converged or diverged between 2000 and 2004, which suggests that firms are not significantly changing the way that they are investing in intangible assets.

Industries and Nation Effects on Corporate Asset Structure

In order to determine whether differences in the importance of intangibles are related to a particular industry or home nation, we again utilized the three types of analyses that were used above. The analyses were run specifically on corporations grouped into their particular industries and home nations, in order to compare and assess them against the other industries, home nations, and the overall sample. First, the non-parametric median testing methodology was used to examine differences in performance between particular nations or industries and the rest of the study sample. This analysis was used to examine differences in risk-management performance between industries and home nations in 2004 and to look for change in performance between 2000 and 2004 (see Tables 5.4 and 5.5). Second, beta and sigma indicators of convergence were employed to examine each industry and nation for differences in convergence in the relative amount of investment in intangible assets.

The empirical results suggest that there are few national differences in the importance of intangible assets, but that industries differ widely in the importance of intangible assets. For home nations, France scored significantly higher on the goodwill % of plant indicator (73.48*** over a total median of 33.62) and Belgium lower (with a score of 22.26*) in the sample of 164. Finland was the only nation in the sample of 274 to be significantly different from the median, with a score of 8.02** compared to the overall median of 27.58.

For industries, banks (56.29**), capital goods (83.09**), media (122.45***), food, beverage, & tobacco (138.88**), and insurance (193.26*) fell well over the median for significance of intangibles for the sample of 164 (33.62). Falling significantly below the median were energy firms (3.93***), automobiles & components (4.71***), and utilities (8.47**). In the sample of 274, the score for consumer services (92.92*) and materials (32.23*) was significantly different from that of the overall sample median of 27.58.

The results of the findings for change in importance of intangibles during the study period (2000 to 2004) support the above results, and further suggest that importance of intangibles is more dependent on its industry than home nation.

For home nations, only the scores for France (34.05**, compared to an overall median of 17.57 in the sample of 164) and Italy (25.45**, compared to an overall median of 5.30 in the sample of 274) were significantly different from the median of their respective samples.

For industries, in the sample of 164 food, beverage, & tobacco (684.13***), insurance (160.20*), and technology, hardware, & equipment (62.30*) fall well above the sample-wide median of 17.57. While automobiles & components (1.47**), diversified financials (0.00**), and energy (-2.20*) had the least, or a decrease in the level of importance of intangibles. In the sample of 274, telecommunication services (153.92**) had the largest growth in intangibles, followed by food & staples retailing (71.68*), compared against an overall median of 5.30. For this sample, software & services (1.10*) changed the least.

Table 5.4. Median Intangible Values by Nation and Industry.

	N = 164	N = 274
Median	33.63	27.59
Nation		
Belgium	22.26*	98.72
Denmark	0.14	432.14
Finland	4.97	8.02**
France	73.48***	57.09
Germany	37.90	47.69
Ireland	37.77	48.41
Italy	21.70	33.17
Netherlands	16.01	24.07
Norway	0.97	0.97
Spain	13.60	31.73
Sweden	86.79	23.42
Switzerland	44.58	32.15
United Kingdom	28.64	23.18
Industry		
Automobiles & components	4.71***	17.03
Banks	56.29**	17.43
Capital goods	83.09**	32.63
Commercial services & supplies	28.55	14.52
Consumer durables & apparel	36.38	10.18
Consumer services	214.80	92.92*
Diversified financials	0.00	0.00
Energy	3.93***	27.40
Food & staples retailing	20.89	59.68
Food, beverage, & tobacco	138.88**	43.47
Health-care equipment & services	106.94	35.83
Household & personal products	13.11	0.38
Insurance	193.26*	35.16
Materials	27.40*	32.23*
Media	122.45***	32.71
Pharmaceuticals & biotechnology	24.99	175.12
Real estate retailing	0.00	10.53
Retailing	75.31	45.37
Semiconductors & semiconductor equipment	1.77	8.58
Software & services	101.66	27.50
Technology, hardware, & equipment	52.26	30.23
Telecommunication services	37.89	24.42
Transportation	4.28	14.69
Utilities	8.47**	13.92

Calculations are based on data provided by CFSB Holt, Innovest, and Deminor Rating.
Note. Significance at 10% (*), 5% (**), and 1% (***).

Table 5.5. Change in Intangible/Tangible Values by Nation and Industry.

	$N = 164$	$N = 274$
Median	17.57	5.30
Nation		
Belgium	0.00	183.35
Denmark	0.06	524.58
Finland	130.76	8.99
France	34.05**	23.00
Germany	18.33	52.28
Ireland	508.02	980.00
Italy	14.56	25.45**
Netherlands	0.00	0.00
Norway	0.22	0.22
Spain	2.80	33.78
Sweden	20.34	54.63
Switzerland	51.97	26.75
United Kingdom	1.89	7.63
Industry		
Automobiles & components	1.47**	15.74
Banks	26.81	5.44
Capital goods	90.24	17.94
Commercial services & supplies	41.51	15.49
Consumer durables & apparel	39.52	9.38
Consumer services	−438.97	22.37
Diversified financials	0.00**	50.22
Energy	(−)2.20*	107.90
Food & staples retailing	11.44**	71.68*
Food, beverage, & tobacco	684.13***	42.90
Health-care equipment & services	223.52	−0.32
Household & personal products	34.61	12.75
Insurance	160.20*	20.43
Materials	23.75	11.06
Media	63.55	10.16
Pharmaceuticals & biotechnology	15.46	−70.02
Real estate retailing	NA	−0.95
Retailing	1807.30	0.00
Semiconductors & semiconductor equipment	11.85	6.75
Software & services	140.47	1.10*
Technology, hardware, & equipment	62.30*	12.30
Telecommunication services	17.36	153.92**
Transportation	8.38	3.91
Utilities	9.70*	8.93*

Calculations are based on data provided by CFSB Holt, Innovest, and Deminor Rating.
Note. Significance at 10% (*), 5% (**), and 1% (***).

The empirical results for convergence of relative importance of intangibles between 2000 and 2004 did not vary between home nations and industrial sectors. There were no statistically significant findings suggesting differences in the convergence of intangibles between particular nations or industries and the overall sample medians.

Conclusions and Implications

This research assessed the relationship between intangible assets and differences in corporate risk-management practices – an issue that has had no previous empirical examination. A summary of the major findings of this research is listed below and is followed by the overall implications of this research.

There is an indirect and limited relationship between level of importance of intangibles and proactive management of risk. The bivariate analysis resulted in no direct correlations between the importance of intangibles indicator and the ratings of corporate governance and environmental performance. However, using a non-parametric median test methodology, four instances were identified where firms with a greater importance of intangibles scored significantly higher than those with a lower importance of intangibles. There was only one case where low intangible firms scored higher than high intangible firms, for industry-specific risks. However, another one of the findings explains this by showing that particular industries have greater dependence on intangible assets.

The importance of intangibles as a part of firm value is growing but not converging over time. The relative significance of intangibles grew overall in both samples (increased 17.57 in the sample of 164 and 5.3 in the sample of 274 between 2000 and 2004). However, there was no significant evidence that the calculated intangibles metric converged between 2000 and 2004. In fact, in the sample of 164, the Spearman's rho beta indicator suggested a slight divergence in intangibles. This was contradicted by the sigma indicators, which were highly negative, suggesting convergence was occurring. Overall, it is reasonable to conclude that neither significant convergence nor divergence of importance of intangibles was happening for all the firms in the sample. This conclusion is not surprising, as it would be expected that firms from industries with greater dependence on intangibles would continue to increasingly value their importance, while firms from other industries with little dependence on intangible assets would continue not to need to invest in them as significantly.

Firms from specific industries tend to have similar levels of intangibles, but that is not true of firms from particular home nations. The difference in levels of intangibles between industry groups was statistically significant in nine cases within the sample of 164 and in two within the sample of 274. This finding suggests that a firm's industry is strongly related to how important intangible assets are to the firm's financial well-being. Industries that had a high significance of intangible assets were banks, capital goods, consumer services, media, food, beverage & tobacco, and insurance. Industries with low importance of intangibles include utilities, automobiles & components, and energy.

The change in importance of intangibles between 2000 and 2004 differs by industry, but not by home nation. The argument that particular industries differ in how important intangible assets are to them is supported by the results for change in intangible assets between 2000 and 2004. Whereas the results for home nations only had two occurrences where change in intangibles were significantly different from the overall sample median, there were twelve significant occurrences when grouped by industry. The industries with the greatest growth in importance of intangibles were technology, hardware & equipment, insurance, telecommunication services, and food, beverage & tobacco. Industries with the least or negative growth in intangible/tangible ratio were automobiles & components, diversified financials, software & services, utilities, and energy.

There is no clear evidence of convergence or divergence of the intangible/tangible ratio between 2000 and 2004. There were no statistically significant findings that suggested that convergence or divergence of the intangible/tangle ratio changed between 2000 and 2004.

In summary, this research found that a growing number of corporations are depending on intangible assets to help them sustain their financial success (supporting the findings of Boulton et al., 2000) and that the corporations included in this research are investing escalating amounts of their resources into developing their intangible assets (confirming the finding of Blair & Kochan, 2000). These findings support the theory that management is beginning to focus on developing and protecting intangible assets. The results suggest that it is likely that increasing numbers of corporations either will be created with a new paradigm financial structure or will transition to the proactive new paradigm risk-management style.

The results have also shown that the financial structure and significance of intangible assets may affect the risk-management practices of firms. In each case where there are multiple statistically significant findings, the higher intangible class managed risk more effectively (with the exception of the industry-specific risk for the reasons given previously). Therefore, this quantitatively suggests that a dependency on intangible assets makes firms more likely to mitigate risks that threaten corporate reputation and brand image. In a sense, this important finding is not surprising, as firms with a greater brand image or highly visible corporate reputation have more to lose from the negative signals that poor corporate governance or environmental performance release to the market.

A number of important implications arise when one considers that more firms are transitioning towards the new paradigm financial structure and, therefore, new paradigm proactive style of risk management. This agrees with the conclusions of past research that has shown that performance standards for corporate governance and environmental performance have been improving in recent years (for example, see Salo, 2005b, and Wójcik, 2006). The results also suggest that new paradigm firms may be becoming more responsive to the demands of outside actors/stakeholders (institutional investors, media, public opinion, etc). This has implications for the potential success of shareholder resolutions filed against firms at annual general meetings. The findings suggest that filing resolutions against firms for aspirational reasons (high volume of intangible assets and relatively strong financial performance) would have a greater chance for success than those filed for remedial reasons – the targeting of firms with high levels of tangible assets and relatively poor financial performance (see Clark et al., 2006).

The rise in importance of intangible assets within general business is a recent phenomenon. It is likely that the relationship between the significance of a firm's intangible holdings and its risk-management practices will become stronger as the understanding of the importance of intangibles grows within firm management, as the investment in intangibles increases and as the measurement of intangibles improves within the marketplace. This strengthening of the relationship supports Salo (2005a), who suggests that an information market for non-financial corporate performance ratings will continue to grow. Management and investors alike will use the performance rating data from this information market to assess risks to intangible assets and corporate reputation. With the increased availability and use of these sources of non-financial performance ratings, the promotion of environmental and corporate governance standards then have potential to accelerate.[27] This acceleration of the relationship between disclosure and performance, in regard to environmental performance, supports the notion that increased disclosure and measurement promotes higher standards of performance, following Lowenstein's (1996) 'What gets measured gets managed' theory on corporate performance.

In addition, it was found that for the sample of firms covered by this research, typical classical model firms and new paradigm firms are from different industries within the marketplace. Typical classical model firms tended to be from tangible heavy industries like industrial manufacturing and utilities. The majority of new paradigm firms, on the other hand, were from modern industries like media, banking/investment, and consumer goods and services. This is an important finding, as the high intangible industries tend to be the 'future economy industries,' the firms that are rising in power in the 'new economy' as intangibles become more important. The fact that a firm's industry is related to the firm's level of dependence on intangibles is also significant. It suggests that outside pressures, which intangible assets make firms more vulnerable to, are not geographically bound or dependent on an individual nation's legal regimes.

The implications that have been developed here are considerable and significant. Cumulatively, they suggest that intangible assets can cause market pressures to promote higher global standards of corporate governance and environmental performance, while also pushing for strong corporate reputation, shareholder value, and financial performance. These findings support the case for a win-win scenario where firm value is increased (because risk is decreased) and global standards of governance, as well as environmental and social performance, are increased, regardless of geographical and legal boundaries, and without a global governance system.

Notes

1 Risk is also increasing as actors external to corporations are gaining power. In particular, financial and non-financial rating agencies, the media, regulators, and institutional investors have each, in their own way, taken control away from managers and added to the complexity of risk that managers face.
2 For a review of the empirical findings on how strong brands provide firms with competitive marketing advantages, see Hoeffler and Keller (2003).

3 One recent study has showed that consumers internationally choose one brand over another because of its social responsibility, because in addition to its association with cultural ideals and differences they signal in product quality (Holt et al., 2004). We would also expect institutional investors to be interested in reputation, as there is evidence that corporate image is an important strategic factor that needs to be managed in order to maximize long-term shareholder value (Gregory, 2001).

4 Recent studies have shown a positive relationship between corporate environmental and corporate financial performance (Edwards, 1998; Environmental Capital Markets Committee, 2000; Kiernan & Lievinson, 1998). A meta-analysis of the research findings of 52 past studies (which represent the population of prior quantitative inquiry) by Orlitzky, Schmidt, and Rynes (2003) found that corporate virtue in the form of social and environmental responsibility is likely to lead to stronger financial performance. While there have been limited studies examining the connection between corporate governance and financial performance, the studies that have been conducted have generally found a positive relationship (see Black, 2001; De Jong, De Jong, Mertens, & Wasley, 2002; Derwall, Günster, Bauer, & Koedijk, 2004; Drobetz, Shchillhofer, & Zimmermann, 2003; Gompers, Ishii, & Metrick, 2003; La Porta, Lopez-De-Silanes, Shleifer, & Vishny, 2002). These performance improvements may be seen in greater firm profits, reduced costs, improved employee satisfaction and retention, consumer loyalty, and brand reputation in domestic and broadly international markets (Dowell, Hart, & Yeung, 2000; Environmental Capital Markets Committee, 2000; Gomper et al., 2003; Porter & van der Linde, 1995). In addition, investors, including institutional investors, are willing to pay more for firms with strong governance practices (McKinsey, 2000) and will avoid firms they know have poor corporate governance practices (Russell Reynolds, 2000).

5 This has become increasingly true with the growing frequency of firms' poor governance practices or environmental failings appearing in the press. It seems that the media now target corporate governance and environmental performance practices, particularly since the recent massive failures epitomized by Enron and *Exxon Valdez*. Companies that have had crises of reputation, such as Exxon, after the *Valdez* oil spill, and Texaco, after being accused of race discrimination, have seen the market value of their shares drop by billions of dollars (Zingales, 1998). Companies with strong corporate reputations recover financially from these crises more quickly than firms that do not have solid reputations (Knight & Pretty, 2000).

6 Firms are also likely to act because CEOs and management strongly dislike having their names associated with wrongdoing in the media (Fama & Jensen, 1983).

7 For more on this emerging information market, see Salo (2005a).

8 For example, firms like Pearlfisher (http://www.pearlfisher.com), Misukanis & Odden (http://www.misukanisodden.com) and Brunswick Group (http://www.brunswickgroup.com).

9 As discussed in Clark, Hebb, and Salo (2006), agency problems cause shareholders to risk chronic economic underperformance of cash flow compared with the total value of productive assets, higher-than-justified retained earnings by corporate managers for use in self-investment, and finally lower-than-expected dividends or rates of appreciation of corporate stock's market price. This principal-agent problem is of central importance to the modern corporation and to capitalism in the marketplace today (see Pratt & Zeckhauser, 1987).

10 The struggle between owners and managers for corporate power has a long history in both legal and economic literature (Roe, 1994).

11 This observation is true, since institutional investors act on behalf of their beneficiaries, whose primary interest is the maximization of shareholder value of the corporations.

12 For example, the Council of Institutional Investors is made up of 140 pension fund members with assets of over US$3 trillion, who pressure firms on a number of issues to promote shareholder value (Council of Institutional Investors, 2005). The Carbon Disclosure Project is supported by a group of 155 institutional investors representing investment groups holding over US$21 trillion, which asks firms for information to allow them to assess the potential economic risks and opportunities to the corporation relating to climate change (Carbon Disclosure Project, 2005).

13 See Clark (2000) for more on the rise of institutional investors, and Clark and Hebb (2004) and Hawley and Williams (2000) on these institutions' effects on collective welfare. Also, a recent UNEP report (2005) reviews the scale and scope of the institutional investment industry, with particular focus on the potential role that social and environmental considerations could play in investment decision-making.

14 For a comprehensive overview of corporate engagement, its growth, and the factors driving it, see Clark and Hebb (2005).

15 Shareholder resolutions and their effect on corporate performance are examined in detail in Clark et al. (2006).

16 These 'sunk costs' are costs that 'are irrevocably committed to a particular use, and therefore not recoverable in the case of exit' (Mata, 1991). There-

fore, while acting as a protective barrier deterring competition from entry, or facilitating firm-specific expertise, they can also limit the extent of corporate flexibility of capital for use providing products and services.

17 Transitioning from the 'classical model' to the 'new paradigm' might occur following exterior events, such as reputation disasters, or because of visionary leadership/management.

18 Of particular interest to Holt's clients is its financial evaluation of firms, which uses a cash flow methodology that allows for a more accurate assessment of firm value.

19 Deminor's Corporate Governance Rating Service was recently sold to Institutional Shareholder Services (ISS).

20 The use of these databases has been justified in past work (see Salo 2005b) and used successfully in other research (see Clark et al., 2006; Salo, 2005b; Wójcik, 2006).

21 These data are available upon request from the authors.

22 This method was chosen following initial analysis that found that the distribution of ratings in our sample is not normal or symmetric.

23 The statistical significance for the median test results was calculated by using an asymptotic significance value that shows how often a chi-square value is expected to be at least as large as the calculated value in similar repeated samples when there is no relationship between the medians. For example, an asymptotic significance of 0.02 shows us that the probability that the medians are equal is 2 in 100. This method has been used successfully in research utilizing rating data in a similar way (see Wójcik 2006 and Salo 2005b).

24 Researchers have successfully used these three analysis types in the same way that this research utilizes them (see, for example, Wójcik 2006).

25 It is worth pointing out that the median score for "medium" intangible firms was 0.17 below the overall median.

26 For example, a low intangible industry may also have low industry specific environmental risk (for example Software & Services), or a high intangible industry may have a high industry specific environmental risk (for example Consumer Services).

27 We would also expect this to become increasingly true as the managerial understanding of the threat that poor corporate governance and environmental performance pose to corporate reputation and brand image will grow, paralleling management's increased understanding of intangibles. This is in addition to the potential financial performance advantages from corporate governance and environmental performance (Edwards, 1998; EPA, 2000; Kiernan & Lievinson, 1998; McKinsey & Company, 2000; Russell Reynolds Associates, 2000).

References

Bakan, J. (2004). *The corporation: The pathological pursuit of power and profit*. New York: Vintage.

Berle, A., & Means, B. (1933). *The modern corporation and private property* (rev. ed.). New York: Harcourt, Brace and World.

Black, B. (2001). Does corporate governance matter? A crude test using Russian data. *University of Pennsylvania Law Review, 149*, 2131–50.

Blair, M., & Kochan, T. (2000). *The new relationship: Human capital in the American corporation*. Washington: Brookings Institution Press.

Bogle, J.C. (2005). *The battle for the soul of capitalism*. New Haven: Yale University Press.

Boulton, R., Libert, B., & Samek, S. (2000). *Cracking the value code: How successful businesses are creating wealth on the new economy*. Toronto: HarperCollins.

Carbon Disclosure Project. (2005). *About the Carbon Disclosure Project (CDP)*. Retrieved 17 December 2005 from CDP website: http://www.cdproject.net/

Clark, G.L. (2000). *Pension fund capitalism*. Oxford: Oxford University Press.

Clark, G.L., & Hebb, T. (2004). Pension fund corporate engagement: The fifth stage of capitalism. *Relations industrielles / Industrial Relations, 59*, 142–71.

Clark, G.L., & Hebb, T. (2005). Why should they care? The role of institutional investors in the market for corporate global responsibility. *Environment and Planning A, 37*(11), 2015–31.

Clark, G.L., Hebb, T., & Salo, J. (2006). Shareholder activism in the public spotlight: Social investors' resolutions at U.S. corporate annual general meetings, 2001–2004. Retrieved 17 December 2006 from Pensions at Work website: http://www.pensionsatwork.ca/english/pdfs/clark_wpg06_02.pdf

Council of Institutional Investors. (2005). *Welcome*. Retrieved 17 December 2006 from Council of Institutional Investors website: http://www.cii.org/

Credit Suisse First Boston – Holt. (2006). *About Holt*. Retrieved 10 February 2006 from Credit Suisse website: http://www.csfb.com/institutional/csfb_holt/about_holt.shtml

Davis, E., & Steil, B. (2001). *Institutional investors*. Cambridge: MIT Press.

De Jong, A., De Jong, D., Mertens, G., & Wasley, C. (2002). *The role of self-regulation in corporate governance: Evidence from the Netherlands*. Working report. No. FR 00-20. Tilburg: Simon School of Business.

DeLoach, J. (2000). *Enterprise-wide risk management*. London: Financial Times, Prentice Hall.

Derwall, J., Günster, N., Bauer, R., & Koedijk, K. (2004). The eco-efficiency premium puzzle. *Financial Analysts Journal, 61*(2), 51–63.

Doukas, J., & Padmanabhan, P. (2002). The operational hedging properties of intangible assets: The case of non-voluntary foreign asset selloffs. *Journal of International Financial Management and Accounting, 13*(3), 183–213.

Dowell, G., Hart, S., & Yeung, B. (2000). Do corporate global environmental standards create of destroy market value? *Management Science, 46*(8), 1059–74.

Drobetz, W., Shchillhofer, A., & Zimmermann, H. (2003). *Corporate governance and expected stock returns: Evidence from Germany.* Paper presented at the EFMA 2003 Helsinki Meetings, WWZ, Department of Finance, University Basel, Basel, Switzerland.

Edwards, D. (1998). *The link between environmental and financial performance.* London: Earthscan.

Environmental Capital Markets Committee. (2000). *Green dividends? The relationship between firms' environmental performance and financial performance.* Washington, DC: U.S. Environmental Protection Agency, National Advisory Council for Environmental Policy and Technology. Retrieved 7 September 2007 from http://www.epa.gov/ocempage/nacept/green_dividends.pdf

Fama, E. (1965). The behaviour of stock market prices. *Journal of Business, 38*(1), 34–105).

Fama, E., & Jensen, M. (1983). Separation of ownership and control. *Journal of Law and Economics, 26*, 301–25.

Gompers, P., Ishii, J., & Metrick, A. (2003). Corporate governance and equity prices. *Quarterly Journal of Economics, 18*(1), 107–55.

Gregory, J. (2001). The bottom-line impact of corporate brand investment: An analytical perspective on the drivers of ROI of corporate brand communications. *Journal of Brand Management, 8*(6), 405–16.

Haapaniemi, P. (2000, March). What's in a reputation? *Chief Executive*, 48–51.

Hawley, J., & Williams, A. (2000). *The rise of fiduciary capitalism.* Philadelphia: University of Pennsylvania Press.

Hebb, T. (2006). The economic inefficiency of secrecy: Pension fund investors' transparency concerns. *Journal of Business Ethics, 63*(4), 385–405.

Hill & Knowlton. (2006). *Return on reputation.* Retrieved 28 June 2007 from Hill & Knowlton website: http://www2.hillandknowlton.com/crw/home/asp

Hoeffler, S., & Keller, K. (2003). The marketing advantages of strong brands. *Journal of Brand Management, 10*(6), 421–45.

Holt, D., Quelch, J., & Taylor, E. (2004). How global brands compete. *Harvard Business Review, 82*(9), 68–75.

Interfaith Center on Corporate Responsibility. (2006). March 2006 ICCR electronic newsletter. Retrieved March 2006.

Jensen, M. (2000). *A theory of the firm: Governance, residual claims, and organizational forms.* Cambridge: Harvard University Press.

Jensen, M., & Meckling, W. (1976). Theory of the firm: Managerial behavior, agency costs, and ownership structure. *Journal of Financial Economics, 3*(4), 305–60.

Kiernan, M., & Lievinson, J. (1998). Environment drives financial performance: The jury is in. *Environmental Quality Management, 7*(2), 1–7.

Knight, R., & Pretty, D. (2000, 20 June). Day of judgment: Catastrophe and the share price. *Financial Times.*

La Porta, R., Lopez-De-Silanes, F., Shleifer, A., & Vishny, R. (2002). Investor protection and corporate valuation. *Journal of Finance, 57*(3), 1147–70.

Lev, B. (2001). *Intangibles: Management, measurement, and reporting.* Washington: Brookings Institute.

Lowenstein, L. (1996). Financial transparency and corporate governance: You manage what you measure. *Columbia Law Review, 96,* 1335–73.

Mata, J. (1991). Sunk costs and entry by small and large plants. In P. Geroski & J. Schwalbach (Eds.), *Entry and market contestability.* Oxford: Blackwell.

McKinsey. (2000). Investor opinion survey. Retrieved 27 February 2007 from McKinsey website: http://www.oecd.org/dataoecd/56/7/1922101.pdf

Monks, R. (2001). *The new global investors.* Oxford: Capstone.

Orlitzky, M., Schmidt, F., & Rynes, S. (2003). Corporate social and financial performance: A meta-analysis. *Organization Studies, 24,* 403–11.

Porter, M., & van der Linde, C. (1995). Green and competitive: Ending the stalemate. *Harvard Business Review, 73,* 120–34.

Pratt, J., & Zeckhauser, R. (Eds.). (1987). *Principals and agents.* Boston: Harvard Business School Press.

Roberts, J. (2004). *The modern firm: Organizational design for performance and growth.* Oxford: Oxford University Press.

Roe, M.J. (1994). *Strong managers, weak owners: The political roots of American corporate finance.* Princeton: Princeton University Press.

Russell Reynolds. (2000). *Corporate governance in the new economy: 2000 international survey of institutional investors.* Author.

Salo, J. (2005a, April 8). *Corporate governance & environmental performance: An assessment and empirical analysis of the relationship using two proprietary databases.* Paper presented at the American Association of Geographers, Annual Conference, Denver, CO.

Salo, J. (2005b). The emergence of non-financial rating agencies for the promotion of global standards: An assessment and empirical analysis of two proprietary databases. Retrieved 1 August 2007 from Pensions at Work website: http://www.pensionsatwork.ca/english/pdfs/salo_rating_agencies.pdf

Teece, D. (2000). *Managing intellectual capital.* Oxford: Oxford University Press.

Teece, D. (2002). Dynamic capacities. In W. Lazonick (Ed.), *The handbook of economics* (pp. 156–71). London: Thompson.

United Nations Environment Program. (2005). *A legal framework for the integration of environmental, social and governance issues into institutional investment.* Geneva: Author.

Wójcik, D. (2006). Convergence in corporate governance: Evidence from Europe and the challenge for economic geography. *Journal of Economic Geography, 6*(5), 639–60.

Zingales, F. (1998). What's a company's reputation worth? *Global Finance, 12*(2), 1.

Zingales, L. (2000). In search of new foundations. *Journal of Finance, 55*, 1623–53.

6 Social Accounting and Reporting for Economically Targeted Investments: The Expanded Value Added Statement

LAURIE MOOK

This chapter presents a social accounting model called the expanded value added statement for reporting the economic, social, and environmental impact of an organization. After introducing social accounting, the chapter outlines the expanded value added statement, which is applied to a hypothetical real-estate development case as an example of an economically targeted investment. The chapter concludes with a discussion of the model.

An Introduction to Social Accounting

Social accounting provides a way of looking at how well an organization is performing economically, socially, and environmentally. It expands the range of criteria that are taken into consideration when measuring performance, by looking at the organization in relation to its role in the larger community. To do this, it looks at the organization's impact on a number of stakeholder groups, such as employees, customers, owners, society, and the environment.

Social accounting can also be applied to a community, as is being done in Nova Scotia and Newfoundland. In both areas, a system of community accounts attempts to measure the security and well-being of the area, using residents' feedback on their feelings of safety, incidence of crime, volunteering, health, social supports, time use, and other socioeconomic factors.

Typically, social accounting focuses on three interrelated components: economic, social, and environmental:

1. economic: of, relating to, or based on the production, distribution, and consumption of goods and services

2. social: of or relating to human society, the interaction of the individual and the group, or the welfare of human beings as members of society
3. environmental: the complex of physical, chemical, and biotic factors (as climate, soil, and living things) that act upon an organism or an ecological community and ultimately determine its form and survival.[1]

The definition of *social accounting* followed in this chapter is 'a systematic analysis of the effects of an organization on its communities of interest or stakeholders, with stakeholder input as part of the data that are analyzed for the accounting statement' (Quarter, Mook, & Richmond, 2003, p. xix). This can be contrasted to definitions of conventional accounting, which focus on only the reporting of financial items for economic decision-making:

> Accounting is a service activity. Its function is to provide quantitative information, primarily financial in nature, about economic entities that is intended to be useful in making economic decisions of action. (American Institute of Certified Public Accountants [Accounting Principles Board], 1970, s. 1023)

Thus, social accounting differs from conventional accounting in its focus on community impact, on stakeholders, and on its wider scope than on financial items alone.

The Expanded Value Added Framework

Along the line of earlier researchers (for example, Abt, 1974; Belkaoui, 1984; Estes, 1976; Linowes, 1972), Mook developed several social accounting statements that integrate financial and social information (Quarter et al., 2003). One model in particular will be applied in this chapter: the expanded value added statement, or EVAS. The EVAS is based on a conventional accounting statement called the value added statement, but it is modified to include social and environmental items.

Value added is a measure of wealth that an organization creates by adding value to raw materials, products, and services using labour and capital. It is not a new concept; rather it has been used since the turn of the twentieth century in the calculation of the gross national product.

Figure 6.1. A graphic illustration of profit.

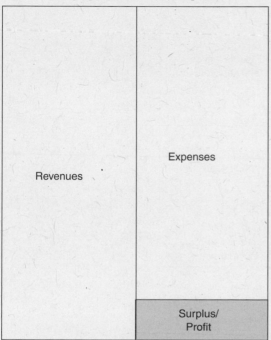

The value added statement also is not new; it was proposed in 1954 by Suojanen and has been used in the United Kingdom since the 1970s. It is also used in other European countries and South Africa.

In contrast to profit, which is the wealth created for only one group – the owners or shareholders – value added represents the wealth created for a larger group of stakeholders (Riahi-Belkaoui, 1999). Thus, the value added statement focuses on the wider implications of an organization's activities beyond its profits or losses. It emphasizes that the organization also employs people, contributes to societal costs through taxes, rewards investors and creditors for risking their funds, and contributes to the community.

Figures 6.1 and 6.2 depict the difference between profit and value added. Figure 6.1 presents a simple graphic illustration of an income statement that equates wealth with profit – or revenues less expenses. The expenses may include payments for such items as external goods and services, wages and benefits to employees, interest on loans, taxes,

Figure 6.2. A graphic illustration of value added.

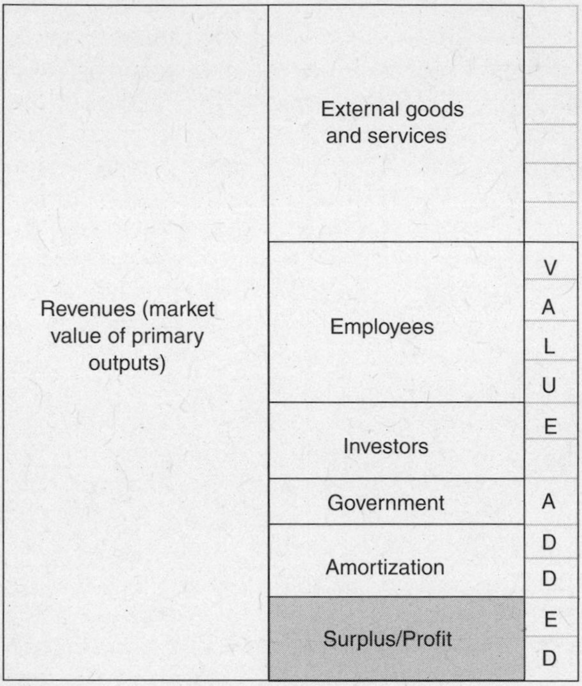

	External goods and services	
Revenues (market value of primary outputs)	Employees	V
		A
		L
		U
	Investors	E
	Government	A
	Amortization	D
		D
	Surplus/Profit	E
		D

and depreciation.[2] Revenues received (which is also the market value of the organization's outputs) are shown on the left-hand side of Figure 6.1, while the expenses and profit that correspond to those revenues are shown on the right.

Value added, on the other hand, is a much broader definition of wealth. As can be seen in Figure 6.2, value added looks beyond the wealth (profit) created for shareholders and includes the wealth for a wider group of stakeholders such as employees, creditors, government, and the organization itself. Thus, value added can be thought of as revenues less purchases of external goods and services. Materials and supplies are purchased from suppliers and turned into different goods and services using labour and capital.

To use a simple example, the value added created by a furniture-making company is calculated by taking the difference between the price the furniture was sold for and the cost of the materials that went into making the furniture (wood, screws, glue, etc.). So if you were making a table that sold for $300, and the wood and materials cost $100, the value added would be $300 minus $100, or $200. Another way of looking at value added is that labour and capital transformed the raw materials into another form, such as the table, and as a result, the value of the materials increased by $200. That value added, $200, is then distributed to the stakeholders of the company – its employees, creditors, government (taxes), and shareholders.

However, one limitation of the value added statement is that it focuses on financial items only and pays no attention to intangibles and items that do not pass through the market. The organization has social and environmental impacts as well as economic ones. The impacts may be intended or unintended, and may occur in the short term (up to three years), medium term (four to six years), and long term (seven years or more). In the expanded value added statement, we want to consider all impacts that have occurred as a result of turning those externally purchased goods and materials into something else. To overcome these limitations, the expanded value added statement was developed to incorporate social and environmental value added (or subtracted) by an organization.[3]

The overall concept used to guide the application of the model is sustainability. Sustainability has many definitions, but most arise out of the 1987 United Nations report, *Our Common Future*, also known as the Brundtland Report, which called for 'a form of sustainable development which meets the needs of the present without compromising the ability of future generations to meet their own needs' (UNWCED, 1987, p. 8). In other words, development should focus upon improving quality of life for all while not destroying the environment, and not upon increasing profits and the standard of living for a few.

The EVAS is not intended to replace existing financial statements but rather to be presented alongside them. By synthesizing traditional financial data with social and environmental data, the EVAS is another mechanism for understanding the dynamics of an organization and one that shows great potential for focusing attention on value creation and use. As such, it generates an additional set of questions that can guide investment decisions. It challenges us to think about organizations in a different way – as creators or destroyers of value to a wide group of stakeholders. As an organizational tool, it shifts from a narrow focus on how to maximize profit to a wider focus on how to maximize value creation that is sustainable. This involves a two-step analysis. First, the contributions of each activity are determined across three dimensions: economic, social, and environmental. Second, each dimension (economic, social, and environmental) is evaluated by stakeholders to measure the entire contribution of the organization (program, community) to sustainability.

The utility of the EVAS will be illustrated by applying it to an economically targeted investment, based on several sources including an actual real-estate development. Using key features of this existing community built as an economically targeted investment of pension funds, I developed a composite case study (Community Village) to demonstrate the utility of the expanded value added statement. Overall, the purpose of this exercise is to demonstrate what can be learned by using the expanded value added statement to assess the economic, social, and environmental aspects of this type of development over a period of 10 years.

Applying the Expanded Value Added Statement: Community Village

Community Village was developed as an economically targeted investment by several pension plans located in a large city in Canada. The community has a population of 5,000 residents and is located within a larger municipal community with a population of 40,000. It was developed on brownfield land in close vicinity to a rapid transit station. The development consists of four rental and six condominium buildings, along with a community centre and community policing centre. Throughout the development, there are several parks with green space accounting for about one quarter of the total land area.

The development used only union labour, and over the course of the 10 years, 3.3 million hours of employment were created: 2.4 million hours in the construction of the buildings, 159,000 in the operations of the buildings, 727,000 in the community centre, and 21,000 in the community policing centre. In addition, 238,000 hours of volunteer opportunities were also created.

The next section outlines the specifics of construction, operations, community centre, and community policing centre – characteristics that will then be brought together in the expanded value added statement. While previous analyses using this model have been applied at the program and organization levels, this application goes one step beyond, using the community as its unit of analysis.

Table 6.1. Breakdown of Expenses of Rental Buildings as
Percentage of Revenues.

Expenses		% of revenue
	Advertising	0.78
	Insurance	1.21
	Professional	0.26
	Management	5.76
	Property taxes	8.03
	Repairs	12.61
	Utilities	4.88
	Wages & benefits	5.22
	Miscellaneous	0.17
	Office	0.33
Total		39.26
	Net income	60.74

Construction

Although the construction of Community Village occurred over a period of 10 years, to keep the example simple, it is assumed that each building is constructed in a period of one fiscal year. The costs of construction of the rental buildings and amenities are capitalized and amortized over 40 years, including interest charges incurred during the time of construction. Half of the financing for Community Village comes from private lenders, and the other half from pension funds: 25% in the form of equity investments and another 25% through an investment trust.

Operations

RENTAL MANAGEMENT

Expense categories and percentage of revenues to manage the four rental buildings are outlined in Table 6.1. The percentage of specific expense categories as compared to revenues is based on a study of five apartment buildings.[4] The rental rate in the first year is based on actual rental rates of similar buildings in Vancouver: $1.15 per square foot per month, and increased yearly by the cost of living adjustment set by the provincial government.

Table 6.2. Breakdown of Expenses of Condominiums.

Expenses	%
Utilities	39.9
On-site wages/contract	17.1
Repairs & maintenance	22.9
Other operating expenses	3.6
Administrative expenses	1.3
Management fees	5.1
Current reserve appropriation	10.1
	100.0

CONDOMINIUM MANAGEMENT

Fees paid monthly by condominium owners cover costs associated with common areas in their buildings and provide funds for a reserve for future capital expenditures. For this example, condominium fees are calculated at $0.20 per square foot per month. Expense categories and reserve appropriations are shown in Table 6.2.

Community Centre

A 30,000 square foot community centre was in full operation by Year 3 of the development. Over the seven-year period covered in this example, it employed an average of 50 full-time employees and 50 half-time employees yearly. It also provided volunteer opportunities for 15 people yearly (the Board of Directors). The average yearly budget for the community centre is $3 million.

Community Policing Centre

The community policing centre also came into full operation in Year 3. It is run by two full-time paid staff and 200 volunteers. Its average yearly budget is $175,000, with $100,000 coming from government funding.

Taxation

The impact of taxation is felt at all three levels of government: municipal, provincial, and federal. At the municipal level, the development contributes to an increased property tax base. In this example, the property tax rate of condominium properties is estimated to be 0.005% of property value. At the provincial level, provincial sales tax of 7% is charged on the sale of new condominiums. A federal goods and services tax of 7% is also collected on the sale of new condominiums. For first-time homebuyers, a rebate is available of 2.52%. In this example, it is estimated that 50% of the condominium buyers are first-time buyers. Employment also provides taxes to government, in this case estimated to be 25% of wages net of contributions.

Statement of Operations

The statement of operations for the 10 years covered in this example is shown in Table 6.3. It brings together four key groups: the development group responsible for constructing and running the housing units, the non-profit community policing office, the community centre, and the government. Over the 10 years, the net surplus to the group is $45.6 million.

Value Added Statement

Another way of looking at the performance of this development is to estimate the value added it created over the 10 years and how it was distributed to its primary stakeholders (Table 6.4).[5] In the case of Community Village, $201 million of value added was created and distributed to employees, government, creditors, investors, unions, condo owners, and a portion retained by the organizations. The portion distributed to each stakeholder can also be shown in a pie chart (see Figure 6.3). However, as we noted previously, the creation of wealth is not just economic; it can also be social (related to human society and its members) and environmental (related to factors that influence ecological survival).

Identifying Social and Environmental Impacts

Even though there may be disagreement on the specifics of assigning a value to social and environmental outputs, placing a value on them recognizes their presence and their relative importance to economic performance. As mentioned previously, the key concept leading the development of this model is sustainability, integrating economic, social, and environmental issues with a long-term view to planning and

Table 6.3. Community Village Statement of Operations.

	Development group	Neighbourhood house	Community policing centre	Government	All
Production					
Sale of residential properties	197,671,925			31,077,093	228,749,018
Self-constructed assets					
Rental buildings	90,713,060			4,819,205	95,532,265
Amenities	12,399,000				12,399,000
Condo management fees	12,398,400				12,398,400
Payroll taxes received				23,159,330	23,159,330
Rent	59,981,896				59,981,896
Government grants		15,000,000	1,000,000		16,000,000
Other grants		15,000,000	750,000		15,750,000
In-kind donations	(240,000)		240,000		0
	372,924,280	30,000,000	1,990,000	59,055,629	463,969,909
Expenses					
Materials and supplies	205,874,218	5,650,000	1,290,000		212,814,218
Wages and benefits	84,142,287	24,000,000	700,000		108,842,287
Payroll taxes					
Grants				16,000,000	16,000,000
Depreciation	18,043,182	350,000			18,393,182
Property taxes	4,819,205				4,819,205
	312,878,893	30,000,000	1,990,000	16,000,000	360,868,893
Subtotal (production minus expenses)	60,045,387	0	0	43,055,629	103,101,016
Dividends	12,511,656				12,511,656
Interest	43,759,500				43,759,500
Condo reserve	1,252,238				1,252,238
Net income	2,521,993	0	0	43,055,629	45,577,622

Table 6.4. Value Added Statement for Community Village, for the 10 Years Ending 31 December 2004.

Value of outputs	435,991,373
Externally purchased G&S	210,818,087
Value added	225,173,286
Employees	83,792,399
Unions	1,890,558
Condo owners	1,252,238
Society	16,000,000
Creditors	45,755,630
Investors	12,511,656
Organizations	20,915,176
Government	43,055,629
Value added	225,173,286

development. Significant problems such as rapid population growth, atmospheric change, persistent pollutants, the beginning of the end of the oil economy, loss of species and habitats, poverty, war, disease, and social instability contribute to the extreme necessity that we change our perspectives on how corporations, cities, and households are managed (Greater Vancouver Regional District, 2004).

The degree of sustainability achieved depends upon both individual and community supports. By providing opportunities for individuals to help communities move towards sustainability, and making the impact of exercising these opportunities visible, we are able to track our progress (or lack of progress) towards these goals. The next section highlights some of the social and environmental characteristics of Community Village that could be accounted for in an expanded value added statement: the impact of transit-oriented development, opportunities for an active lifestyle, crime prevention measures, and the impact of making environmentally conscious decisions in purchases energy-using devices. These items are not meant to be exhaustive; rather, they are illustrative and meant to trigger thought on other types of impacts that could be included.[6]

TRANSIT-ORIENTED DEVELOPMENT
Because Community Village is located on the rapid transit line, residents can quite easily leave their car at home when they commute to work. Some even choose not to have a car at all. The impact of this

Figure 6.3. Distribution of value added.

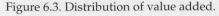

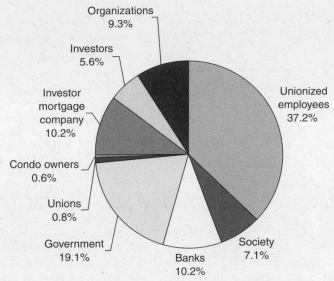

reduced car use affects both the individual and wider society. An extensive study of these impacts isolated individual and societal transportation cost factors, as shown in Table 6.5 (Litman, 2005).

Using these figures, the impact of one person from 25% of the adult residents (assuming an average of 1.5 adults per unit) switching from car use to rapid-transit use for the daily commute to work is calculated on the basis of an average 20-kilometre round-trip commute, five days a week, 48 weeks a year. At $0.5659 per kilometre (Table 6.5), the 1996 dollar value associated with this switch is $2,716 per person per year. Breaking this down into individual and societal impacts, the rate per kilometre is $0.248 and $0.3178, respectively (in 1996 U.S. dollars). When these figures are adjusted for cost of living and converted to Canadian dollars, over 10 years the total impact of this switch amounts to $18.3 million, with $8.0 million in actual savings to the residents who have switched (individual impacts) and $10.3 million in economic, social, and environmental benefits to the wider society (societal impacts). This calculation also takes into consideration the population growth over the 10 years in Community Village as new buildings were constructed.

Table 6.5. Transportation Cost Factors (in 1996 US$).

Cost	Definition	Average car	Rideshare passenger	Shift (per mile)	Shift (per km)
Individual					
Vehicle ownership	Fixed vehicle expenses	0.1873	0.0000	0.1873	0.1124
Internal parking	Parking costs borne by users	0.0455	0.0000	0.0455	0.0273
Vehicle operation	User expenses that are proportional to travel	0.1336	0.0030	0.1306	0.0784
User travel time	Time spent travelling	0.2300	0.1800	0.0500	0.0300
Internal accident	Vehicle accident costs borne by users	0.0500	0.0500	0.0000	0.0000
Total individual		0.6464	0.2330	0.4134	0.2480
Societal					
External accident	Vehicle accident costs not borne by users	0.0318	0.0000	0.0318	0.0191
External parking	Parking costs not borne by users	0.1091	0.0000	0.1091	0.0655
Congestion	Delay each vehicle imposes on other road users	0.1545	0.0000	0.1545	0.0927
Barrier effect	The disamenity roads and vehicle traffic imposes on pedestrians and bicyclists. Also called 'severance'	0.0136	0.0000	0.0136	0.0082
Road facilities	Road expenses not paid by user fees.	0.0145	0.0000	0.0145	0.0087
Municipal services	Public services devoted to vehicle traffic	0.0136	0.0000	0.0136	0.0082
Roadway land value	Opportunity cost of land used for roads	0.0218	0.0000	0.0218	0.0131
Option & equity value	Reduced travel choices, especially for disadvantaged people	0.0045	0.0000	0.0045	0.0027
Air pollution	Costs of motor vehicle emissions	0.0564	0.0020	0.0544	0.0326
Noise	Costs of motor vehicle noise	0.0091	0.0000	0.0091	0.0055
Resource consumption	External costs resulting from resource consumption	0.0264	0.0010	0.0254	0.0152
Water pollution	Water pollution and hydrologic impacts of vehicles & roads	0.0118	0.0000	0.0118	0.0071
Waste disposal	External costs from motor vehicle waste disposal	0.0018	0.0000	0.0018	0.0011
Land use impacts	Economic, environmental, and social costs resulting from low density, auto oriented land use	0.0636	0.0030	0.0636	0.0382
Total societal		0.5327	0.0030	0.5297	0.3178
Total overall		1.1791	0.2360	0.9431	0.5659

ACTIVE LIFESTYLE

In 1997, almost two thirds of Canadians were found to be physically inactive (Craig, Russell, Cameron, & Beaulieu, 1999). Katzmarzyk, Gledhill, and Shephard (2000), in a study on the effects of physical inactivity on coronary artery disease, stroke, colon cancer, breast cancer, type 2 diabetes mellitus, and osteoporosis, estimated that physical inactivity has resulted in a cost in 1997 to the Canadian health-care system of $2.1 billion, or 2.5% of all health-care costs. The same study found that reducing physical inactivity by 10% has the potential to reduce these expenditures by $150 million a year.

In the case of Community Village, several elements come together to promote a physically active lifestyle: proximity to public transit, pedestrian-friendly walkways, provision of bicycle racks, and recreational and sports facilities. Extrapolating the figures above, if we estimate that the physical inactivity rate in Community Village (population 5,000) was reduced by 10% as recommended by the Katzmarzyk, Gledhill, and Shephard study (from 62% to 55.8%), the impact on health-care costs would amount to about $88,684 in the 10-year period. If the impact is calculated for the community surrounding Community Village (population 40,000) who have access the amenities of Community Village, the amount would increase many fold. This would be reported in the social column of the expanded value added statement. Although this may seem minor in the context of the development as a whole, it does bring attention to the issue of a healthy, active lifestyle and its impact on health promotion and quality of life.

CRIME PREVENTION

Two initiatives of Community Village have an impact on crime prevention: the creation of a community policing centre and the application of planning principles known as Crime Prevention through Environmental Design. It is possible to put a value on this impact and include it in the expanded value added statement, using studies that estimate the direct cost of crimes to victims and the cost of pain and suffering associated with these crimes. Using data from Statistics Canada (Table 6.6), the average direct cost of property crimes in Canada, in 1996 $, was $2,390 (Brantingham & Easton, 1998). The cost of pain and suffering associated with these crimes has been estimated in 1999 dollars to be $11,563 (1996 $ = $11,076, Leung, 2004). These amounts result in a total of $13,466 in 1996 $.

Table 6.6. Average Cost of Property Crime to
Victims, by Type of Crime (1996 $).

Theft	2,131
Mischief	638
Break and enter	2,309
Motor vehicle theft	6,649
Robbery	2,857
Fraud	3,531
Overall average	2,390

Prior to the development of Community Village, property crime rates in the area, as reported by the city, were 50 per 1,000 people per year. With a population of 40,000, this amounts to 2,000 crimes per year. Since the development and the Community Policing Centre were established, crime rates have gone down by 5%. Using these figures, the overall impact over 10 years amounts to $7.5 million.

IMPACT OF PURCHASING DECISIONS

The expanded value added model makes explicit the economic, social, and environmental impacts of purchasing decisions, which is especially useful if these impacts are realized in the long term. One example is in the choice of energy-saving devices. In a housing development, the impact of choosing energy-efficient equipment can be significant. One example illustrates the impact of two such devices: exit signs and compact fluorescent light bulbs (Table 6.7). In both cases, the initial cost outlay is significantly more for the ENERGY STAR[7]-rated devices than for the non–ENERGY STAR ones. However, this cost is recouped fairly quickly. Indeed, over the 10 years, the total cost (including energy costs) for the ENERGY STAR–rated devices is $278,914, while the cost of the non–ENERGY STAR ones is $955,453. In other words, as a result of a purchasing decision, the organization is providing extra value to its customers of $676,539.

Energy savings are not the only impact of using these energy-efficient devices. There is also an impact on the creation of carbon dioxide gases, the production of which is linked to global warming. By choosing to use the ENERGY STAR–rated devices in these two examples, CO_2 emissions are reduced by almost 2,000 tonnes for 10 years. This impact is also shown in the expanded value added statement using a shadow price of $45.79/tonne of CO_2, based on the estimated cost of an interna-

Table 6.7. Comparison of ENERGY STAR and Non-ENERGY STAR Devices.

Item	Number required	ENERGY STAR			Non-ENERGY STAR		
		Initial cost	Maintenance (yearly)	Energy use	Initial cost	Maintenance (yearly)	Energy use
Exit signs	573 (3 per floor)	$75 each	$0	44 kWh	$45 each	$10	193 kWh
Compact fluorescent lights	4,584 (24 per floor)	$15 each	$0	42 kWh	$0.50 each	$10	146 kWh

tional emission-trading permit (Wigle, 2001). This is only one method of assigning a cost (and a fairly conservative one), but allows it to be included in the statement.[8] Use of these two items alone – exit signs and compact fluorescent lights – would result in a value to society of almost $90,000 over the 10 years.

Whereas in a conventional value added statement the impact of purchasing energy-efficient devices would not be shown, the expanded value added statement highlights the social and environmental impacts of purchases of external goods and services. In this case, the additional value added created is distributed to customers: to condominium owners in the form of lower condominium fees and to renters in the form of lower rents. These future savings can be thought of as self-created intangible assets and carried at cost on the balance sheet, and amortized over the useful life of the device. With major advances made in the last 15 years in the energy use of appliances, and the increasing importance of addressing the use of non-renewable energy sources and their impact on global warming, the expanded value added statement can make visible the 'secondary costs' of these items, especially if the initial cost of energy-efficient devices is higher than less energy-efficient ones.

Putting It All Together

Combining all of these elements – building construction, amenities, and social and environmental impacts – in the expanded value added statement (Table 6.8) shows that Community Village created almost $228 million of value added over the 10 years covered in this example. If only the financial items were considered, as they are in conventional accounting, the value added would be $201 million. The expanded value added statement highlights the additional value added created because of deliberate social and environmental considerations taken into account, and provides a way of communicating this information to a wider public. It also makes explicit how this value added was distributed and the primary stakeholders involved in keeping this community viable.

Discussion

The expanded value added statement for Community Village (Table 6.8) shows that financial information alone does not tell the organiza-

Table 6.8. Expanded Value Added Statement for Community Village.

	Financial	Social and environmental		Combined
		Individuals	Society	
Productions for the period	435,991,373			435,991,373
Volunteer contributions			1,912,500	1,912,500
Additional value added created by CPC			5,691,753	5,691,753
Additional value added created by purchase decisions		676,519	88,890	765,409
Transit-oriented development		8,009,822	10,264,621	18,274,443
Active lifestyle			88,684	88,684
Value of outputs	135,991,373	8,686,341	19,156,919	462,724,162
Externally purchased G&S	210,818,087			210,818,087
Value added	225,173,286	8,686,341	18,046,448	251,906,075
Employees	83,792,399			83,792,399
Unions	1,890,558			1,890,558
Condo owners/Renters	1,252,238	8,686,341		9,938,579
Society	16,000,000		18,046,448	34,046,448
Creditors	45,755,630			45,755,630
Investors	12,511,656			12,511,656
Organizations	20,915,176			20,915,176
Government	43,055,629			43,055,629
Value added	225,173,286	8,686,341	18,046,448	251,906,075

tion's whole performance story. The expanded value added statement focuses on value creation and creates greater awareness of at least two areas:

1. The role of stakeholders in creating financial, social, and environmental wealth
2. The interconnectedness of the economic, social, and environmental dimensions of organizational activities.

Some of the limitations of the expanded value added statement are imposed by the selection of items to be included and by the methods available to put a monetary value on them. In this regard, the challenges faced by the expanded value added statement are shared by other forms of alternative accounting and economics: identifying, measuring, quantifying, standardizing, and placing a value on key social and environmental indicators that could measure and encourage sustainable performance (Ranganathan, 1999; White & Zinkl, 1999).

Another challenge is to assess not only value added but also value subtracted, as it is important for accounting statements to illuminate both positive and negative impacts on sustainability. These are areas that require continued development and discussion (see (Bennett, Rikhardsson, & Schaltegger, 2003; Gray & Bebbington, 2001; Rikhardsson, Bennett, Bouma, & Schaltegger, 2005; Schaltegger & Burritt, 2000).

The strengths of the expanded value added statement lie in its ability to take a broader look at the organization and the role of stakeholders and to put them into a larger socio-economic perspective. It starts with existing financial information but presents it in such a way as to emphasize the contribution of labour and capital to production. It also includes non-monetary items, to present a more encompassing picture of an organization's economic, social, and environmental dimensions, and their interdependence. Although more work has to be done on providing acceptable valuation methods, and not everything can be monetized, the change of focus from a profit-oriented bottom line to an integrated economic, social, and environmental bottom line provides an opportunity for organizations and society to think about impacts in a much broader sense. Accounting is a driver of behaviour and can be conceived of as an explicit change agent in order to move organizations towards economic, social, and environmental goals.

By synthesizing financial data with social and environmental data, the expanded value added statement is one mechanism for understanding the dynamics of an organization and the inter-related economic-social-environmental implications of choices made in day-to-day operations. In making these relationships more visible, the expanded value added statement can help us look at the world differently and as a result act differently in a way that responds to the needs of workers, retirees, communities, and the environment.

Notes

1 Merriam-Webster Online. Retrieved 30 July 2007 from http://www.m-w
  .com/dictionary/
2 Depreciation or amortization is the process of matching the cost of an asset
  against revenues based on its estimated useful life. Thus, instead of expensing the entire cost of an asset when it is purchased, it is expensed according to
  how long it is estimated to be useful in producing value. In a simple example,
  if the asset were estimated to last 5 years, one fifth of its cost would be
  expensed every year for 5 years.
3 A detailed explanation on how to put the statement together can be found in
  Mook et al. (2003).
4 http://www.canfedapts.org/TaxStudy.htmU.K.intro
5 Stakeholders are those that are affected by the organization's activities, positively or negatively. Primary stakeholders are those groups that are essential
  to the ongoing operation of the enterprise. Typically, these are customers,
  employees, investors, community, government, and suppliers. If any one
  of these groups fails to support the organization, the organization will cease
  to function. Secondary stakeholders are those that are influenced by or
  affected by the organization's activities, but do not engage in transactions
  with the organization. They are also not essential for its survival (Clarkson,
  1995).
6 In order to determine which outputs to include in social accounting, it is
  helpful to think about outputs at three levels: primary, secondary, and tertiary (Richmond, 1999, p. 1). Primary outputs are the direct effects of the
  organization's activities on its primary stakeholders. In the example of Community Village, this includes the provision of housing. Secondary outputs are
  the indirect effects of the organization on its primary stakeholders. This
  might be the impact of increased physical activity because of the design of the
  development. Tertiary outputs are the effects of the organization's activities
  on those other than primary stakeholders. This could include wider environmental impacts of the development.

7 ENERGY STAR is an international standard for consumers that identifies the most energy-efficient products on the market.
8 Estimates go as high as US$835 (1992) per tonne (Wigle, 2001).

References

Abt and Associates Inc. (1974). The Abt model. In D. Blake, W. Frederick, & M. Meyers (Eds.), *Evaluating the impact of corporate programs* (pp. 149–57). New York: Praeger.

American Institute of Certified Public Accountants (Accounting Principles Board). (1970). *Basic concepts and accounting principles underlying financial statements of business enterprises*. New York: Author.

Belkaoui, A. (1984). *Socio-economic accounting*. Westport: Quorum Books.

Bennett, M., Rikhardsson, P.M., & Schaltegger, S. (Eds.). (2003). *Environmental management accounting: Purpose and progress*. Dordrecht: Kluwer.

Brantingham, P., & Easton, S.T. (1998). The cost of crime: Who pays and how much? *The Fraser Institute Critical Issues Bulletins*. Retrieved 23 July 2006 from Fraser Institute website: http://www.fraserinstitute.ca/shared/readmore.asp?sNav=pb&id=229.

Clarkson, M. (1995). A stakeholder framework for analyzing and evaluating corporate social performance. *Academy of Management Review, 20*(1), 9–117.

Craig, C.L., Russell, S.J., Cameron, C., & Beaulieu, A. (1999). *Foundation for joint action: Reducing physical inactivity*. Ottawa: Canadian Fitness and Lifestyle Research Institute.

Estes, R. (1976). *Corporate social accounting*. New York: Wiley.

Gray, R., & Bebbington, J. (2001). *Accounting for the environment* (2nd ed.). London: Sage.

Greater Vancouver Regional District. (2004). *The social components of community sustainability: A framework*. Retrieved 30 August 2006 from GVRD website: http://www.gvrd.bc.ca/growth/pdfs/SocialComponentsofCommSus UsersGuide.pdf

Katzmarzyk, P.T., Gledhill, N., & Shephard, R.J. (2000). The economic burden of physical inactivity in Canada. *Canadian Medical Association Journal, 163*(11), 1435–1440.

Leung, A. (2004). *The cost of pain and suffering from crime in Canada*. Retrieved 23 July 2006 from Department of Justice Canada website: http://www.justice.gc.ca/en/ps/rs/rep/2005/rr05-4/index.html

Linowes, D. (1972). An approach to socio-economic accounting. *Conference Board Record, 9*(11), 58–61.

Litman, T. (2005). *Transportation cost analysis spreadsheets*. Retrieved 7 June 2006 from Victoria Transport Policy Institute website: http://www.vtpi.org/tca/tca.xls

Mook, L., Quarter, J., & Richmond, B.J. (2007). *What counts? Social accounting for nonprofits and cooperatives*. London: Sigel.

Quarter, J., Mook, L., & Richmond, B.J. (2003). *What counts: Social accounting for nonprofits and cooperatives*. Upper Saddle River: Prentice Hall.

Ranganathan, J. (1999). Signs of sustainability: Measuring corporate environmental and social performance. In M. Bennett & P. James (Eds.), *Sustainable measures: Evaluation and reporting of environmental and social performance* (pp. 475–95). Sheffield: Greenleaf.

Riahi-Belkaoui, A. (1999). *Value added reporting and research: State of the art*. Westport: Quorum Books.

Richmond, B.J. (1999). Counting on each other: A social audit model to assess the impact of nonprofit organizations. PhD diss., University of Toronto.

Rikhardsson, P.M., Bennett, M., Bouma, J., & Schaltegger, S. (Eds.). (2005). *Implementing environmental management accounting: Status and challenges*. Dordrecht: Springer Kluwer.

Schaltegger, S., & Burritt, R. (2000). *Contemporary environmental accounting*. Sheffield: Greenleaf.

Soujanen, W.W. (1954). Accounting theory and the large corporation. *Accounting Review, 29* (3), 391–398.

UNWCED. (1987). *Our common future: A report of the World Commission on Environment and Development*. New York: Oxford University Press.

White, A., & Zinkl, D. (1999). Standardisation: The next chapter in corporate environmental performance evaluation and reporting. In M. Bennett & P. James (Eds.), *Sustainable measures: Evaluation and reporting of environmental and social performance* (pp. 117–31). Sheffield: Greenleaf.

Wigle, R. (2001). *Sectoral impacts of Kyoto compliance*. Ottawa: Industry Canada.

7 Economically Targeted Investments, Union Pension Funds, and Public–Private Partnerships in Canada

JOHN LOXLEY

Economically targeted investments (ETIs) are a form of socially responsible investment and are 'designed to produce a competitive rate of return commensurate with risk, as well as to create collateral economic benefits for a targeted geographic area, group of people, or sector of the economy' (Harrigan, 2003, p. 241). As Manley, Hebb, and Jackson stress in chapter 8, 'Targeted investments focus on achieving both a financial and a social return.' While the concept may appear straightforward, it is anything but, as there may be conflict between maximizing financial returns and maximizing a broader social/economic rate of return (Carmichael, 2003a). Furthermore, it is even unusual for these broader returns to be measured, though it has been done in Canada (Carmichael, 2003b). This chapter examines union pension investments in Canadian infrastructure through the vehicle of public–private partnerships (PPPs), in which private businesses undertake functions traditionally performed by governments, to ascertain whether these investments qualify as ETIs. Certainly, investments in infrastructure constitute a targeted sectoral investment with a social and economic usefulness that goes beyond immediate returns. However, the question arises whether union pension–sponsored PPP investment in this sector is driven by any broader considerations than maximizing financial returns.

The chapter commences by outlining how PPP arrangements differ from conventional approaches to building and operating public infrastructure. It then examines the rising infrastructure gap in Canada. It goes on to outline and to critically examine the reasons advanced for using PPPs to help fill that gap, as opposed to employing conventional approaches to building and operating public assets. The attraction of PPPs to the private sector and to pension funds is that they offer a higher rate of return than do conventional bond financing. However, the central dilemma is that these enlarged returns might be achieved directly or indirectly at the expense of workers in the public sector or at the expense of taxpayers.

The rest of the chapter examines the experience of union pension funds with PPPs in the infrastructure sector. This is mainly, but not entirely, a history of involvement by the Ontario Municipal Employees Retirement System (OMERS). The chapter traces and analyses the involvement of OMERS in the building and operating of public schools, the Confederation Bridge, nuclear power facilities in Ontario, other energy-related infrastructure projects, nursing homes, and, most recently, hospitals. It should be noted that some of these PPP initiatives were operated at arms length through a subsidiary in which, for some years, the Canada Pension Plan also held an interest. The chapter also looks at the sorry experience of the Ontario Teachers' Pension Plan investment in the Hamilton-Wentworth water and sewage treatment plant, and notes the aspiration of the Labourers Pension Fund to enter the controversial hospital PPP business.

The chapter assesses these experiences. It concludes that there is no evidence that these pension plans ever undertook infrastructure investment as part of a deliberate ETI strategy in which broader considerations other than narrow financial returns were considered. On the contrary, it appears that bottom-line financial returns were the motivation in these ventures. While this may, in some cases, have put pressure on jobs and wages of those working on the PPP project, usually the high returns were the result of lucrative lease arrangements, monopoly pricing, or obtaining public assets at bargain basement prices. The chapter then examines alternative approaches to the financing of infrastructure.

The Movement towards Public–Private Partnerships (PPPs) in Canada

The private sector has always played an important role in providing public infrastructure in Canada. Traditionally, governments have raised money for investment in infrastructure through taxation or through sales of bonds to private banks, finance houses, or pension funds. The actual building of infrastructure projects is usually left to private contractors who submit competing tenders for the work. Government planners, engineers, and architects plan, design, regulate, and supervise, working alongside private-sector professionals. Once built, the infrastructure is generally operated and maintained by the public sector.

Since the early 1990s, there has been a growing trend in Canada towards the use of PPPs in infrastructure. This has occurred in two different ways (Loxley & Loxley, 2008). The first involves the private sector in more than one aspect of designing, building, financing, owning, and operating 'public' infrastructure. Usually, the public sector invites a private-sector company to bid on a range of these operations, leasing the infrastructure back from the company over a specified period, usually 20 to 30 years. This arrangement allows the private partner to service the debt and make a profit on both the building and the operation (and finance!) of the project. The private partner thus handles the finance and acts as contractor as well as operator. It often designs the project as it builds it (design-build), though this feature could be built into traditional procurement approaches. In this way, risks associated with construction are borne, it is said, by the private partner instead of the government.

The second way in which PPPs have been used is in permitting the private sector to operate publicly owned infrastructure. In this case, the government simply hands over the operating budget, or a portion of it, to a private partner who is then charged with the responsibility of running it.

The Infrastructure Gap in Canada

One of the major driving forces behind the embracing of PPPs as a vehicle for delivering public investments is the widely acknowledged, but difficult to calculate, deficiency in the addition, maintenance, and replacement of Canadian public infrastructure stock. That stock, which includes roads, water and sewage treatment facilities, as well as housing, education, health, and recreation facilities, was estimated at $500–600 billion in 2004 (TD Bank Financial Group, 2004, p. 2). This figure, however, does not appear to include public buildings, land, and public enterprise assets, such as assets of public utilities. It must be taken, therefore, to be a very conservative estimate.

Estimates of the infrastructure 'gap' are even more tenuous, as they include not only shortfalls in past maintenance and replacement but also the amount by which new infrastructure growth has fallen behind some, necessarily subjective, view of 'need.' The TD Bank argues that estimates of this gap are 'all over the map' as a result of different methodologies and assumptions, but concludes, 'The consensus is that the gap is massive – as high as $125 billion or 6–10 times annual investment flows' (TD Bank Financial Group, 2004, p. 4). The problem is not that public spending on infrastructure has not increased in recent years. On the contrary, public spending on buildings, machinery, and equipment increased from $1.3 billion per annum in the early 1960s to $18 billion in 2002, or to $3.0 billion in real, 1960s terms. Public spending on civil engineering rose from $1 billion to about $9 billion over the same period, or to $1.4 billion in real terms. The problem is that these increases have not kept pace with maintenance needs and with population and income growth. In fact, as a percentage of GDP, public investment fell from the 2–3% range in the 1960s and 1970s, to only around 0.5% in the 1990s, so that the capital stock as a percentage of GDP is $180 billion lower than it was in those early years (Mackenzie, 2004). The gap is, therefore, real and large and is acknowledged both by those advocating PPPs, such as TD Bank, and by those opposing them, such as the Canadian Union of Public Employees (Canadian Union of Public Employees [CUPE] – Ontario Division, 2004).

The existence of an infrastructure gap is not, in itself, a sufficient reason to pursue the PPP route. In theory, the gap could be filled simply by devoting more resources to infrastructure and by using traditional procurement and operating methods, without recourse to arrangements by which the private sector becomes involved in owning, leasing, or operating these facilities. The infrastructure could also be financed in the traditional way through taxes, user fees, or regular government bond issues, without necessitating the raising of private equity or loan finance that characterizes many PPP arrangements.

The arguments for taking the PPP route are threefold. First, there is a point of view that government is inefficient at building infrastructure, and maintaining and operating it, and that this is better left to the private sector though a PPP arrangement. Furthermore, even if infrastructure is to be built and owned by the public sector, the private sector will be more efficient at operating it. The second argument is that governments face a fiscal constraint that PPP arrangements can overcome. The PPP approach is said to offer governments 'upfront access to a deep pool of funds, without which necessary projects may remain a distant dream' (TD Bank Financial Group, 2004, p. 34). Third, PPPs are said to offer the opportunity for governments to shift certain types of risk onto the private sector.

The Arguments for PPPs Considered

The efficiency argument for PPPs has its theoretical basis in claims that the private sector has access to economies of scale or scope, can draw on greater experience or learning effects, or has lower agency costs (Loxley, 1996; Vining, Boardman, & Poschmann, 2005, pp. 202–3). However, attempts to quantify these efficiencies are rare and, even then, rife with inconsistencies and unreliability. Thus, in the United Kingdom, it is claimed that PPPs save an average of 17% over conventional projects. This argument is widely quoted without any qualification (International Monetary Fund, 2004, p. 39), even though it does not stand up to careful scrutiny (Pollock & Vickers, 2000). In the absence of empirical verification, the claim to greater efficiency becomes, in effect, an ideological one used to further commodify state activities, opening them up to both the market and private profit.

The fiscal argument for PPPs is in many respects a self-serving one, as governments are in large measure responsible for the fiscal straitjacket they claim they face. Thus, a number of provincial governments have introduced balanced budget legislation, which hinders their ability to undertake capital projects that might otherwise be debt financed (Loxley, 2003). The same governments have been aggressively reducing taxes in recent years, further impeding their ability to finance capital projects. This then creates an environment in which PPPs become particularly attractive as private financing reduces up-front budget expenditures, replacing them with annual lease payments.

In recent years, however, the implementation of generally accepted accounting principles (GAAP)[1] and the movement towards summary accounting[2] have made it more difficult for governments to use this form of off-book financing. However, GAAP aside, all forms of lease payment are in effect debt, the size of which can be calculated as the present value (discounted value) of payments over the life of the lease. Normally, these would be treated as debt in bond rating assessments by investment houses, regardless of how they are treated in the books of the government.

Using PPPs for fiscal purposes is, therefore, no longer as attractive in Canada as it was in the early days of PPPs. They may still generate beneficial fiscal impact, however, if they shift risk to the private sector – the third attraction listed above. Lease payments on PPP arrangements are generally much higher than interest payments on public debt because the public sector can borrow money more cheaply than can the private sector. Therefore, for the public sector to undertake the PPP route makes sense only if transfer of risk from the public to the private sector offsets the higher financing costs. In that case, PPPs may still have a positive fiscal impact.

Infrastructure risks take many forms,[3] and if some of them are to be transferred, they must first be identified and quantified. Then an assessment can be made of whether the additional financing costs of PPPs are, in practice, offset by quantified risk transfer. Ideally, PPP bids should be evaluated at the outset against a detailed public-sector comparator, which documents what it would cost the public sector to undertake the project, including the cost of various types of risk.

Financing PPPs and Its Attractions

PPPs offer a number of profit-making opportunities to the private sector. Private consultants are used to develop the PPP case. The PPP would normally be registered as a company and its equity owned by the private sector. This company would own the assets and be responsible for construction and operations, or it might hire a different company to operate the PPP. An operations PPP would manage the publicly owned assets. Public assets may be sold to the private sector at less than market value. Debt financing for the PPP might come from privately owned financial institutions, such as banks, trust companies, insurance companies, or pension funds. The private sector may also make profits out of refinancing a PPP once the asset is built and operational, since by that time most of the up-front risk will have been incurred.

The attraction to the private sector of providing finance to capital asset PPPs, as opposed to financing government bond borrowing for infrastructure directly, is that it offers the prospects of higher returns through equity and loans. Part of this higher return is associated with the higher risks involved in preparing, building, and operating an infrastructure entity. Part of it would be to offset the high transactions costs involved in putting together and implementing PPP proposals. Part of it would also be associated with PPPs being used to overcome perceived fiscal constraints, often self-imposed, so that the volume of finance and profit might be higher than otherwise. Where a PPP involves operating a service, relatively high returns to equity or loan investments might have other origins, such as monopoly control over pricing or the ability to restructure the terms and conditions of employment to significantly reduce labour costs. These two possibilities warrant further inspection.

Monopoly pricing power in the hands of private partners might result from the PPP introducing new pricing systems, or from the closure or prevention of competing services. The pricing of public services, such as water, road tolls, or energy consumption, can be quite complex. Demand is difficult to predict, as are operation and maintenance costs, and initial estimates might prove to be highly inaccurate, resulting either in losses or in much higher profits than initially anticipated. If losses are incurred, the PPP will seek higher charges or it will threaten closure, usually prompting a supportive reaction from the government. If inaccurate assumptions lead to excess profits, this might become a permanent feature of the provision of service through a PPP unless the initial contract specifically addresses this possibility. The selling of public assets to a PPP arrangement also raises questions about the valuation of those assets and whether the private partner is paying a fair market price for them.

If charges for public services are set relatively close to what they had been before the PPP, then the private sector is likely to achieve or exceed its targeted return only if it can reduce operating costs. Indeed, contracts are often drawn up that reward the private partner for reductions in operating costs. Usually, labour constitutes a high proportion of such costs so that an essential element of the logic of handing over the service to a PPP is a desire to reduce labour costs that the public entity might otherwise have had difficulty doing. Thus, the creation of the new operating entity might make it possible to replace unionized by non-unionized workers, in the process reducing wages and possibly important benefits such as pensions or supplementary health care. It might enable the re-drawing of job descriptions so that fewer workers are needed or so that part-time workers replace full-time workers, thereby saving again on wages and benefits.

Herein lies the potential dilemma for union pension funds. PPPs hold out the promise of higher returns on their investments than do government bonds and other conventional financial assets, even after adjusting for risk. This is appealing to pension-fund managers, given their fiduciary responsibility to maximize pension-fund returns. However, often this promise is based on the prospects that PPPs hold out for adversely affecting the lives of working people, by reducing their wages and benefits, by undermining their job security, or by significantly changing their working environment or terms of employment. Alternatively, these above average returns might be the result of the PPP being in a position to charge monopolistic fees to workers as consumers. They might also be the result of the opening up of the provision of public services to new environmental or public health threats by reductions in the quality of service that profit maximization might entail.

Furthermore, if risk transfer to the private partner does not materialize, the higher costs of leases over normal public borrowing will have negative implications for other aspects of the budget. This, in turn, might lead to pressure on the level or quality of service, the incomes or jobs of public employees, or the need for taxes. Additionally, high returns might simply indicate transference of public assets to the private partner at less than market value. Hence, the added returns that workers enjoy in their pension fund might be the result of a variety of added social and economic costs that they face as workers, consumers, and taxpayers.

So, how active are union pension funds in financing PPPs in Canada and how real, in practice, is this potential dilemma? The next section describes the involvement of three union pension funds.

Pension-Fund Involvement in PPPs in Canada

The Ontario Municipal Employees Retirement System (OMERS)

OMERS has been the pension fund most active in PPP investments in Canada. This fund manages the pension contributions of 92,000 pensioners and 260,000 employees of municipal governments, school boards, and other public entities. Its total assets exceed $41 billion (OMERS, 2005c), and in 2002 it had approximately $1.2 billion invested in PPPs (Drury, 2002), though, as we shall see, the amount has risen substantially since then. The PPP investments of OMERS are all managed through Borealis Infrastructure Management Inc., of which it is the sole shareholder. In 2001, Borealis acquired Dorset Partners, a private equity fund, and renamed it Borealis Capital, which became a platform for the OMERS investments in PPPs. OMERS owned 26% of Borealis Capital, as did the Canada Pension Plan (CPP), the balance being held by private partners (Chenery, 2001). The CPP also committed to bringing in funds in addition to its $20 million equity holding, in the amount of $170 million (FPinfomart, 2006). In 2004, however, amid claims of waste and mismanagement, OMERS bought out the other partners, and Borealis Capital was dissolved (Reed, 2004). OMERS now routes its PPP investments directly through Borealis Infrastructure Management Inc., though it continues to partner in specific projects with the Canada Pension Plan.

SCHOOLS

The first of those involvements has also been the most controversial. It consisted of the building of 15 schools in Nova Scotia on a build-finance-lease-operate scheme, plus acquisition of one already built, at a cost of $162 million, which was bond financed (Bowman, 2000). The original intent of the PPP approach, which was planned to cover 55 schools, was to shift schools' capital financing off budget. This was thwarted after the auditor general declared that insufficient risk transfer had taken place to the private sector to warrant the leases being termed operating leases. Accordingly, 'the entire cost of leased assets acquired would have to be included in the calculation of net debt' (Auditor General, 1998, p. 67).

Evaluating the financial aspects of the PPP schools deal is not easy, as public-sector comparators were not developed at the outset of the deal, and no proper analysis was made of risk transfer. Accordingly, it is impossible to know precisely what net benefits or costs might have been incurred. The PPP approach to school building was severely curtailed by the Conservative government of John Hamm in 2000, to only 33 schools, amid allegations of cost overruns. It was claimed that the budgeted $350 million cost of the schools had already been exceeded by $32 million. CUPE-Ontario (2003b, p. 9) has suggested that this curtailment was probably very expensive for OMERS in terms of bid preparation and contract negotiations, for which they would have received no compensation.

Other criticisms of the PPP schools approach were that construction quality was often inadequate, while the province was left carrying all operating and maintenance charges and the private partner often deferred maintenance. Community access to school facilities was transferred to the discretion of a private company and fees for community use of schools became high and unregulated. A number of issues were raised concerning the commercialization of schools, with regard to design of facilities (specialist for educational purposes versus multi-use, which is more profitable for the private partner), access to firms wishing to advertise, and control of vending machine receipts. In addition, it was claimed that financing costs were often higher than the province's cost of borrowing and that the reversal to conventional approaches saved some $2 million per school (Shaker, 2003).

This expedition into PPP financing was not carefully planned or thought through, and the public sector did not exercise due diligence in entering into contracts. Indeed, in several cases, building commenced even before lease contracts were signed or financing was put in place, the province making advances of dubious legality to the private partners (Auditor General, 1998, ss. 8.54–8.62). While in New Brunswick PPP schools used non-unionized labour, this appears not to have been the case in Nova Scotia. However, unions did complain about pressure being put on workers for layoffs or wage concessions and that collective agreements last for only 2–4 years while PPP leases last for 20–30 years (Canadian Union of Public Employees [CUPE] – National, 2004, pp. 22–3).

Thus, the Nova Scotia experience has become 'a cautionary tale' (Dobbin, 2002) in alternative approaches to school funding. Since no detailed evaluation of that experience has been conducted, it is not possible to know to what extent the OMERS schools were complicit in these problems. The assumption is, however, that they were party to bad deals and bad public policy (Canadian Union of Public Employees [CUPE] – Ontario Division, 2003b, pp. 9–11). There is some evidence that borrowing costs were higher for Borealis than those of the province, at 6.35% (Bowman, 2000) versus 5.6% (Shaker, 2003). This would certainly have added costs to the province, given the minimal risk transfer reported by the auditor general. However, without access to the lease agreements, it would be impossible to ascertain the exact amount. What seems clear is that these investments were made by OMERS for strictly financial reasons and that there is no suggestion that they considered them ETIs.

TOLL BRIDGE OPERATION

OMERS also has money tied up in the operation of the Confederation Bridge, which links Prince Edward Island and New Brunswick, through its majority ownership in BPC Maritime Corporation, which acquired a 34% holding in Strait Crossing Development Inc. in 2003 and a 65% holding in July 2006. Strait Crossing Development Inc. built the bridge between 1993 and 1997 and will operate it until 2032 on a 35-year lease. The bridge was financed by an issue of real interest rate bonds, in the amount of $661 million. The financing was taken up mainly by pension funds (Abdel-Aziz & Russell, 2001, p. 902), secured by a commitment of the federal government to continue paying subsidies it had previously paid to the ferry system that the bridge replaced. The federal government agreed to pay the subsidies for 35 years until the financing had been repaid and the bridge transferred back to the public sector. The subsidy was fixed at $41.9 million in 1992 dollars and indexed to the annual rate of inflation (Loxley, 1999a, p. 19). Strait Crossing Development Inc. was given access to all tolls, which were set about 10% above the ferry crossing charges, with increases being limited to no more than 75% of the annual rate of inflation. Government agreed to compensate Strait Crossing Development Inc. if toll revenues were to fall below the $13.9 million (in 1996 dollars), which the ferry service earned in 1992, but there is no upper limit to the revenues it can earn (Loxley, 1999a, p. 21).

Strait Crossing Development Inc. has little equity in the project, which is essentially debt financed and in a way that presents very little risk to the pension funds holding the bonds. There appear to be only two major risks for Strait Crossing Development Inc. on the operating side. The first pertains to the demand to use the bridge, which is slight, since Strait Crossing Development Inc. also negotiated a no-competition clause with the government and since the government has also guaranteed a minimum level of revenue. The second pertains to risk of bridge damage or closure due to storms. This risk is real, larger than expected but, ultimately, not measurable (Loxley, 1999a). Again, however, Strait Crossing Development Inc. would have the minimum revenue deal to fall back on, should the risk materialize. Therefore, Strait Crossing Development Inc. offers OMERS a steady, reliable, and long-term source of earnings, the details of which are not publicly available. These earnings are more the result of monopoly than they are of labour oppression that often accompanies PPPs, since Strait Crossing Development Inc. employs only about 30 workers and all are unionized. The bridge did, however, replace about 650 ferry workers (Loxley, 1999a). Again, this project was undertaken by OMERS for (sound) financial reasons, and not as an ETI with broader social or economic purposes.

ENERGY PROJECTS

OMERS is engaged in a number of energy related PPPs, including holding a 31.6% interest in the lease of two nuclear power facilities operated by Bruce Power, through the BPC Generation Infrastructure Trust. This investment cost OMERS $376 million in 2003, partnering with TransCanada Pipelines Ltd. and Cameco, each with the same share, and two small unions representing staff: the Power Workers Union (4%) and the Society of Energy Professionals (1.2%). This consortium replaced British Energy, which had held the lease since 2000 (Ontario Power Generation, 2002). Bruce Power supplies Ontario with 20% of its electricity and employs some 3,700 workers.

As in the case of the Confederation Bridge, OMERS avoided most of the controversy surrounding the deal by becoming a partner only several years after the contract was signed. However, controversy has plagued provincial energy policy in Ontario for some time now, as consumer prices have risen strongly and energy delivery has been problematic. Opponents of the Bruce lease agreement forecast that this would be the case and opposed the deal on the grounds that it constituted a giveaway of public assets at much less than their market value and also that it moved Ontario steadily along a continuum of integration with U.S. markets in which consumer prices are, by and large, much higher. The original lease was for 18 years with the possibility of a 25-year extension. It saw British Energy pay $625 million plus an annual fee of $150 million over 17 years. Proceeds of the agreement would be used for the eventual decommission of the nuclear plants, for disposing of spent fuels, and for helping retire the 'stranded debt' of Ontario Hydro (Alphonso & Mackie, 2000). Critics argued that these lease costs were grossly inadequate and would not even cover the costs of eventually decommissioning the plants, which remain a public responsibility. British Energy should make an operating profit of $435 million per annum, simply by selling energy at 5% above the then prevailing price. Furthermore, if it invested $4 billion in refurbishing the nuclear plants, as the consortium now plans to do, it could easily make profits of $800 million per annum for 20 to 30 years. Selling energy at U.S. prices would bring in much higher profits, estimated by critics to be a staggering $68 billion over that period (Gordon & Wilson, 2001). The agreement with British Energy, therefore, grossly underestimated the value of the Bruce facilities, shifting surpluses from the public to the private sector and increasing energy costs to the consumer.

Since the details of what OMERS earns from Bruce through the BPC Generation Infrastructure Trust are not made public, it is impossible to say with any precision whether the profit forecasts of Gordon and Smith have proven accurate. However, the OMERS share in Bruce Power is the same as that of Cameco – 31.6% – hence one can gain some insights into OMERS profits from Bruce Power by examining those of Cameco. These appear to have been $108 million in 2003, $121 million in 2004, and $165 million in 2005 (Cameco, 2005). These numbers suggest that total annual returns to equity in Bruce Power amounted to about $522 million, or even more than projected by Gordon and Wilson.

It appears that the OMERS investment in Bruce has risen considerably since 2003 and is now estimated at $1.3 billion. OMERS plans to provide about $2.1 billion towards the restart and refurbishment program up to 2011, at which time Bruce Power is expected to supply approximately one quarter of Ontario's electricity (OMERS, 2005a). It appears, then, that the Bruce Power investment is a highly lucrative one for OMERS. Again, this has less to do with the PPP enabling greater exploitation of labour than with Bruce Power's relative monopoly position in a situation of scarce capacity. This is in addition to a gross undervaluation of the assets on which the lease is based. It also has little to do with ETIs, as the investment is strictly for financial returns.

OMERS also has a 10% equity interest in Enersource Corporation through BPC Energy Corporation, the other 90% being owned by the City of Mississauga. Enersource supplies electricity to 175,000 clients. It had an equity capital of about $201 million in 2005, suggesting that the OMERS share is about $20 million. Net income after corporate tax and other adjustments was $13.4 million, suggesting that OMERS earned $1.3 million (Enersource, 2005). The company is unionized and OMERS was requested to become a partner in order to provide some outside quality assurance. Borealis also helped arrange bond financing for the company (Borealis Infrastructure, 2006).

OMERS also partners with the City of Toronto in Enwave, which delivers heat and cooling to a number of buildings in downtown Toronto. OMERS has 53% of the total equity, or $98.8 million, and the City 47%, or $74.5 million in 2005, producing net income for OMERS of $1.6 million and for the City, $1.2 million (City of Toronto, 2005).

HEALTH-CARE FACILITIES

Through Borealis, OMERS has also invested in PPP health-care facilities. It has delivered 12 long-term care facilities, providing 1,700 beds, to private health-care providers such as Extendicare and other non-profit licensed providers. No financial information on these involvements is published either by OMERS or by Borealis. Extendicare, a U.S./Canadian health-care company, with assets exceeding $1.6 billion, reports that it entered into 25-year capital lease agreements with a BCP Long-Term Care Facilities, which provided it with about $125 million in 2001 to build eight nursing homes and $14.4 million in 2003 to build an additional one, at interest rates in the region of 8% per annum (Extendicare, 2005, p. 17). It is not clear, however, whether this company is owned by Borealis, but this appears to be the case (see Chenery, 2001, for cross-referencing). The very least one can say is that the OMERS investment in 12 such facilities likely cost about $190 million, but we have no details on the origin of that money, on how much was equity, or on how much was loans raised from others.

Private investment in long-term care facilities has come under sharp attack in recent years from a number of organizations, including the Ontario Health Coalition, and especially so since the Conservative government announced in 1998 the building of an additional 20,000 long-term care beds. The Coalition argues that two thirds of these beds were awarded to the private sector, most to just three corporations, including Extendicare, with the result that 'Ontarians are paying the private corporations and capital costs to build long term care beds that these companies will run for profit' (Ontario Health Coalition 2004). This gives Ontario one of the highest proportions of beds in the for-profit sector and, as fees rise, issues of accessibility are becoming more pronounced.

Even more controversially, OMERS is funding the building of two PPP hospitals in Ontario in conjunction with Carillion and EllisDon, in a consortium called the Healthcare Infrastructure Company of Canada Inc. Borealis is the major partner (75%) in the building and leasing for 25 years of the 608-bed William Osler Hospital in Brampton. It is also involved in the building and 20-year leasing of the Royal Ottawa Hospital, a 188-bed psychiatric hospital. In both cases, OMERS and the private companies will be involved in the financing, designing, and building of the facilities, as well as in the provision of non-clinical services. These projects are controversial for a number of reasons. To begin with, Carillion, a British company with experience in six similar projects in the United Kingdom, has a chequered history. It has been criticized for cost overruns on its hospitals. The Swindon hospital, which it financed and built, was $720 million on completion instead of the planned $330 million. Poor design and inadequate capacity were features of both the Swindon and the Dartford hospitals. Refinancing of the latter hospital on completion netted Carillion a windfall profit of $45 million and placed the hospital in the hands of investors 'who don't know and don't care about the patients or the hospital staff' (Unison, 2005), causing a public outcry. Carillion has a poor health and safety record and a reputation for paying low wages. Carillion hospitals have also failed inspections for basic standards in hygiene, trolley waits, cancelled operations, and breast cancer referrals (Mehra, 2005).

Secondly, both projects are already well over budget. The Brampton Hospital has risen in cost from about $350 million to over $550 million.

The Royal Ottawa has risen from $100 million to $125 million. The construction of both hospitals has also been significantly behind schedule.

Thirdly, there are clear disagreements over the relative costs of the PPP approach versus the traditional public-sector approach. The Royal Ottawa Health Care Group claims that the agreement with the Healthcare Infrastructure Company of Canada Inc., which blends the financing for the capital and facility management services, will cost $256 million over the course of the 20-year, eight-month arrangement. This figure compares favourably to that of a traditionally built and operated facility, which would have cost $273 million for the same product, a present value savings of $17 million (Canadian Health Reference Guide, 2005, ¶11).

It is not clear how these numbers were arrived at. Calculations by economist Hugh Mackenzie demonstrate that had the hospital been funded through government debt, the cost in present value terms would have been $174 million lower (Ontario Health Coalition, 2005). The concern is that although this is typical of PPP arrangements, in a hospital context these additional costs may in future put pressure on day-to-day hospital operations. This appears to be the case in the United Kingdom, where such hospitals operate with fewer beds, doctors, nurses, and support staff than do public hospitals. Frequent legal disputes also add to the expense of PPPs, putting further pressure on clinical and maintenance operations (Ontario Health Coalition, 2005).

The ambiguity about the financial aspects of these hospital deals results, in large measure, from the fourth point of controversy, which is the secrecy surrounding them. Once the private sector enters the picture, information that had previously been available to the public about hospital capital and operating costs suddenly becomes subject to commercial interests and hence inaccessible to the public. The financial aspects of both agreements have not been made publicly available, even though taxpayers' money is funding them. There is no way, therefore, that an objective evaluation of these agreements can be made by third parties – a serious deficiency in the funding of public services and infrastructure (Auerbach, 2002).

Some efforts have, however, been made to avoid two potential problems with the William Osler deal that were encountered in the United Kingdom. First, provision has been made for the private partners to assume responsibility from the William Osler Health Centre for the continued employment of unionized labour under the pre-existing collective agreement. This gives some protection to workers, though it would not prevent pressure on jobs and wages that often accompanies hospital deals. Second, the private partners may not refinance the hospital without prior approval of the Centre and only then on condition that the Centre shares 50% share of any refinancing gains (William Osler Health Centre, 2004). Neither of these provisions, however, transforms these investments from purely financial ones to ETIs.

FUTURE INTENTIONS

OMERS is the Canadian pension fund most heavily involved in PPPs in Canada. The attraction to OMERS of PPPs is that they expect to earn a return on these types of investment of 10–15% (Borealis Infrastructure, 2006d; Daw, 2004). These investments are relatively risk free, given that governments underwrite them. This is well in excess of what they can earn from government bonds of similar duration (30-year Canada bonds are yielding in the region of only 4.44% [Bank of Canada, 2006]). In fact, in 2005, Borealis Infrastructure, which includes but is not restricted to PPPs, earned a 23.3% return on capital, well in excess of its targeted long-run rate of return (Borealis Infrastructure, 2006a)! OMERS has also made it clear that it intends to become even more heavily involved. It is committed to increasing its ownership of public infrastructure to as much as 15% of its total assets. Its CEO, Paul Haggis, is quoted as saying that if governments or trade unions in Canada make this difficult, then it will go overseas (Norris, 2004). Indeed, that is exactly what OMERS has done, in conjunction with the Ontario Teachers' Pension Plan Board, in investing $1.2 billion in a consortium buying Southern Energy PLC in the United Kingdom (Ontario Teachers' Pension Plan, 2004).

There has, indeed, been pressure on OMERS from Canadian unions not to invest in PPPs, and especially from CUPE. Paul Moist, the national president of CUPE, has argued, 'We don't want our own money being used in schemes by other public–sector employers to privatize work of public employees' (Norris, 2004, ¶8). The significance of this statement is that CUPE represents the biggest proportion of OMERS membership, some 46% (OMERS, 2005b), and it is also the union that has consistently challenged the claims being made for PPPs and has undertaken most of the research on PPP policy and projects in Canada. The Ontario Public Service Employees Union (OPSEU), the Ontario Nurses' Association, and the Ontario Secondary School Teachers' Federation (Canadian Union of Public Employees [CUPE] – Ontario Division, 2003a), which, together, represent another 9% of OMERS membership, have also joined it in its campaign against OMERS involvement in PPPs. Recent changes to the governance structure of OMERS, through the *Ontario Municipal Employees Retirement System Act*, 2006, give stakeholders a much greater say in the administration of OMERS and appear to have doubled CUPE's representation on the Administrative Corporation Board, which deals with investments (OMERS, 2006c). It remains to be seen what kind of impact this might have on OMERS's interest in PPPs.

The Ontario Teachers Pension Plan

Apart from OMERS, there has been relatively little documented activity by Canadian pension funds in PPPs. The Ontario Teachers Pension Plan, which has $79 billion in assets and represents 250,000 active teachers, made one brief foray into this area. It held a 30% share in Philip Utilities Management Corporation, established in 1994, which was given responsibility for the operation, management, and maintenance of the water and sewage plants of the Hamilton-Wentworth Region for a 10-year period. This gave Philip Utilities Management Corporation control of the municipally owned water treatment plant, three waste water treatment plants, and 129 pumping and outstations.

The contract stipulated that Philip Utilities would be paid an annual fee of about $18 million, which was the Region's previous budget for services, less $0.5 million saving to the Region (Loxley, 1999b). The first $1 million of any savings Philip Utilities might make would accrue to the company and any further savings would be split 60:40 and eventually 80:20 between the company and the Region. This was a straight operations agreement, as ownership of the capital assets continued to reside with the Region. There were major problems with this agreement, which gave the company an incentive to reduce its wage bill. Despite short-term employment guarantees, it appears the labour force was eventually halved, compromising the quality of service (Loxley, 1999b). In 1996, there was a serious sewage spill, the costs of which had to be borne by the Region. There were several legal disputes about the origins of cost savings, as Philip Utilities claimed a portion of savings resulting entirely from Regional initiatives. There were delays in reporting on operations and concerns about the loss of access to information. Senior Regional staff who negotiated the deal found employment in Philip Utilities, raising important ethical questions, and the promised economic development spin-offs did not materialize (Loxley,

1999b). This project was taken back into public-sector hands in January 2005 (Mehra, 2005).

The Labourers' Pension Fund of Central and Eastern Canada

The Labourers' Pension Fund of Central and Eastern Canada (2003), representing over 37,000 members and with assets in excess of $1.1 billion, partnered with Carillion Canada and EllisDon, in Hospital Infrastructure Partners Inc., to bid on two Ontario hospital PPPs (Carillion Health, 2006a, 2006b; EllisDon, 2004). Through its wholly owned subsidiary CPF Realty, the Fund successfully bid on the Sault Area Hospital (Infrastructure Ontario, August 2007), a 289-bed facility, and unsuccessfully on the North Bay Regional Health Centre (Infrastructure Ontario, January 2007), which will have 275 acute-care beds and 113 long-term mental health beds (Canadian Council on Public–Private Partnerships, 2006).

Assessment

The history of Canadian union pension-fund activity in PPPs has, therefore, been essentially a history of OMERS, which probably has in the region of $2.5 billion invested in them.[4] These investments have, largely, been quite lucrative for OMERS. Most, however, have serious flaws in them from an ETI perspective. In a few cases, the Nova Scotia schools in particular, these involvements have had direct negative impacts on labour, supporting the main concern of unions opposed to PPPs. This issue was more central to the Ontario teachers' investment in the Hamilton-Wentworth PPP. The new foray into health PPPs seems to warn of many future problems in this area, notwithstanding any interim agreements or the OMERS commitment to socially responsible investment, which acknowledges that 'well-managed companies are those that demonstrate respect for their employees' (OMERS, 2006). Other concerns of PPP opponents, which might have huge indirect implications for public-sector workers, seem to have played a larger role. These concerns include the selling off of public assets at less than market value (Bruce), the granting of monopoly power to the PPP over user charges (Confederation Bridge, its various energy investments), the handing over of public facilities for expensive long-term leases (schools, hospitals, care homes), and the failure to realize risk transfer to the private sector – capital cost overruns being large in many instances while in others operating risks being retained by government. Each of these reduces resources available to the public sector and hence impinges on public-sector service, wages, or employment levels. At the same time, PPPs do contribute to high rates of return – a clear clash between socially responsible investment and the bottom line.

While it can be argued that investments that help close the infrastructure gap will unquestionably produce broader social or economic returns, there is no evidence that OMERS or any the other pension funds sought out investment in PPPs for other than narrow financial reasons. Nowhere does there appear to be any published reflection on any collateral returns these projects might yield, and certainly no reflection on any of the damage they might be causing to workers, taxpayers, or recipients of other public services. Borealis's investment criteria are strictly financial, investing in PPPs because they provide 'reliable and superior risk-adjusted long-term investment returns compared with more conventional investments like stocks and bonds' (Borealis Infrastructure, 2006c). In announcing a new social investment policy, OMERS itself has stressed, 'We do not use social screens to reject companies considered to have unacceptable products or business practices, nor do we give precedence to non-financial considerations over risk and return considerations. Our fiduciary responsibility to our plan members comes first' (OMERS, 2006). Collateral impacts of projects are of interest to OMERS, therefore, only if they affect long-run financial returns.

Thus, while investments by OMERS and other pension funds in PPPs are unquestionably targeted to the specific sector of infrastructure, and various sub-sectors within it, it would be incorrect to categorize them as ETIs in the sense that Carmichael (2003b), Harrigan (2003), and others are using that term. Pension funds are here simply and unequivocally maximizing financial returns from their PPP ventures.

The question arises, then, why other union pension funds have not followed suit in pursuing these lucrative investments. The explanations given are the lengthy negotiations with governments. This can be explained by the complicated nature of the agreements, though some segments of the private sector see in this a reluctance of civil servants to part with authority (Bray, 2003) or a failure of governments to simplify and standardize agreements (Chenery, 2001) – charges that still appear to have some currency. Opposition from trade unions is a political factor that some pension-fund managers are said to be reluctant to confront. Perhaps more convincing is the argument that small pension funds simply do not have the expertise or the necessary experience to enter into these complex contractual arrangements and the negotiations surrounding them. As Morgan Eastman, of OPSEU, has argued, 'Most pension funds, apart from the very large ones, generally do not have the staff to analyze these infrastructure investments: they rely on consultants ... It is a very specialized market' (Chenery, 2001, p. 3). Even OMERS has set up a subsidiary to specialize in PPPs and it too operates in conjunction with other private partners with specialist expertise in infrastructure construction and finance. As Chenery (2001) argued six years ago, if more union pension funds are to become involved in infrastructure PPPs, as is likely, it will be through the creation of consortia, such as the ones emerging in health care in Ontario, or it will be the result of the establishment of a specialist infrastructural fund that will, itself, hire the necessary expertise.

Alternative Approaches to Financing Infrastructure

Opponents of PPPs argue that there are alternative ways of financing the infrastructure so badly needed in Canada. First, balanced budget legislation could be eased to exempt legitimate capital spending from spending constraints. Second, instead of taxation being regarded as a burden, it should be considered the necessary price to pay for modern, efficient, public services. Third, since much of Canada's infrastructure is the responsibility of municipalities, which often face higher borrowing costs because of their small scale, the creation of pooled municipal infrastructure funds, along the lines of the Municipal Finance Authority in BC, and its counterparts in Nova Scotia, New Brunswick, and Newfoundland, should be entertained for the whole country (Calvert, 2005). Fourth, Townson (2003) has also suggested the creation of a Green Infrastructure Fund financed by bonds issued by senior levels of government, which would provide union pension funds with a risk-free return on an investment in environmentally sound infrastructure.

If PPP financing of infrastructure is to continue, as it likely will, then there must be clear rules put into place to protect the interests of both workers and taxpayers. First, the true costs of PPP alternatives should be entered on the books of governments as debt, regardless of accounting conventions. Second, the rights of workers to organize and be protected under collective agreements must be explicitly acknowledged and provided for in PPP agreements. Their pension benefits must also be made portable to the PPP entity. Third, these agreements must be open for scrutiny by pension contributors, their unions, and members of the public. They should be subject to public discussion before being signed, and any private company wishing to access public funds through the PPP mechanism must agree to such disclosure in advance. Finally, the full economic and social consequences of these investments, both positive and negative, should be taken into account by pension-fund managers and their arms length subsidiaries.

None of this will eradicate opposition to PPPs or protect workers or consumers entirely from the pressures that inevitably arise when public services are commodified, but it would, perhaps, help prevent some egregious shortcomings. Ultimately, the struggle over PPPs is not a technical or economic one. It is, essentially, a political one. In that respect, the recent reorganization of the governance structure of OMERS might prove to be the biggest single determinant of union pension-fund activity in PPPs in the coming years.

Notes

This paper draws heavily on research into public–private partnerships that the author and Salim J. Loxley have been conducting for some years now, the manuscript for which has been submitted for publication. The research assistance of Jesse Hajer and Andrew Donachuk is gratefully acknowledged. Funding provided by the Global Political Economy Research Fund of the Faculty of Arts, University of Manitoba, is also gratefully acknowledged.

1 GAAP requires that any lease arrangement that gives the lessee effective ownership of the asset over its useful life must be considered a capital lease and be shown on the books at full present value (Canadian Institute of Chartered Accountants, 2004). Only lease arrangements that allow use without effective ownership can be classified as operating leases and expensed annually. The trick for governments wishing to shift infrastructure expenses off the books is, therefore, to structure them in such a way that they qualify as operating leases or channel them through arms-length organizations.

2 Summary accounting includes the financial transactions, including lease liabilities, of all public-sector entities such as special operating agencies and crown corporations, and this prevents any attempt to shift liabilities off government books by running them through arms-length public entities

3 Project risk refers to cost overruns due to construction problems. Operating risk refers to projects not operating as planned, and can be broken down into market risk, financing risk, technical risk, and environmental risk. Other

risks that might affect projects are the risk of regulations or public policy/
laws changing, 'acts of God' (force majeure), and residual risk affecting the
price of the asset at the end of any lease. See Grimsey and Lewis (2002) for a
discussion of such risks and their measurement. See Calvert (2005) for risks
facing pension funds engaging in PPPs.

4 It should be remembered, however, that the Canada Pension Plan was a partner with OMERS in Borealis Capital in 2001–4, and was, therefore, equally
heavily involved in PPP investments in infrastructure in those years.

References

Abdel-Aziz, A.M., & Russell, A.D. (2001). A structure for government requirements in public–private partnerships. *Canadian Journal of Civil Engineering*,
28(6), 891–909.

Alphonso, C., & Mackie, R. (2000, July 12). British Energy to run Ontario
Power's Bruce plants. *Globe and Mail*, p. B1.

Auditor General. (1998). *O'Connell Drive Elementary School lease*. Halifax:
Department of Education and Culture.

Auerbach, L. (2002). *Issues raised by public private partnerships in Ontario's hospital sector*. Ottawa: CUPE.

Bank of Canada. (2006). Rates and statistics. Retrieved 10 September 2007 from
Bank of Canada website: http://www.bank-banque-canada.ca/en/rates/
bonds.html

Borealis Infrastructure. (2006a). *Borealis Infrastructure caps off successful year with
return of 23.2% in 2005*. Retrieved 5 January 2007 from Borealis Infrastructure
website: http://www.borealisinfrastructure.com/news/newsreleases
.aspx#march12006

Borealis Infrastructure. (2006b). *Energy*. Retrieved 5 January 2007 from Borealis
Infrastructure website: http://www.borealisinfrastructure.com/assets/
energy.aspx

Borealis Infrastructure. (2006c). *Infrastructure opportunities*. Retrieved 5 January
2007 from Borealis Infrastructure website: http://www.borealisinfrastruc-
ture.com/approach/infrastructureopportunities.aspx

Borealis Infrastructure. (2006d). *Investment criteria*. Retrieved 5 January 2007
from Borealis Infrastructure website: http://www.borealisinfrastruc-
ture.com/approach/investmentcriteria.aspx

Bowman, L. (2000). P3 – Problem, problem, problem. *Project Finance*, *206*, 25–8.

Bray, R. (2003). On the edge. *Summit*, *6*(3), 16.

Calvert, J. (2005, Winter). Pensions and public–private partnerships: A cautionary note for union trustees. *Just Labour*, *5*, 1–3.

Cameco. (2005). *Annual report: Financial information*. Retrieved from Cameco website: http://www.cameco.com/investor_relations/annual/2005/pdf/cameco_AR_Financial_Information.pdf

Canadian Council on Public–Private Partnerships. (2006). *PPP project tracker*. Retrieved 5 January 2007 from Canadian Council on Public–Private Partnerships website: http://www.pppcouncil.ca/resources_project_tracker.asp

Canadian Health Reference Guide. (2005). *Construction on New Royal Ottawa Hospital and Research Institute begins*. Retrieved 5 January 2007 from CHRG website: http://www.chrgonline.com/news_detail.asp?ID=30690

Canadian Institute of Chartered Accountants. (2004). Leases. In *Handbook* (section 3065, subsection 3060.3003). Toronto: Author.

Canadian Union of Public Employees (CUPE) – National. (2004). *P3 schools: Public interests vs. public profits*. Ottawa: Author.

Canadian Union of Public Employees (CUPE) – Ontario Division. (2003a). *Don't use our pension money against us, unions tell OMERS, Borealis*. Retrieved 4 January 2007 from CUPE website: http://cupe.ca/media/ART3f1ec66fe2014

Canadian Union of Public Employees (CUPE) – Ontario Division. (2003b). *P3 presentation for members of the OMERS Board of Directors*. Toronto: Author.

Canadian Union of Public Employees (CUPE) – Ontario Division. (2004). *Rebuilding strong communities with public infrastructure*. Retrieved 4 January 2007 from CUPE website: http://cupe.ca/updir/infrastructure_p3_sub.pdf

Carillion Health. (2006a). *Case study: Royal Ottawa Hospital, Ontario, Canada*. Retrieved 5 January 2007 from Carillon website: http://www.carillion-health.com/our_services/case_studies/case_study_royal_ottawa.asp#TopOfPage

Carillion Health. (2006b). *Case study: William Osler Hospital, Brampton, Ontario, Canada*. Retrieved 5 January 2007 from Carillon website: http://www.carillionhealth.com/our_services/case_studies/case_study_william_osler.asp#TopOfPage

Carmichael, I. (2003a). Fiduciary responsibility: A tool to control workers or an opportunity to build community wealth? In I. Carmichael & J. Quarter (Eds.), *Money on the line: Workers' capital in Canada*. Ottawa: Canadian Centre for Policy Alternatives.

Carmichael, I. (2003b). It's our jobs, it's our money: A case study of Concert. In I. Carmichael & J. Quarter (Eds.), *Money on the line: Workers' capital in Canada*. Ottawa: Canadian Centre for Policy Alternatives.

Chenery, J. (2001). *Financing the future: Building Canadian infrastructure*. Retrieved 4 August 2007 from Summit website: http://www.summitconnects.com/Articles_Columns/Summit_Articles/2001/special_focus/PPP/financing_future.htm

City of Toronto. (2005). *Financial annual report*. Toronto: Author.

Daw, J. (2004, 12 June). OMERS chief mulls new investment model. *Toronto Star*, p. D06.

Dobbin, M. (2002). *Warning: The P3s are coming*. Retrieved 7 September 2007 from National Union of Public and General Employees website: http://www.nupge.ca/news_2002/news_au02/n23au02a.htm

Drury, G. (2002, September/October). The pension fund approach to PPP. *Strategic Direct Investor: SDI*, 11.

EllisDon. (2004). *ROH signs deal for new public hospital*. Retrieved 10 August 2007 from EllisDon website: http://www.ellisdon.com/ed/press/news/?id=70

Enersource. (2005). *2005 annual review*. Retrieved 7 January 2007 from enersource website: http://www.enersource.com/pdf/2005-report.pdf

Extendicare. (2005). *2005 Annual report*. Retrieved 10 August 2007 from Extendicare website: http://www.extendicare.com/investor/ExtendicarAR05_Full.pdf

FPinfomart. (2006). Borealis capital corporation [Electronic Version]. *Financial Post Crosbie mergers and acquisitions in Canada*. Retrieved 10 August 2007 from FPinfomart website: http://www.fpinfomart.ca

Gordon, M., & Wilson, J. (2001). *'Tories' electricity plan spells financial disaster*. Retrieved 7 September 2007 from Ontario Tenants Rights website: http://www.ontariotenants.ca/electricity/ontario-hydro.phtml

Grimsey, D., & Lewis, M.K. (2002). Evaluating the risks of public private partnerships for infrastructure projects. *International Journal of Project Management, 20*(2), 107–18.

Harrigan, S. (2003). Economically targeted investments: Doing well and doing good. In I. Carmichael & J. Quarter (Eds.), *Money on the line: Workers' capital in Canada*. Ottawa: Canadian Centre for Policy Alternatives.

Infrastructure Ontario. (2007, August). Contract awarded for the Sault Area Hospital Project. News release.

Infrastructure Ontario. (2007, January). *Preferred proponent selected for the North Bay Regional Health Centre*. News release.

International Monetary Fund. (2004). *Public–private partnerships*. Washington, DC: Author.

Labourers' Pension Fund of Central and Eastern Canada. (2003). *Financial highlights*. Retrieved 4 January 2007 from http://www.lpfcec.org/portal/page?_pageid=114,1221038&_dad=portal&_schema=PORTAL

Loxley, J. (1996). *The economic and financial analysis of public–private partnerships*. Ottawa: Canadian Union of Public Employees – National Office.

Loxley, J. (2003). *Alternative budgets: Budgeting as if people mattered*. Halifax: Fernwood Books and Canadian Centre for Policy Alternatives – Manitoba.

Loxley, J., & Loxley, S.J. (2008). *The economics and finance of public–private part-nerships: Theory and Canadian policy and practice*. Manuscript submitted for publication.

Loxley, S.J. (1999a). *An analysis of a public–private sector-partnership: The Confederation Bridge*. Ottawa: Canadian Union of Public Employees.

Loxley, S.J. (1999b). *An analysis of a public–private sector-partnership: The Hamilton-Wentworth-Philips Utilities Management Corporation PPP*. Ottawa: Canadian Union of Public Employees.

Mackenzie, H. (2004). *Financing Canada's hospitals: Public alternatives to P3s*. Toronto: Ontario Health Coalition.

Mehra, N. (2005). *Flawed, failed, abandoned: 100 P3s; Canadian and international evidence*. Retrieved 10 August 2007 from CUPE website: http://cupe.ca/updir/Flawed_Failed_Abandoned_-_Final.pdf

Norris, G. (2004, 11 June). OMERS committed to infrastructure investment, might go outside Canada: Haggis. *Canadian Press*.

OMERS. (2005a). *Borealis Infrastructure to increase investment in Bruce Power*. Retrieved 10 August 2007 from OMERS website: http://www.omers.com/Newsroom/News_releases/Borealis_Infrastructure_to_increase_investment_in_Bruce_Power.htm

OMERS. (2005b). *Affiliation summary 2005*. Retrieved 10 August 2007 from OMERS website: http://www.omers.com/Plan_Governance/OMERS_Member_affiliation_summary/Affiliation_summary_2005.html

OMERS. (2005c). *Annual report 2005*. Retrieved 10 August 2007 from OMERS website: http://www.omers.com/AssetFactory.aspx?did=7672

OMERS. (2006). *Statement of investment beliefs*. Retrieved 10 August 2007 from OMERS website: http://www.omers.com/Investments/Corporate_governance/Statement_of_Investment_Beliefs.html

Ontario Health Coalition. (2004). *Long term care facilities*. Retrieved 4 January 2007 from Ontario Health Coalition website: http://www.web.net/ohc/LTC%20background.htm

Ontario Health Coalition. (2005). *Fact sheet: Public–private partnerships*. Retrieved 10 August 2007 from Ontario Health Coalition website: http://www.web.net/ohc/P3s/p3factsmay05.pdf

Ontario Power Generation. (2002). *TransCanada PipeLines and BPC Generation Infrastructure Trust join Cameco and unions in revised Bruce Power partnership*. Retrieved 4 January 2007 from Bruce Power website: http://www.brucepower.com/uc/GetDocument.aspx?docid=450

Ontario Teachers' Pension Plan. (2004). *Ontario Teachers', OMERS and Scottish and Southern Energy win $7.5 billion infrastructure bid for gas distribution networks in UK*. Retrieved 6 January 2007 from Ontario Teachers' Pension Plan

website: http://www.otpp.com/web/website.nsf/web/National_Grid_
Transco

Pollock, A., & Vickers, N. (2000, 14 April). Private pie in the sky. *www.
PublicFinance.co.uk*. Retrieved 10 August 2007 from Chartered Institute of
Public Finance and Accountancy website: http://www.cipfa.org.uk/
publicfinance/search_details.cfm?News_id=4718&keysea

Reed, J. (2004). OMERS in the public eye. *The Advocate*. Retrieved 7 January
2007 from http://www.oasbo.org/admin/eZeditor/files/f_9_OSBB0204
.pdf

Shaker, E. (2003, April). The devil in the details: The P3 experience in Nova
Scotia schools. *Our schools: Our selves*. Retrieved 10 August 2007 from Canadian Centre for Policy Alternatives website: http://www.policyalternatives
.ca/index.cfm?act=news&call=950&do=article&pA=BB736455

TD Bank Financial Group. (2004). *Mind the gap: Finding the money to upgrade
Canada's aging public infrastructure*. Toronto: Author.

Townson, M. (2003). *The role of pension funds in financing investment in public
infrastructure*. CUPE.

Unison. (2005). NAO report into Darent Valley PFI hospital 'proof positive' of
company profiteering says UNISON. Retrieved 10 August 2007 from
UNISON website: http://www.unison.org.uk/asppresspack/pressrelease_
view.asp?id=596

Vining, A.R., Boardman, A.E., & Poschmann, F. (2005). Public–private partnerships in the U.S. and Canada: 'There are no free lunches.' *Journal of Comparative Policy Analysis, 7*(3), 199–220.

William Osler Health Centre. (2004). Summary of the William Osler Health
Centre Project Agreement with the Healthcare Infrastructure Company of
Canada Inc. Retrieved 4 January 2007 from http://www.williamoslerhc
.on.ca/workfiles/project_agreement.pdf

8 Economically Targeted Investing: Financial and Collateral Impact

KATHRYN MANLEY, TESSA HEBB, AND
EDWARD T. JACKSON

This chapter argues that pension funds can earn attractive risk-adjusted rates of return on targeted private equity investments that seek to fill capital gaps in the market, and that by doing so they can benefit their communities as a whole. Targeted investments focus on achieving both a financial and a social return. The terminology that is used to refer to targeted investing ranges from 'economically targeted investments' to 'investments in underserved capital markets' or 'investing with intent.'

Although targeted investing may be done with any type of investment, the focus of this chapter is on targeted investments in private equity instruments. It is clear that there are inefficiencies in the private equity market. Theory suggests that these inefficiencies can be exploited to create appropriate returns. At the same time, such investments can create collateral benefits, such as urban revitalization and increased employment opportunities. There are a number of targeted investment approaches within the private equity field, including funds-of-funds and commingled funds. The key is to find best practices that pension funds can use in order to implement targeted investment programs that can benefit both the fund and the community. This chapter therefore examines two environments where targeted investing has been used and draws implications from them.

We first examine a best practice example from the United States. In 1992, the California Public Employees Retirement System (CalPERS) began to target investment in the State of California as part of its overall investment policies. One of the programs adopted as part of this goal is the private equity California Initiative. We examine the California Initiative as a model of targeted investment. We conclude that best practice in pension-fund targeted investment is achieved through geographic rather than social targeting. We believe that when investors limit themselves to a strictly geographic focus, their primary concern is market rates of return, with collateral impacts as a secondary result from the investment.

Second, we examine some empirical data from Canada. We test the impact of geographic targeting on investment portfolios using MacDonald and Associates data on Canadian private equity investments exited between 1999 and 2005. We compare exited deals where at least one of the investment partners had a stated geographic target against investments with no geographic targeting. The findings indicate no difference between targeted and untargeted firms in terms of age of firm at the time of investment, industry sector, market capitalization (at time of IPO), exit type, and time between investment and exit. From this case study, we draw lessons for Canadian pension funds interested in pursuing targeted investing.

This chapter is organized in the following manner. Section two examines the theoretical arguments in favour of targeted investing and urban economic development strategies. Section three presents an overview of current pension-fund involvement in private equity in general and in underserved capital markets in particular. Section four situates the U.S. case study by looking at the involvement of CalPERS in underserved capital markets, while section five focuses on the California Initiative. Section six looks at the best practice results that can be drawn from this case study. Section seven moves to Canada to test the impact of geographic targeting on investment portfolios. Lastly, section eight draws implications for Canadian pension funds and public policy and provides some concluding arguments.

Theoretical Argument

Michael Porter has noted that the North American system of allocating investment capital is failing. This system, as compared to the Japanese or German systems, is less supportive of equity investment overall, favours those forms of investments for which returns are most easily measurable, and encourages investment in some sectors while limiting investment in others (Porter & Wayland, 1992). In particular, Porter has argued that institutional sources of equity capital have often ignored inner city opportunities and minority owned businesses (Porter, 1995). In the *Harvard Business Review,* he noted, 'Access to debt and equity capital represents a formidable barrier to entrepreneurship and company

Figure 8.1. Equity capital for entrepreneurs.

Stage	Pre-seed	Seed/start-up	Early	Later	
Source	Founders	Angels/angel alliances		Venture funds	
Demand	$25 K	$100 K	$2,000 K	$5,000 K	> $5,000 K
Supply		Funding gap	Secondary funding gap		

Source: Centre for Venture Research – University of New Hampshire, as presented in Sohl, 2003.

growth in inner city areas' (Porter, p. 64). In essence, he describes an important urban capital gap.

Similarly, Jeffrey Sohl (2003) notes that the U.S. private equity market in particular does not meet the standards for market efficiency. He describes two major capital gaps in the private equity industry: one at the $100,000 to $2 million range, and the other at $2–5 million (see Figure 8.1).

For those unfamiliar with the private equity market, it is perhaps useful to explain that there are two major types of private equity investors: angels and venture capital firms. Angels are high net-worth individuals who invest a small proportion of their own wealth in small and medium enterprises; venture capital firms create funds, raising capital in order to invest in specified investment situations (Mason & Harrison, 2004). As seen in Figure 8.1, angels are the primary source of external equity financing at the high-risk, early stages (seed and start-up) of an entrepreneurial venture's existence, whereas venture capital funds invest in larger ventures and make little impact on the early stage financing of entrepreneurial ventures (Freear, Sohl, & Wetzel, 2002; Sohl, 1999).

Porter and Sohl are not alone in the view that capital gaps are present in the private equity market. Other authors have found different types of capital gaps, which explain why underserved capital markets exist. While Porter describes inner city capital gaps relative to other regions, Lipper and Sommer (2002) describe 'have' versus 'have-not' states with respect to the availability of venture capital investments. The capital gaps described by Sohl are related to the amount of capital required by the business, as are those described in articles by Davis (2003), Freear et al. (2002), and Mason and Harrison (2003). Other reasons why underserved capital markets exist include prejudice, making it more difficult for minority business owners to obtain capital (Garvin, 1971); information gaps, both for businesses seeking capital and for capital providers (Freear et al., 2002; Sohl, 1999); and capital provider preferences for some sectors over others (Patterson, 1993; Porter & Wayland, 1992). Evidence of capital gaps has been found in many countries, and this phenomenon is well documented in the United States, Canada, and the United Kingdom (Davis, 2003; Freear et al., 2002; Harrison & Mason, 2000; Sohl, 1999).

The existence of such underserved capital markets is, in fact, one of the strongest arguments in favour of economically targeted investments (ETIs). Indeed, ETIs are often defined as investments that fill a capital gap or infuse capital into an underserved market, while both delivering an appropriate risk-adjusted rate of return and providing collateral benefits (Quarter, Carmichael, Sousa, & Elgie, 2001; Read, 1997; Zanglein, 2001). Porter's arguments, in particular, support the creation of urban economic development strategies, such as the California Initiative. He described four major advantages to inner city investing: strategic location, since they offer proximity to business areas; local market demand, since these markets have not yet been saturated; integration with regional clusters; and the availability of human resources (Porter, 1995). Similarly, all of the different types of capital gaps described represent opportunities for pension funds to achieve desirable returns through targeted investing.

Opponents of ETIs insist that there is little evidence to suggest that markets are inefficient (Barth & Cordes, 1981) and they assert that investments that are not already being funded must be inferior (Notsinger, 1998). Although Barth and Cordes argue that markets are not inefficient and that therefore ETIs are not useful, they also note, 'If capital markets actually failed to efficiently allocate funds to such activities, pension funds might actually earn higher returns by diverting a larger share of their portfolios to, say, venture capital or urban housing investments' (p. 236).

In fact, the widely documented existence of capital gaps as found in the general private equity literature, and as described above, suggests that the private equity market is not efficient. There are currently many imperfections in the private equity market (Sohl, 2003), which can hurt the economic development of a region (Lipper & Sommer, 2002).

Arguments of market efficiency aside, the major concern for pension funds and other institutional investors when considering investment in ETIs is that of their fiduciary duty to provide a reasonable risk-adjusted rate of return to their beneficiaries. For this reason, many researchers have looked at the ability of ETIs to provide a reasonable rate of return. Unfortunately, evidence on whether it is possible to consistently realize an appropriate return has been divided. For example, Gregory (1990) found that the performance of ETIs was indeterminate; one third of the public employee pension plans with ETIs that he studied met their benchmark returns, 4% failed, and 3% exceeded benchmarks. The rest either did not know or did not answer the question.

Notsinger (1998) notes that even if the market to finance these investments is inefficient, fund managers may be unable to distinguish between good investments and those that are overpriced. His research examined a number of pension funds both with and without ETIs and found that, overall, those without ETIs earned statistically higher abnormal returns than funds with ETIs. However, the difference in returns between those that invested in ETIs and those that did not was not statistically significant when divided into the three individual annual surveys. He concluded, 'Pension funds that invest in ETIs experience lower risk-adjusted rates of return than funds that do not invest in ETIs.' However, referring to the amount of the differences, he also noted, 'These estimates are probably too large to blame solely on ETIs because these investments typically make up only 5% of a pension fund's portfolio' (p. 94). In another study, Marr, Trimble, and Nofsinger (1994) concluded that pension fund ETIs had consistently underperformed accepted benchmarks.

In contrast, Watson (1994) found that ETIs might improve the performance of pension funds. In another study, Doran and Bannock (2000) investigated examples of locally targeted funds that institutional investors were supporting. They found that there were local gaps in the availability of venture capital and concluded that locally targeted private equity can be a profitable investment opportunity for public-sector funds. The performance of the funds they examined was at least comparable with that of private venture capital funds. They noted that there need be no compromise between the objective of supporting local economic development and that of seeking the highest financial returns.

Although the evidence on whether or not ETIs have been able to provide adequate risk-adjusted rates of return remains divided, theory suggests that this should be possible. Porter argued that, following the principles of competitive advantage, inner city businesses would allow investors to receive appropriate returns on their investments (Porter, 1995). Capital gaps based on amount of funding, prejudice, location, sector, etc. represent opportunities for pension funds to address market inefficiencies. Given that there are documented capital gaps in the market for private equity, pension funds should be able to use ETIs to fill these gaps while earning an attractive risk-adjusted rate of return, thus fulfilling their fiduciary duties.

Overview of Current Pension Funds Involvement in Underserved Capital Markets

Private Equity and Pension Funds

Pension-fund involvement in private equity and other non-traditional investments has increased in recent years (Davis, 2003; Greenwich, 2002). Pension funds are turning to alternative investments such as private equity because this type of investment is often able to outperform more traditional investments (Healy & Hardy, 1997). Another reason that alternative investments may be attractive is the additional portfolio diversification that they provide; for instance, venture capital is not closely correlated to the broad stock market (Healy & Hardy, 1997).

However, although involvement in the private equity market by pension funds in both Canada and the United States is increasing and is large in terms of dollar value, it remains small as a percentage of total pension-fund portfolio assets (Chemla, 2004; Greenwich, 2002). Healey and Hardy (1997) found that, in 1995, the largest funds in the United States and Canada had almost $70 billion committed to private equity. Nonetheless, Chemla (2004) found that, although over half of the investments in venture capital funds in 2001 came from pension funds, this number represented less than 5% of pension-fund assets. There is also clear evidence that American pension funds contribute more capital to venture capital and private equity than do Canadian pension funds (Chemla, 2004; Davis, 2003; Industry Canada, 2004).

The hesitance of many pension funds to participate in these alternative investments may be attributed to a number of challenges. For instance, private equity investments are essentially illiquid and exits may be difficult (Chemla, 2004; Healy & Hardy, 1997). In addition, they may be perceived as inherently 'more risky,' even when this is not the case (Healy & Hardy, 1997). Pension-fund trustees may also be concerned about the due diligence requirements for these investments, the need for expert advice, and the fact that reliable data may be difficult to obtain (Healy & Hardy, 1997; Industry Canada, 2004). In particular, small and medium size institutions have structural limitations in terms of gathering this information and performing due diligence (Industry Canada, 2004).

Davis (2003) notes in his overview of the Canadian venture capital market that, in the United States, 'VCs and pension fund managers developed best practices, third-party pools, private placement databases providing market information, and a human resources component producing diverse investment specialists, intermediaries, market experts (known as gatekeepers) who act solely on behalf of fiduciary interests, and deal-making agents (Falconer 2000)' (p. 201). He suggests that Canada can learn from the U.S. experience. A recent Industry Canada report seconds this sentiment, noting that funds of funds, gatekeepers, and other tactics can help pension funds to overcome structural barriers to private equity investing (Industry Canada, 2004).

These suggestions should apply not just to Canadian pension funds looking to emulate the more experienced American market. The fact remains that private equity and other alternative investments are not widely invested in by pension funds in either country. There are, however, a few American funds, such as CalPERS, that do have a lot of experience in these areas, specifically in serving underfunded capital markets. It is to these funds that we can look to for best practices.

Pension Funds and Underserved Markets

Urban economic development strategies have undergone a dramatic transformation over time, making them increasingly attractive to savvy pension-fund investors. Initially conceived as economically targeted investments (ETIs), urban economic development was valued as a collateral benefit exogenous to investment returns. This first generation of projects focused on capital preservation combined with collateral benefits as the principle aim of the investment, with acceptable low rates of return guaranteed through government involvement. By the mid-1990s, first-generation ETIs coexisted with second-generation projects. In these new projects urban economic development is endogenous to the rates of return, with resulting investment risks managed through the structure of the private partnerships rather than a reliance on government guarantees. While risks are higher in these projects, so are the potential returns from investment. A third generation of urban economic development investment projects is now being entered and is potentially the most dynamic phase along this continuum. Urban development in this phase is regarded as an economic opportunity, and the investment is a pure venture capital structure determined solely by potential rates of return. The spillover from the impact of urban revitalization is a positive but not essential driver (Figure 8.2). Current estimates of U.S. pension-fund investment in third-generation urban development projects are $6 billion (Hagerman, Clark, & Hebb, 2006; Hebb, 2006). The CalPERS California Initiative modelled on the second- and third-generation approaches to urban economic development offers interesting lessons for these kinds of engagements.

Methods and Vehicles for Urban Economic Development

Pension funds can participate in urban economic development through private equity in many ways. The level of involvement required by the fund ranges anywhere from a simple investment in a previously established outside fund that meets their development goals to an internally managed direct private placement of equity in a specific firm (Cross, 1993). However, for the most part investments fall between these two extremes. Commingled funds with professional management are one of the most successful ways of structuring ETIs. These funds are pooled investments that have participation from several pension funds and are run by hired outside managers (Calabrese, 1999).

Consortiums are useful way to overcome structural barriers, by pooling the resources of several pension funds to undertake investments (Yago, Zeidman, & Schmidt, 2003). Partnering with private investors is also beneficial, as it provides a way for pension-fund managers to confirm that risk-adjusted returns, diversification, and due diligence are comparable to what might be achieved using other investments (Calabrese, 1999). Partnerships with intermediaries allow the funds to avoid dealing directly with the details of due diligence, etc., while still ensuring that the investments are well managed (Yago et al., 2003). Bringing private management to investments with a public benefit can help to ensure that both the direct financial goals and the collateral economic development benefits are achieved.

One example of how consortiums and partnerships can work is through the creation of pooled funds that allow investors to spread their risk over more companies while still achieving economic development goals in their own community (Yago et al., 2003). For instance, the Department of Housing and Urban Development worked in cooperation with six pension funds to establish a program enabling pension funds to invest in low-income housing (Rosentraub & Shroitman, 2004). Similarly, Levine (1997) described a study sponsored by the International Foundation of Employee Benefits Plans and the University of Wisconsin-Milwaukee Center for Economic Development, which called for the creation of a private intermediary to help pension funds invest in ETIs. This intermediary, representing a cross section of pension funds, assisted them in identifying ETI opportunities and in soliciting proposals from outside investment mangers to carry out their plans. The private intermediary also helped the pension funds with their co-investment strategies and their investment monitoring activities.

Securitization of products by an intermediary is another way of making an equity investment while overcoming some of the difficulties associated with ETIs. One example is the packaging of individual small business loans that meet the economic development goals of the fund into a security, converting illiquid individual loans into more liquid securities (Yago et al., 2003). Another example is that of NYCERS, which makes investments in fixed-income instruments that offer loans to small business for export finance with resultant small business growth and export expansion (Levine, 1997).

Other common characteristics of successful ETIs include geographic diversification with reciprocal targeting, risk reduction strategies such as wide diversification of venture capital funds, comparability to benchmarks, clear collateral benefits, and cost reduction strategies such as economies of scale (Calabrese, 1999).

CalPERS Involvement in Underserved Capital Markets

In 1992, the California Public Employees Retirement System (CalPERS), the largest public pension fund in the United States (assets of US$206 billion as of 31 March 2006), began to target investment in the State of California as part of its overall investment policy. This long-standing policy of the CalPERS Board began with their allocation decision to invest $375 million in the development of affordable single-family homes in California as part of their real-estate portfolio. The investment was expected to generate 22% returns to the pension fund, provide construction jobs, and fill a capital gap in the market, while increasing the supply of moderately priced homes in the state.

In 1998, CalPERS decided to raise its exposure to venture capital and to help expand the venture capital industry in California. This resulted in a fund-of-funds called California Emerging Ventures, which has now expanded to include other types of private equity investments. Since 1998, two more generations have been added to this fund and over 130 companies have received financing. Table 8.1 describes the performance of these funds thus far (as of 2004). It is important to note that, although net internal rate of return is negative, the funds are at the early stages of the J-curve at this point[1] (see Figure 8.3). In other words, since the funds were five years old or fewer at the time these data were collected, they have not yet moved into the profitable part of the curve. However, examining the internal rates of return (IRR) provided, it is clear that the pattern is as expected, with the older funds approaching the zero IRR or break-even point and expected to continue to increase over the next few years.

By 2004, the CalPERS total in-state California investments were valued at approximately $20 billion or 11% of the fund. As of 31 October 2004, 19.5% of the California portfolio was allocated to the AIM Program,[2] 41.25% to real estate, 13% to public equity, and 6.8% to fixed income (see Figures 8.4 and 8.5). Now the AIM Program had $9.1 billion in commitments that either were headquartered in or had a major presence in California.

It must be remembered that with a GDP of $1.33 trillion, California is the fifth largest economy in the world. As a result, CalPERS does not lose portfolio diversification with this geographic focus in their investments. CalPERS policy on risk/return criteria is clear: they do not make concessions on risk-adjusted return, asset allocation, or diversification guidelines (Harrigan, 2003).

Within this large in-state portfolio, approximately 2% of the fund is earmarked specifically for ETIs that include private equity, real estate, and fixed income investments. With full recognition of the fiduciary duty of CalPERS to its plan members, the CalPERS Board of Trustees adopted a policy statement in 2000 that clearly laid out the parameters of the ETI program. This document was revised in 2002 and again in 2004. The February 2000, four-page document titled *Statement of Investment Policy for Economically Targeted Investment Program* states, 'An Economically Targeted Investment is defined as an investment which has collateral intent to assist in the improvement of both national and regional economies and in the economic well being of the State of California, its localities and residents. Economic stimulation includes job creation, development and savings; business creation; increases or improvement in the stock of affordable housing; and improvement of the infrastructure.' It goes on to say, 'By strengthening the State's econ-

Table 8.1. California Emerging Ventures.

Fund description	Vintage year	Capital committed	Cash in	Cash out	Cash out & remaining value	Net IRR	Investment multiple
California Emerging Ventures I, LLC	1999	958,064,006	739,020,813	261,973,793	672,224,324	−4	0.90x
California Emerging Ventures II, LLC	2000	1,356,275,465	813,738,318	121,986,186	702,510,264	−8.4	0.90x
California Emerging Ventures III, LLC	2001	466,500,904	93,097,127	4,113,160	70,987,052	−24.8	0.80x

Figure 8.2. Public-sector pension plans and urban revitalization.

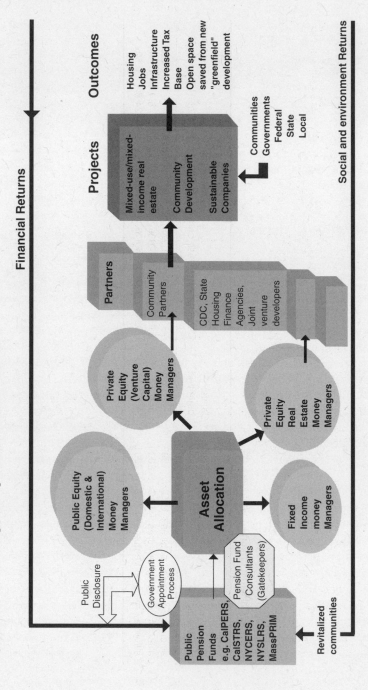

Source: Hagerman (2007) modified from original Clark and Hebb 2004

Figure 8.3. The private equity J-curve.

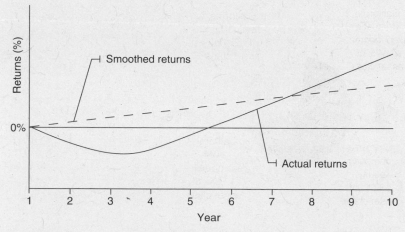

omy and the well being of employers, ETIs help promote the continued maintenance of employer contributions to the System.' However, it is clear in the policy statement that the pension fund will not sacrifice returns to meet these objectives. 'The system will consider only ETIs which when judged solely on the basis of economic value, would be financially comparable to alternatively available investments. Comparability will be judged on a risk adjusted basis with the System being willing to accept no less in return and incur no additional risk or cost.' Nor will the system take responsibility for the collateral benefits generated from the investment decision.

In 2002, the ETI policy was revised to include a major section (section V) titled 'California Emerging Markets Investment Policy.' This policy further targeted CalPERS investments into underserved capital markets in the state: 'The objective of this policy is to discover and invest in opportunities that may have been bypassed or not reviewed by traditional, more mainstream sources of investment capital.' Such markets include rural and urban areas undergoing or in need of revitalization where there are assets (e.g., an available labour pool, underutilized infrastructure) conducive to business development. The long-term goal of the policy is 2% of the total portfolio of CalPERS (valued at $4 billion as of March 2006). This does not imply a mandate to invest in underserved capital markets, 'but rather should be viewed as an additional set of suggested parameters within which to consider such invest-

Figure 8.4. California commitments, 2004.

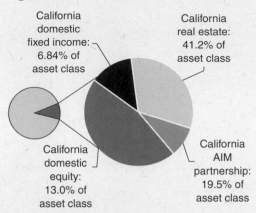

Figure 8.5. California investments, 2004.

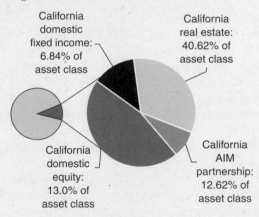

ments.' These investments include fixed income, private equity, and real-estate asset classes. Despite the fact that these investments target underserved capital markets, they 'shall be priced at least at market prices and shall be subject to applicable performance measures.' These investments must also receive prudent levels of due diligence, and as part of that process 'staff shall consider the current economic condition of the State of California and the prudence of committing assets to under-served areas given that economic condition.'

Two investment programs are key components of CalPERS investments in California's emerging markets. The first is the California Initiative, a $500 million investment program targeting small business and emerging and developing companies in underserved urban and rural California communities. This Initiative falls under the AIM Program, which makes up about 5% of the CalPERS portfolio. The AIM Program explicitly includes a California-oriented component that is designed to take advantage of '(a) the unique size characteristics of the California economy; (b) the existence of a 'capital gap' for certain business segments within the state; and (c) the ability to construct a diversified array of investment vehicles that reflects the state's large number of business entities' (CalPERS, 2004c).

The second program is the California Urban Real Estate (CURE) program, which is part of the real-estate asset allocation. This case study focuses on the private equity California Initiative.

The California Initiative

Early Development

The California Initiative moved the CalPERS long-standing targeted in-state private equity investment program toward a more focused set of investments specifically aimed at California's underserved capital markets (also known as domestic emerging markets). Because of the perceived risks, uncertainty about the market, and lack of knowledge at the Board and staff level, this shift in focus required both a Board-level champion and an external feasibility study in order to raise the comfort level and knowledge about this market for the full CalPERS Board and staff. The Board-level champion was Phil Angelides, California state treasurer, who used his Board position at both CalPERS and the California State Teachers Retirement System (CalSTRS), as well as his role as treasurer, to advance the ideas associated with investment in underserved capital markets. In May 2000, he released a 36-page report, *The Double Bottom Line: Investing in California's Emerging Markets*,[3] which detailed the advantages of investment in California's underserved capital market. Drawing from Michael Porter's work at the Harvard Business School, he outlined the competitive advantage of these communities. He reinforced the decisions of CalPERS and CalSTRS to enter these markets with corresponding programs at the California State Treasury. Angelides persuaded fellow Board members to look seriously at the opportunities for investment that underserved capital markets present.

While Angelides provided the catalyst for the California Initiative, the CalPERS Board and staff needed additional outside resources to assure themselves of the validity of this approach for the pension fund. The California Initiative was to be part of the private equity asset class or AIM program at CalPERS. In 2000, the CalPERS Board asked staff for a detailed, external, expert study of AIM including its targeted commitment to underserved capital markets. CalPERS staff turned to McKinsey Consultants for such a study. This step allowed time for both investment staff and Board members to become more familiar with underserved capital markets and to be reassured that outside experts agreed that there were indeed untapped investment opportunities in these markets. The whole CalPERS private equity asset class was itself a young portfolio, having been started in 1990 and having an average age of 3.7 years for its investments. Overall, this asset class had an asset allocation target of 7%.

By June 2000, the California Initiative was approved by the Board as part of the Economically Targeted Investment Program, opening up the search for suitable investment partners for this program. Its mission statement (adopted May 2001) reads, 'The California Initiative will invest in traditionally underserved markets primarily, but not exclusively, located in California. The objective is to discover and invest in opportunities that may have been bypassed or not reviewed by other sources of investment capital' (CalPERS, 2004a).

Initially 67 firms responded to a CalPERS request for proposal for the California Initiative. CalPERS staff and consultants went through rigorous due diligence. By May 2001, 10 private equity firms[4] were selected to partner with CalPERS in this endeavour and a capital commitment of $475 million was allocated to the Initiative. CalPERS uses multiple fund managers to cover a range of strategies, such as corporate partnerships, co-investments, funds of funds, and funds that target minority-owned enterprises (Yago et al., 2003). Investment structures used by the CalPERS California Initiative are illustrated in Figure 8.6. Although CalPERS structures its investment partnerships in a number of ways, in all cases it looks for the partner vehicle to also invest their own capital in the project.

The largest investment was and still is with Yucaipa Corporate Initiatives Fund, with an initial capital commitment of $200 million. The second largest commitment was to Bank of America Fund of Funds at $100 million. Three funds were already existing general partners of CalPERS, while several others were new, innovative small funds with whom CalPERS was prepared to partner. Most of these investments were small by CalPERS standards, between $10 and $25 million. Given

Figure 8.6. Investment structures used by the CalPERS California initiative, July 2003.

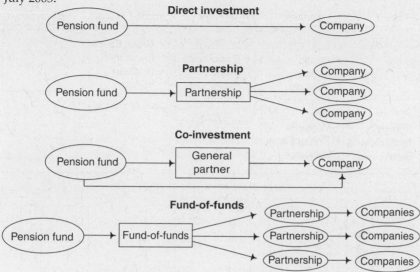

that the due diligence required is the same as that for a large investment, it was important that the AIM investment staff shared the Board's commitment to the program. The investment funds themselves covered the spectrum of private equity from early stage seed funds to corporate funds (see Figure 8.7). As of June 2005 the California Initiative had invested in 83 companies.

Not only were the investment partners providing different structures and private equity investment styles, they were also geographically dispersed throughout California and across the United States. In all cases, CalPERS expectation is that the partner vehicles work closely with community and economic development groups as well as city, county, state, and federal agencies.

Key criteria that determine investment decisions in underserved capital markets by these investment funds are:

- that the company is located in a region with limited access to investment capital
- that there is diversification of company management (either women or ethnic minority)
- that the company employs workers from low- and moderate-income areas.[5]

Figure 8.7. California Initiative investment partners by private equity type.

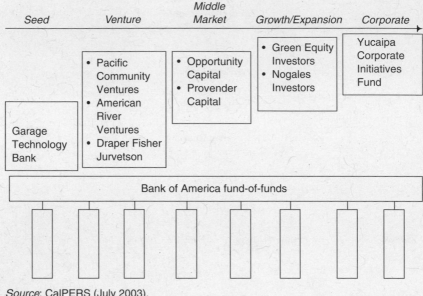

Source: CalPERS (July 2003).

Impact

The California Initiative is in the early stages of its growth. Much of the capital allocation remains to be invested. The impact on California's underserved capital market is already noticeable. The $475 million of the CalPERS capital allocation has leveraged commitments for a further $725 million from other investors. The role of CalPERS as the lead (or first) investor is key. In February 2006 CalPERS issued an extensive report on the activities in its California Initiative portfolio. It identified three benchmarks for the program: companies that have limited access to capital, companies that employ workers who reside in economically disadvantaged areas, and companies that have female and/or minority management. Of the 68 California Initiative companies invested by 2006, 65 met at least one of the benchmarks, 39 met at least two, and 18 met all three. Forty-eight of the companies are based in California, 51 employ a significant proportion of their workforce in California, and 37 have been in the program's portfolio for one year or more.

CalPERS estimates that these companies have created almost 2,500 jobs, including nearly 600 in California, since investment. They employ more than 5,000 Californians, about 2,000 of whom live in economically disadvantaged areas.

Returns on the assets of the four-year-old program are an annual return of 16% as of 30 September 2005. CalPERS is aiming for returns of up to 20%, and the California Initiative is delivering returns in that range.

Many different types of investments are represented within this portfolio. For instance, the Bank of America fund is actually a fund of funds, which is diversified across a wide number of industries (Banc of America, 2006). On the other hand, the Pacific Community Ventures Investment Partners directly invests in businesses such as Evergreen Lodge – a San Francisco lodging business that also has the social goal of helping at-risk Bay Area youth to develop stable careers and lives. Another investment that Pacific Community Ventures has made is that of Beacon Fire & Safety, which provides sales and service of fire safety equipment while employing low-income workers from at least six different communities in California (Pacific Community Ventures, 2006). Provender Capital has provided financing for Carver Bancorp, Inc., the largest African-American-operated savings bank in the United States (Provender, 2006). Yucaipa has invested in a restaurant chain called Picadilly Cafeterias, Inc., which was facing bankruptcy, thus saving jobs. This business's workforce is made up of 65% minorities, and 74% of the restaurants are located in underserved communities. The California Initiative investments have varying structures and represent a wide diversity of industries (see Figure 8.8).

The California Initiative as a Best Practice Case Study: Results

It is important to note that the role of pension funds should not be to create the market that they invest in. They simply provide liquidity to the market and then exit the opportunities after the first stage of risk-taking. Investing in targeted private equity should be a profitable endeavour, following best practices drawn from the California Initiative and other pension funds' experience.

CalPERS undertook the California Initiative as an intentional investment strategy that achieves both a market risk-adjusted rate of return and invests in California's underserved capital markets. CalPERS hopes to gain strong performance from its long-term investments by being an early entrant into these markets (Porter, 1995). Additionally the fund hopes to strengthen the economic health of California and by extension to underpin the ability of employers to maintain their contri-

Figure 8.8. California Initiative portfolio diversification by industry, as of September 2004.

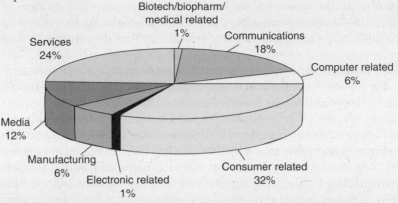

Industry	Actual Company Examples
Consumer related	Pool supply retail chain. Clothing and apparel company
Services	Hotel, restaurant chain, and relocation service company
Communications	Wireless internet services and telecom company
Media	Spanish-language format radio station
Computor related	Software and enterprise services companies
Manufacturing	Auto parts and container companies

Source: CalPERS (July 2004b).

butions to the pension plan. Finally, CalPERS believes that economically vibrant and healthy communities indirectly benefit the pension plan, its members, and retirees.

The most important best practice result is that of measuring success first by the risk-adjusted rate of return, and only subsequently on other targets. This allows the fund managers to be sure of meeting their fiduciary responsibilities. This is also the best way to benefit the community, since theory suggests that, by filling capital gaps, investors should both receive excess returns and support economic development. If investors do not receive an appropriate return, it is probable that they are not filling a true capital gap (i.e., a gap that an efficient market would have funded), but are instead investing in projects that an efficient market would have left unfunded. Calabrese (1999) lists the comparability of fund returns to an appropriate benchmark as one of the common characteristics of leading successful alternative investment programs.

CalPERS does not make concessions on risk/return criteria (Harrigan, 2003).

Unfortunately, however, the California Initiative is a new program, and the investment portfolio is young. Annual returns on the four-year-old fund were at 16.3% as of September 2005. These returns are indicative of the J-curve effect described earlier. Total investment by CalPERS in the California Initiative is $500 million, representing 0.3% of its total portfolio. CalPERS investment officers bring a long-term investment horizon to this asset class and feel strongly that Board sensitivity to these markets allows CalPERS first-mover advantage, entering the market ahead of other investors and as a result capturing significant returns. This has certainly been the case with the other CalPERS targeted program, the California Urban Real Estate Program (CURE), where performance as of August 2005 had an annual IRR of 22.2% since inception (far superior to that of the core real estate portfolio).

Another best practice is to use geographic rather than social targeting, and to set broad targets. This allows the fund to focus on diversification and return, by allowing for some flexibility in the way that it meets social goals. For instance, CalPERS believes in picking proven fund managers and investment vehicles and allowing these top-quartile vehicles to do their job within broad guidelines. It is important to avoid having too little in-house oversight, but it is equally important to avoid having too much (Calabrese, 1999). CalPERS does not distort established asset allocation and geographic diversification guidelines in order to achieve their social goals (Harrigan, 2003). Having geographic targets, such as focusing on inner cities (as suggested by Porter) or within any particular underserved capital market, makes it easier for both social goals and financial goals to be met.

There are also best practices in the way pension funds structure their targeted investments. One best practice that many successful alternative investment programs use is that of geographical diversification through reciprocal targeting (Calabrese, 1999). This allows pension funds to invest a sum of money into a diversified portfolio with the understanding that the same amount of money will be invested, from the broad portfolio, within their geographical area. Levine (1997) suggests that pension funds work together to create a development foundation, which would allow for diversification of investments and spreading of risk, but still allow some control over the investments by the individual pension funds. Commingled funds with professional management allow for pooling of capital by the pension funds and can help reduce costs and increase economies of scale, while at the same time allowing for direction by professional hired management (Blakely, Lynch, & Skudrna, 1985; Calabrese, 1999). Partnering with private investors is a best practice because it allows fiduciary concerns to be addressed by confirming that risk-return goals, diversification, and due diligence are being appropriately dealt with (Calabrese, 1999). These are all investment patterns that the California Initiative has been using.

While financial concerns are the primary drivers of any investment decision, CalPERS targeted investments have delivered significant collateral benefits that strengthen the economic underpinnings of the state. These collateral benefits are measured in greater employment, opportunities for businesses owned by women and minorities, increased affordable housing, and stronger and healthier communities.

As a public employee pension plan, CalPERS is aware of the political climate in which it operates. When asked, almost all Board and staff of the fund say that the California Initiative will be judged by the financial returns it generates over time. In order to ensure out-performance, CalPERS is extremely careful in its investment manager selection and looks for managers with successful track records. This means it is hard for new investment vehicles to receive CalPERS funding. The biggest obstacle facing the fund will be the patience required for long-term results to be achieved. As several pension-fund officials have stated, there is limited reward for success in non-traditional investment decisions, while failure is heavily punished (primarily through negative media attention). This is particularly challenging when CalPERS is required by law to publicly post its quarterly performance results for all private equity investment managers.

CalPERS has chosen a deliberate targeted investment strategy focused on California's underserved capital markets. It is still too soon to see whether the California Initiative will be a 'best practice' case in its financial contribution to the pension plan, which is the key factor. However, while still a young investment program, the California Initiative does have the potential for long-term returns benefiting the pension plan, its members, and the larger community.

Geographic Targeting in Canada

Testing the Impact of Geographic Targeting

Although the financial impacts of the California Initiative are not yet clear, this case study does demonstrate some potentially useful best

Table 8.2. Location of Firms in Sample.

Province	Number of firms
Alberta	21
British Columbia	40
Manitoba	1
New Brunswick	1
Nova Scotia	5
Ontario	157
Quebec	64
Saskatchewan	1

practices in geographic targeting. In Canada, a number of funds also use geographic targeting criteria. This presents an interesting opportunity to examine the use of geographic targeting through empirical testing. Using MacDonald and Associates data on Canadian private equity investments exited between 1999 and 2005, we compare exited deals where at least one of the investment partners had a stated geographic target, against investments with no geographic targeting. *Exited deals* are investments whose returns have been realized, such as through mergers and acquisitions, because the company went out of business, or through an initial public offering (IPO).

The Sample

We used data on private equity investments exited between 1999 and 2005. These criteria left us with 290 deals to examine. We were able to identify deals in which at least one of the investment partners had a stated geographic target. This allowed a 'targeted' variable to be added to the sample to differentiate between these deals and deals in which no geographic targeting was used. Sixty of the deals had at least one investment partner with targeting criteria and 230 did not. Thirteen of the deals were buyouts, 16 were mezzanine financing deals, and the remaining 261 were venture capital deals.

There were 78 IPO exits in the sample. Eight firms went out of business, and the remaining 204 ended in mergers or acquisitions. The number of investors participating in each deal varied, ranging from 1 investor to, in two cases, 11. The firms in which funds were invested were located throughout Canada. Within the sample there were representatives from eight provinces (see Table 8.2).

Methods

The goal of the analysis was to determine whether targeted or untargeted investments were more likely to be successful, depending on a number of different criteria. The initial step in the analysis was to determine whether the two subsamples (targeted and untargeted investments) were well matched in other possible determinants of success. Factors such as age, sector, and size of firms are known to affect access to capital (Haines, Orser, & Riding, 1999; Madill, Haines, & Riding, 2004). Thus, *t* tests were performed in order to test the comparability of the samples on these predictors.

The second step was to define what was meant by success. For the purpose of this analysis, success was defined in two ways: the amount of time between the initial investment and the exit, and the type of exit.

A shorter time to exit, and thus a quicker return on investment, was considered more desirable in this study. Venture capital firms obtaining shorter times to exit were considered more successful. Often, venture capital investments become the 'living dead' – they have not reached the level of growth or profitability required to produce attractive returns, but are still viable and not losing money (Ruhnka, Feldman, & Dean, 1992). These investments never generate the desired returns for the investor, because they must be held for too long. Thus, a successful deal is one that can be exited within a reasonable time. If targeted and untargeted investments differ greatly in their average time to exit, then probably one type is more successful at avoiding the 'living dead' and at turning over deals more quickly.

With regards to type of exit, it is generally considered that IPOs are the more profitable exit type for venture capital investments (Davis, 2003). This type of exit usually boasts higher returns than acquisitions, for instance, and does not generally result in a loss for the venture capital investors. Balboa and Marti (2004) explain that the ability for firms to participate in an accessible IPO market is essential for the existence of a private equity or venture capital market. Similarly, Bygrave and Timmons (1992) state that venture capital would not be feasible without IPOs. Unfortunately, the Canadian IPO market is more restrictive than the American IPO market (Davis, 2003). For this reason, it is especially important to note any differences between targeted and untargeted investments in type of exit they are able to achieve. Three types of exits were listed in the MacDonald and Associates database (2006): IPO, merger and acquisition, and out of business. Although the following

Table 8.3. Firm Age and Sector.

	Targeted	N	M	SD	SE
Age of firm at first investment	No	146	6.84	11.691	.968
	Yes	43	8.86	22.412	3.418
Industry division	No	230	4.35	4.477	.295
	Yes	60	3.50	4.328	.559

data are old, it is still interesting to note that in a study of 26 funds exiting over 400 investments between 1970 and 1982, Bygrave & Timmons (1992) found that only IPOs made more than one times investment (at 1.95 times). The next highest was acquisitions, with gains of only 0.4 times. Thus, investments exiting via IPO were considered more successful in this study.

In order to determine which of the subsamples was more successful in these two factors, *t* tests were performed to provide a comparison of means for targeted and untargeted investments on the above criteria of success.

RESULTS

The first step, as described above, was to perform *t* tests to determine whether the two subsamples were well matched. Table 8.3 shows statistics for the age of the firm at the time of first investment and the sector (industry division) in which these firms operate. *T* tests confirmed that there were no significant differences between the two samples in the age of the individual firms that received an investment, or in the industries in which they operate.

Ordinarily, a size variable should also be tested. However, the database to which the researchers had access did not provide any information on the size of the firms, either in annual sales or in number of employees. The only variable that could provide any indication of size is the market capitalization factor at IPO for those firms that exited by this method. This is probably not an ideal measure because it is related to rate of return as well as to type of exit. However, a set of *t* tests was performed for the IPO firms only in order to determine if there were any differences. The *t* tests showed no significant differences between the subsample of targeted investments exiting via IPOs and untargeted investments exiting via IPOs with respect to the age of the firm or the market capitalization.

Table 8.4. Investments by Financing Type.

	Frequency	%	Valid %	Cumulative %
Buyout	13	4.5	4.5	4.5
Mezzanine	16	5.5	5.5	10.0
Venture capital	261	90.0	90.0	100.0
Total	290	100.0	100.0	

It appears that the subsamples of targeted and untargeted firms are well matched in traditional predictors of financing like size, sector, and age. There is no significant difference between sector or age for the sample as a whole and there is no significant difference between the two groups in market capitalization at IPO.

Tests of Success Factors

Subsequent to ensuring that the samples were well matched, t tests were performed in order to compare the means of the success factors for targeted and untargeted firms. No significant differences were revealed by the t tests. However, these tests look at the aggregate results. There were three types of financing listed in the sample: buyout, mezzanine, and venture capital financing. Table 8.4 shows the breakdown of investments by financing type.

Most of the deals were venture capital deals, but 16 were mezzanine financing and 13 were buyouts. It is possible that there were differences by type of financing and that this would not appear in the aggregate results, especially since venture capital dominates the sample. For instance, perhaps targeting produces different results when the investment is a venture capital investment as opposed to a mezzanine financing investment. For this reason, the success factors were also examined within each of the types of financing. The t tests for buyouts and mezzanine financing still did not show any significant differences in the success factors of exit type and time to exit.

Lastly, the venture capital deals, which make up the bulk of the investments, were examined. The results are shown in Table 8.5.

It does appear that targeted venture capital deals have invested in firms that are significantly younger than non-targeted firms. However, there are no significant differences between the targeted and untargeted investments in the exit type or the time between investment and exit.

Table 8.5. Results of Independent Samples Test – Ventures Capital Deals.

		Levene's test for equality of variances		t-test for equality of means					Std. error difference	95% confidence interval of the difference	
		F	Sig.	t	df	Sig. (2-tailed)	MD			Lower	Upper
Exit type	Equal variances assumed	1.280	.259	-.564	259	.573	-.075		.133	-.338	.188
	Equal variances not assumed			-.545	77.279	.587	-.075		.138	-.350	.200
Age of firm at first investment	Equal variances assumed	6.933	.009	2.174	168	.031	2.882		1.326	.265	5.499
	Equal variances not assumed			3.189	137.027	.002	2.882		.904	1.095	4.669
Age of firm at exit	Equal variances assumed	5.336	.022	1.750	168	.082	2.372		1.355	-.304	5.047
	Equal variances not assumed			2.470	124.020	.015	2.372		.960	.471	4.272
Time (years) between investment and exit	Equal variances assumed	5.040	.026	-.701	259	.484	-.277		.394	-1.053	.500
	Equal variances not assumed			-.822	102.491	.413	-.277		.337	-.944	.391

These *t* tests do not seem to indicate that untargeted investments are any more or less successful than targeted investments on the criteria of time between investment and exit and the type of exit. This remains true for each subtype of financing deal (venture capital, mezzanine, and buyout). This result implies that targeted firms are not different from untargeted firms in time it takes them to exit a deal or the type of exit that they will ultimately achieve.

Implications

No significant differences were found between targeted and untargeted investments in sector, age, or market capitalization (a proxy for size). This means that the samples were fairly well matched for comparison. When this comparison was completed, it was determined that there are no differences in 'success' between targeted and untargeted firms, at least in time to exit and type of exit. Neither targeting nor failing to target geographically was found to be a predictor of success.

So far in this study, there does not seem to be a difference between targeted and untargeted firms in either the traditional predictors of financing (age, size, and sector), or the 'success' factors selected in this study. This implies that there may not be a trade-off between 'doing good and doing well.' An important caveat to the above implications is that return data are not publicly available for these two groups. However, as noted above, deals exiting sooner and deals exiting via IPO are both more likely to have greater returns. We find no difference between targeted and untargeted portfolios in terms of early exits or IPOs.

Implications for Canadian Pension Funds and Public Policy

The California Initiative case is too young for its final financial success or failure to be determined, and the return results could not be tested for the Canadian data. However, on the basis of theory as well as the initial evidence from these funds, it was found that targeted private equity investments could be beneficial for Canadian pension funds. There is an opportunity for pension funds to fill capital gaps in the market, especially given the broad nature of documented gaps such as the capital gap between $2 million and $5 million. The existence of such capital gaps means that the market for private equity is not efficient and that there is room for pension funds to make attractive rates of return while promoting economic development in their regions.

Figure 8.9. Comparison between American and Canadian plans with positive PE allocation (unweighted).

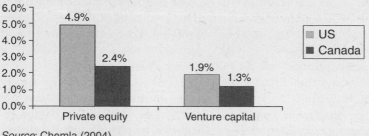

Source: Chemla (2004).

However, many obstacles to this type of investment remain. Canadian pension funds have shown themselves to be less willing to invest in private equity than their American counterparts. For instance, one estimate suggests that, in the United States, pension funds commit 5–8% of their assets to venture capital, while the rate in Canada is closer to 1% (Davis, 2003). Why are Canadian pension funds less likely to invest in private equity than American funds? One reason is that Canadian pension funds tend to have smaller assets, increasing the likelihood of 'structural barriers' to private equity investments (Chemla, 2004). This obstacle, however, could be addressed through commingled or pooled funds and other best practices described above if fund managers were aware of these vehicles. In addition, the size and characteristics of the Canadian financial market play a role. The Canadian private equity and venture capital markets may not be as developed as the American markets (Figure 8.9), and many Canadian funds are still too new or young to have a track record (Industry Canada, 2004). The IPO market in Canada is also less active than that in the United States, making the liquidity problem even greater (Chemla, 2004).

Further, there are few examples of ETIs in Canada, and where they do exist, there is very little research on their rates of return, and what research does exist is mostly anecdotal (Quarter et al., 2001). This adds to the unwillingness of pension funds to invest, since they lack information on which to base informed decisions.

It is clear that, while preliminary evidence supports the idea that pension funds can profit from targeted investing, further work remains to be done. It is important to continue studying the experiences of pension funds in the United States and elsewhere that have already pioneered successful efforts in this area. Canadian funds can learn from mistakes that were made and profit from best practices. In addition, as time passes more information will become available about the financial returns of these endeavours. This will make it easier to assess the risk-return universe that is available within this type of investment and facilitate forecasting.

There is a continued role for public policy to help Canadian pension funds overcome the barriers that they face in targeted private equity investing. Education and availability of information are areas that should be addressed as soon as possible. The availability of, for instance, existing Canadian rate of return data would allow for a clearer understanding of the potential success of future targeted investing programs. Targeting investments to underserved capital markets could be beneficial to Canadian pension funds, as well as to the economic development of the country as a whole, but, clearly, further study is required.

Notes

We would like to gratefully acknowledge the support of the Pensions at Work project of the Ontario Institute for Studies in Education University of Toronto and the Social Sciences and Humanities Research Council in the writing of this chapter. We would also like to thank the Rockefeller Foundation for their support in the California case study. We would like to thank CalPERS for providing access to their organizations for this case study.

1 In the early years, private equity funds will show low or negative returns due to the management fees and expenses and the fact that investments have not yet been exited. However, investment gains are achieved in later years when the companies have matured and returns can be realized. This is known as the J-curve effect.

2 CalPERS calls its private equity asset class its Alternative Investment Management Program or AIM.

3 'Double bottom line' investments are those with both financial and social returns. This is a reference to investments (such as ETIs) that achieve acceptable risk-adjusted rates of return and some type of social ancillary benefit as well; for instance, creating jobs or affordable housing in a low-income area.

4 American River Ventures, Bank of America, DFJ Frontier, Garage Technology Ventures, Green Equity Investors, Nogales Investors, Opportunity Capital, Pacific Community Ventures, Provender Capital, and Yucaipa Companies

5 Low- and moderate-income (LMI) areas are defined as 50% and 80% of median income respectively.

References

Balboa, M., & Marti, J. (2004). From venture capital to private equity: The Spanish experience. *Journal of Private Equity, 7*(2), 54–63.

Banc of America. (2006). *Portfolio.* Retrieved 7 September 2007 from http://www.bacapitalaccessfunds.com/portfolio/index.asp

Barth, J.R., & Cordes, J.J. (1981). Nontraditional criteria for investing pension assets: An economic appraisal. *Journal of Labor Research, 2*(2), 219–47.

Blakely, E.J., Lynch, J., & Skudrna, K. (1985). Creating jobs through pension fund investments in real estate: Innovations from California. *California Management Review, 27*(4), 184–97.

Bygrave, W.D., & Timmons, J.A. (1992). *Venture capital at the crossroads.* Boston: Harvard Business School Press.

Calabrese, M. (1999, April 29–30). *Building on past success: Labor-friendly investment vehicles and the power of private equity.* Paper presented at the Second National Heartland Labor-Capital Conference, Washington, DC.

CalPERS. (2003). *California Initiative Program: Investing in California's underserved markets.* Retrieved from http://www.calpers.ca.gov/

CalPERS. (2004a). *Alternative Investment Management Program quarterly review executive summary, quarter ended September 30, 2004.* Retrieved 30 September 2004 from http://www.calpers.ca.gov/eip-docs/investments/assets/equities/aim/private-equity-review/qrtrly-perf-review.pdf

CalPERS. (2004b). *California Initiative Program: Investing in California's underserved markets.* November 2004. Retrieved 31 August 2005 from http://www.calpers.ca.gov/apps/board/invest/200411/Item05a-01.pdf

CalPERS. (2004c). *Statement of investment policy for economically targeted investment program.* February 2000, revised September 2004. Retrieved 31 August 2005 from http://www.calpers.ca.gov/index.jsp?bc=/investments/policies/alternative/home.xml

Chemla, G. (2004). Pension fund investment in private equity and venture capital in the U.S. and Canada. *Journal of Private Equity, 7*(2), 64–71.

Cross, P.S. (1993). Economically targeted investments: Can public pension plans do good and do well? *Indiana Law Journal, 68*, 931–76.

Davis, C.H. (2003). Venture capital in Canada: A maturing industry, with distinctive features and new challenges. In D. Cetindamar (Ed.), *The growth of venture capital: A cross-cultural comparison* (pp. 175–206). Westport: Praegar.

Doran, A., & Bannock, G. (2000). Publicly sponsored regional venture capital: What can the UK learn from the US experience? *Venture Capital, 2*(4), 255–285.

F.B. Heron Foundation. (2003). *Illustrative deal profiles: Yucaipa Corporate Initiatives Fund.* Retrieved 7 September 2005 from http://www.fbheron.org/stories_03_part3.pdf

Freear, J., Sohl, J.E., & Wetzel, W. (2002). Angles on angels: Financing technology-based ventures – A historical perspective. *Venture Capital, 4*(4), 275–87.

Garvin, W.J. (1971). The small business capital gap: The special case of minority enterprise. *Journal of Finance, 26*(2), 445–57.

Greenwich Associates. (2002). Pension plan, endowment and foundation asset allocation. Greenwich CT: Author.

Gregory, D.L. (1990). Public Employee Pension Funds: A cautionary essay. *Labor Law Journal, 41*(10), 700–705.

Hagerman, L., Clark, G.L., & Hebb, T. (2006). *Pension funds and urban revitalization New York case study: Competitive returns and a revitalized.* Working Paper 05-15. Oxford: Oxford University Centre for the Environment.

Hagerman, L., Clark, G., & Hebb, T. (2007). Investment intermediaries in economic development: Linking public pension funds to urban revitalization. *Community Development Investment Review, 3*(1), 8.

Haines, G.H., Jr, Orser, B.J., & Riding, A.L. (1999). Myths and realities: An empirical study of banks and the gender of small business clients. *Canadian Journal of Administrative Sciences, 16*(4), 291–307.

Harrigan, S. (2003). Economically targeted investments: Doing well and doing good. In I. Carmichael & J. Quarter (Eds.), *Money on the line: Workers' capital in Canada* (pp. 237–52). Ottawa: Centre for Policy Alternatives.

Harrison, R.T., & Mason, C.M. (2000). Editorial: The role of the public sector in the development of a regional venture capital industry. *Venture Capital, 2*(4), 243–53.

Healy, T.J., & Hardy, D.J. (1997). Growth in alternative investments. *Financial Analysts Journal, 53*(4), 58–65.

Hebb, T. (2006). *Pension funds and urban revitalization California case study A: Private equity CalPERS' California Initiative.* Working Paper 05-15. Oxford: Oxford University Centre for the Environment.

Industry Canada. (2004). *Finding the key: Canadian institutional investors and private equity.* Retrieved 1 December 2006 from http://www.cvca.ca/files/Finding_the_Key_Report-_June_2004.pdf

Levine, P. (1997, 10 November). Where there's a will, there's ETI. *Pensions & Investments,* p. 52.

Lipper, G., & Sommer, B. (2002). Encouraging angel capital: What the U.S. states are doing. *Venture Capital, 4*(4), 357–62.

MacDonald and Associates. (2006). *Database of private equity investments in Canada, 1999–2005*. Toronto: Author.

Madill, J., Haines, G.H.J., & Riding, A.L. (2004). A tale of one city: The Ottawa technology cluster. In L. Shavinina (Ed.), *Silicon Valley North: A high-tech cluster of innovation and entrepreneurship*. Oxford: Elsevier.

Marr, M., Trimble, J.L., & and Nofsinger J.R. (1994). Economically targeted investments. *Financial Analysts Journal, 50*(2), 7–8.

Mason, C.M., & Harrison, R.T. (2003). Closing the regional equity gap? A critique of the Department of Trade and Industry's Regional Venture Capital Funds Initiative. *Regional Studies, 37*(8), 855–68.

Mason, C.M., & Harrison, R.T. (2004). Improving access to early stage venture capital in regional economies: A new approach to investment readiness. *Local Economy, 19*(2), 159–73.

Notsinger, J.R. (1998). Why targeted investing does not make sense! *Financial Management, 27*(3), 87–96.

Pacific Community Ventures. (2004). *Community Portfolio*. Retrieved 7 September 2005 from http://pacificcommunityventures.org/portfolio

Patterson, J.D. (1993). Who's counting? ETI returns, economic impact. *Pensions & Investments*, p. 12.

Porter, M.E. (1992). Capital disadvantage: America's failing capital investment system. *Harvard Business Review, 70*(5), 65–82.

Porter, M.E. (1995). The competitive advantage of the inner city. *Harvard Business Review, 73*(3), 55–71.

Porter, M.E., & Wayland, R. (1992). Capital disadvantage: America's failing capital investment system. *Harvard Business Review, 70*(5), 65–82.

Provender Capital Group. (2005). *Provender portfolio*. Retrieved 7 September 2005 from http://www.provender-capital.com/portfolio.html

Quarter, J., Carmichael, I., Sousa, J., & Elgie, S. (2001). Social investment by union-based pension funds and labour-sponsored investment funds in Canada. *Relations Industrielles, 56*(1), 92–115.

Read, A. (1997). Building signposts for the future: Pension fund investment strategy, socially responsible investing, and ERISA. *Journal of Pension Planning and Compliance, 23*(3), 39–55.

Rosentraub, M.S., & Shroitman, T. (2004). Public employee pension funds and social investments. *Journal of Urban Affairs, 26*(3), 325–37.

Ruhnka, J.C., Feldman, H.D., & Dean, T.J. (1992). The 'living dead' phenomenon in venture capital investments. *Journal of Business Venturing, 7*(2), 137–55.

Sohl, J.E. (1999). The early-stage equity market in the U.S.A. *Venture Capital, 1*(2), 101–20.

Sohl, J.E. (2003). The U.S. angel and venture capital markets: Recent trends and developments. *Journal of Private Equity, 6*(2), 7–17.

Watson, R.D. (1994). Does targeted investing make sense? *Financial Management, 23*(4), 68–73.

Yago, G., Zeidman, B., & Schmidt, B. (2003). *Creating capital, jobs and wealth in emerging domestic markets.* Santa Monica, CA: Milken Institute.

Zanglein, J. (2001). Overcoming barriers on the ETI highway. In A. Fung, T. Hebb, & J. Rogers (Eds.), *Working capital: The power of labor's pensions* (pp. 181–202). Ithaca: ILR Press/Cornell University Press.

9 Pension-Fund Management and Socially Responsible Investment

RAN GOEL AND WES CRAGG

As a result of recent shifts in the understanding of fiduciary responsibility, pension funds and their trustees find themselves caught up in a vigorous debate about the development of investment strategies that take into account issues that go well beyond a narrow focus on the maximization of financial returns. What is being debated is first, whether factoring economic, environmental, social, and governance criteria into their investment strategies is consistent with their legally defined fiduciary responsibilities. Gil Yaron addresses this issue in chapter 3, and concludes, 'A modern reading of pension trustee fiduciary duties, supported by the majority of existing jurisprudence from the United States and Britain, suggests that when making investment policy, the law permits pension trustees to take values-based, non-financial criteria into consideration, including screening investments and ETI, provided a prudent process is followed that includes authorization from the plan's investment policy and communication to plan members' (p. 100). Changing times and institutional investment practices, he suggests, require 'an evolution in thinking' that transcends 'the traditional narrow reading of fiduciary law,' a reading whose exclusive focus is maximizing financial returns.

In this chapter, we go beyond the question of whether socially responsible investment practices are legally permissible and therefore compatible with the fiduciary responsibilities of pension-fund mangers to address a second dimension of the current debate: Do pension funds have a positive ethical obligation to plan and evaluate their investment strategies for their economic, environmental, social, and governance (EESG)[1] impacts – impacts that may or may not connect directly to maximizing financial returns? An equally important aspect of this debate is which of the many available tools and strategies responsible investors should employ.

Corporate and Investor Responsibility: Why the Debate?

Why, then, are pension funds faced with these debates at this time? Two broad trends are particularly relevant in response to this question.

The Impact of Globalization

For much of the twentieth century, the private sector engaged in business activities with an understanding that its primary responsibility was to generate profits for shareholders within the framework of the law. It was assumed that the responsibility for shaping the legal environment of business and for ensuring that the economic benefits of economic development were fairly shared rested with government. Under the conditions of increasing globalization, however, this understanding is being re-examined and challenged. Increasingly, corporations engaged in international markets are being asked to go beyond what the law requires and to respect fundamental ethical standards of business conduct. Companies active in countries where human rights abuses are common now find their activities under international scrutiny by vocal civil society critics. Various instruments set out the human rights obligations of corporations. These developments mark a reallocation of ethical responsibilities between government and business of potentially dramatic proportions.

Four interrelated reasons are central to this reallocation of responsibilities: the changing role of the private sector, advances in science and technology in the private sector, the changing power of the state, and the reach of civil liberty. These factors will be dealt with in turn.

THE CHANGING ROLE OF THE PRIVATE SECTOR

Under conditions of globalization, the private sector, dominated by the growth of large multinational corporations, has come to play an increasingly significant role in the economies of the developed world. In the developing and the underdeveloped world, private-sector investment now drives economic development. As Figure 9.1 illustrates, the largest multinational corporations now have revenues that dwarf the total incomes of many countries.[2] Of the 15 companies and governments with the largest budgets, 6 are governments and 9 are companies. Of the

Figure 9.1. Country and company rankings, 2002.

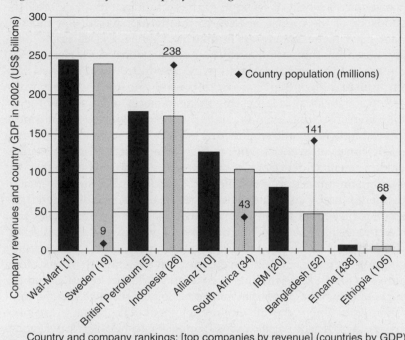

Country and company rankings: [top companies by revenue] (countries by GDP)

Sources: Population figures – CIA (2004); GDP figures – World Bank (2004a);
Company revenues – *Business Week* (2003)

100 largest economies in the world, 51 are now global corporations and
only 49 are countries (Anderson & Cavanagh, 2000). The implications of
decisions taken by multinational corporations for the welfare of the people and the communities of the countries in which they do business are,
on these grounds alone, substantial.

Equally important, corporations have become freer to choose where
the goods and services they provide will be produced and by implica-
tion the legal and regulatory standards that will govern their production. The products that appear on the shelves of a Wal-Mart store, the
produce in the local grocery store, or the call centre voice may originate
anywhere in the world. This factor has greatly expanded the power of
corporations to determine the regulatory environments in which they
do business.

SCIENCE, TECHNOLOGY, AND THE PRIVATE SECTOR

Advances in science and technology have fundamentally altered the relationship of the human species to the natural world. For most of human history, the impacts of human activity on the natural world, while sometimes dramatic, have been local. Modern science has altered that relationship in a fundamental way. Scientific advances have now given human beings the capacity to control and to alter the natural world on a global scale. Harnessing nuclear energy was an early, highly visible, and unsettling expression of this new power. A second more recent example is genetic engineering – the power to change life forms through direct intervention with nature. The most visible and widely discussed recent evidence of this phenomenon is the developments that are having an impact on medicine and human health, such as genetically altered food. Legal battles over patents for genetically altered life forms like the Harvard Mouse are another example.[3] We might say that human beings have acquired the power to change the nature of nature.[4]

Multinational corporations are exploiting that power. Their access to huge pools of capital has allowed them to generate the technology required to put 'nature-altering science' to work. The result is that the impacts of economic development are no longer restricted to the local environments where the developments occur. The impacts are now global in their reach. Applications of nuclear technology have global implications, as Chernobyl demonstrated. The use of fossil fuels in North America and Western Europe is having an impact on the global climate. Science has therefore put in the hands of the modern multinational corporation a kind of power that was the subject of science fiction a few short decades ago.

THE CHANGING POWER OF THE STATE

By contrast, globalization has diminished the power or willingness of national governments to set regulatory standards in important ways. The World Trade Organization (WTO) and regional free trade agreements like the North American Free Trade Agreement (NAFTA) have significantly constrained the regulatory freedom of national governments. In many developing countries, multinational corporations are essentially unregulated, except insofar as they impose environmental and social standards of performance on themselves. Individuals, communities, and indeed entire countries may thus become subject to the ethical standards that these corporations explicitly or implicitly espouse. Competition for private-sector investment has fuelled regulatory competition, leading to what some have described as a 'race to the bottom.' As a result, serious questions about both the capacity and willingness of governments to set appropriate social, economic, and environmental parameters for economic activity in global and local markets have emerged.

Parallel to this development is the fact that multinational corporations are playing an increasingly influential role in the deliberations of international institutions like the United Nations, the World Bank, the International Monetary Fund, and the WTO, to name just a few. That is to say, multinational corporations are involved in shaping the international legal regulatory environments whose purpose, at least in part, is to regulate the conduct of those same corporations in international markets. This involvement in the regulatory activities of international institutions, traditionally the preserve of state governments, is a relatively recent phenomenon.[5]

THE REACH OF CIVIL SOCIETY

Companies and governments now find themselves under critical scrutiny by active civil society organizations. These organizations are committed to sharing information, research, organizational, communication, and political skills, and capacity. Their goal is to raise business conduct standards locally and globally. Their values are human solidarity, the centrality of the human person, justice, and the obligation of corporations to contribute to the common good.[6] Their interventions have proven very influential and their public credibility is high relative to that of leaders in business and government.

Role of Institutional Investors

The intersection of these four developments has fuelled a growing debate about the ethical responsibilities of the modern corporation, including the appropriate allocation of responsibility for ensuring respect for fundamental ethical values and the fair distribution of the benefits and costs of economic development. The debate has assumed an urgent tone in response to corporate scandals, evidence of government corruption, concerns about environmental protection (particularly climate change), the use and abuse of natural resources, the protection and advancement of human rights, and the health and safety conditions under which goods and services marketed globally are produced. Management strategies and investment decisions can have significant economic impacts, both positive and negative. To take just one example, investment in oil, gas, and mining has added immeasurably to the wealth of people and nations, principally in the developed world. As an engine of economic development in the developing world, on the other hand, the dominant impact of investment in extractive industries is frequently described and experienced as a curse.

The strategies of managers are heavily influenced by investment funds looking for financial results often calculated on a relatively short-term period. The proposal that the primary and dominant responsibility of business is to maximize profits for shareholders has become a deeply entrenched principle in mutual fund and pension-fund management. Therefore, the debate over ethical responsibilities of today's large multinational corporations is in many respects inseparable from the debate over the economic, environmental, social, and governance responsibilities of institutional investors, of which public-sector pension funds are among the largest.

Indeed, it is unlikely that corporate management and boards of directors will be persuaded to think seriously about the nature and scope of their responsibilities unless institutional investors are persuaded to broaden their investment strategies and practices to include social, environmental, and economic dimensions, implications, and impacts.[7] As the fiduciaries of investment funds comprising a significant portion of the world's public equity markets, public-sector pension-fund trustees will play a central role in how this debate unfolds.

Labour Pension Funds and the Emerging Debate

Trustees of public-sector pension funds have a particularly salient stake in the current debate surrounding the responsibilities of institutional investors. The reasons are not hard to identify. Labour unions were created to protect and advance not only the financial returns of workers but also their social welfare and the social and economic welfare of the communities in which they lived. Human rights in the form of workers' rights have historically been at the top of their social agendas. Environmental concerns have also factored into labour negotiations and political interventions, though not always in the most enlightened ways. Finally, labour unions have historically understood the importance for their members of policy development and regulatory frameworks at the government level. They have participated actively in political debate, the activities of political parties, labour negotiations, public policy debates, and political campaigns with a view to ensuring that the voice of labour was heard and understood.

A central question for labour unions, therefore, is whether their traditional focus on social, economic, and environmental issues should carry over into pension-fund investment. For much of the history of labour pension-fund management, the answer to this question has been a clear 'no!'[8] As with the investment community more broadly, labour unions have accepted the understanding that has dominated the conduct of business through most of the last century, an understanding that has assigned responsibility for generating wealth to the private sector and the responsibility for ensuring that wealth was generated in morally acceptable ways and then distributed fairly to government.

This chapter addresses two sets of questions confronted by the labour trustees of public-sector pension funds. The first is a threshold question. Should EESG factors that go beyond narrow considerations of only maximizing share value play a role in investment decision-making of public-sector pension funds? Assuming this threshold is passed, what is the role, if any, of the myriad instruments of corporate responsibility currently available in incorporating EESG issues into investment decision-making?

We will argue that international standards that have emerged in the recent past to address the ethical – that is to say, the EESG – responsibilities of corporations, should play a central role in addressing these two questions. In this context, the term *standards* will be used to refer to the ethics codes, principles, guidelines, and other instruments that are aimed at defining the broader ethical (i.e., economic, environmental, social, and governance) responsibilities of corporations and increasingly, institutional investors (McKague & Cragg, 2005).

We begin with an overview of the two broad types of justifications used to persuade institutional investors to pursue a responsible investment approach: the 'business case' and the 'ethics case.' We shall argue that the underlying normative basis of the labour movement is that the labour trustees of public-sector pension funds should ground their investment decisions on an ethical investment strategy insofar as the law permits. We shall then outline the role of what is sometimes referred to as non-financial standards in the pursuit of responsible investment strategies and review briefly the evolution of responsible investment standards over the past three decades. Finally, several priority areas for the further development of these instruments will be explored and the role of labour pension funds discussed.

Trustees and EESG Issues

It should be obvious that EESG factors can affect a company's stock price. The *Exxon Valdez* oil spill, the tobacco industry settlements, the Bhopal disaster, and excessive executive pay at Disney all affected the share prices of the respective companies involved, to say nothing of Enron, WorldCom, and the series of ethical disasters that investors have had to cope with in the past decade.[9] The ethical values of corporations and their managers and directors clearly have financial implications. Responsible investing advocates, while differing in many material respects, are united in insisting that corporations and their shareholders are directing insufficient attention to the EESG aspects of their businesses.

The calls for deeper integration of EESG issues in corporate decision-making are based on two broad sets of justifications. Roughly stated, these approaches are what we shall describe as the 'business case' and the 'ethics case' for responsible investment. The two justifications frequently overlap in their demands of business and indeed have been employed simultaneously by some institutional investors. However, they are distinct in important ways.

The Business Case for Responsible Management Practices

The business case for broadening investment strategy to include EESG criteria in institutional investment strategy accepts the dominant view that the primary responsibility of business is to maximize profits for shareholders. However, it argues that EESG investment standards have an important role to play in achieving that objective. There are many reasons for thinking that the best financial investment strategy is one that is guided by EESG considerations. The most common of those reasons is the potential cost to investors of focusing narrowly on short-term financial returns. A recent exploration of the values underlying the Global Compact, which is set out in a publication entitled *Who Cares Wins* captures this justification well: 'Financial markets are already factoring in environmental and social issues, but often only if they are seen as being material to value creation and risk in the short-term ... CEOs and CFOs recently interviewed by the World Economic Forum, for example, stressed that intangible aspects related to ESG issues play an increasingly important role in value creation but that analysts' short-term focus hinders them in recognizing this trend' (Global Compact,

2004, p. 3). The potential costs of focusing narrowly on financial factors are, first, costs that undermine shareholder value associated with a failure to look beyond short-term financial gains, and second, lost opportunities to create value for investors. Let us look briefly at each in turn.

Unethical conduct and corporate environments generate stress that can undermine management morale and labour relations, leading to reduced productivity. In worst-case scenarios, insensitivity to ethical standards, understood broadly to include economic, environmental, social, and governance concerns, can lead to whistle-blowing (for example, when sound environmental standards are ignored), with consequent negative publicity, loss of internal control (for example, the abuse of expense claims or off-book accounting or corruption), internal conflict in the form of strikes and work stoppages, and conflict with local communities and other engaged stakeholders. At stake here are the hidden costs associated with strained relations with important stakeholder groups. However, risks to reputation can also be significant. Reputations are built over time. In contrast, they can be seriously damaged very quickly through lack of attention to maintaining sound standards of conduct that ensure that risks associated with short-term financial gain are carefully evaluated by employees and the corporation before they are undertaken.

Failure to attend to issues beyond those associated with narrowly defined financial considerations also invites government regulation. If the corporate community is insensitive to the negative social, environmental, or wider economic impacts of its activities, to political pressure, or to the perceived need to correct unsatisfactory impacts of corporate activity, governments may be compelled to intervene. This can sometimes result in onerous costs associated with meeting legislated regulatory standards. The *Sarbanes-Oxley Act* in the United States is a good example of this phenomenon.

Consideration of intangibles is ignored, often because they are so hard to quantify. Indeed, they are most easily identified in hindsight after the damage has been done and the costs tabulated. Attending to them up front requires a discipline and a focus that is justified from a business perspective because proactive evaluation protects shareholder value by avoided costs that are difficult to predict but can be significant.

Failure to build ethical values into strategic planning and corporate operations can also mean missed opportunities to create value for shareholders. Once again, it is intangibles that are at stake – intangibles whose value is by their nature hard to quantify. An example illustrates the point. Serious energy-saving investments by a company can be expensive. It may take several years for investments of this kind to pay off. If the cost is expensed in the current quarter, profits may drop below financial analysts' expectations. This may lead senior management to decide not to undertake the project, even though it improves the underlying fundamentals (such as vulnerability to energy price spikes), contributing to long-term shareholder value. This risk is typically exacerbated by compensation patterns that reward primarily for near-term appreciation of share value, thus pitting the short-term interests of managers and boards of directors against the interests of the corporation and its shareholders.

A recent survey of several hundred chief financial officers illustrates the phenomenon. When asked what they would do if near the end of the financial quarter it became apparent that their company would not meet the market's earnings targets, 80% replied that their companies 'would delay discretionary spending such as R&D, advertising, and maintenance' (Jensen, 2005). What this illustrates is the central role of institutional investors in shaping the business strategies and the decision-making of corporations and their managers (World Economic Forum, 2005).

An account of the value-creation benefits of ethically sound social, environmental, and economic practices would also have to include potentially positive impacts on employee morale, recruitment, quality of management, and stakeholder relationships. Working in a positive ethical environment can result in positive attitudes, reduced sick leave, retention of skilled employees, and visible pride in one's company. Employees who take pride in their place of work are more likely to take pride in the quality of the work they do. In addition, good work standards can be infectious.

Equally important, the positive impacts of a progressive approach to a firm's social, economic, and environment responsibilities can go well beyond company employees. A good reputation for an ethical work environment can influence recruiting. Given a choice, most people prefer working for an ethical company. A reputation for high ethical standards can also affect external stakeholder relations in positive ways. It can reduce the potential for conflict, increase opportunities for cooperation, and enhance communication and understanding. These kinds of benefits are not easily quantifiable. Each, however, can bring significant financial rewards.

The second pillar underpinning the business case is the tangible and more quantifiable risks that unethical conduct carries for share value.

Recent corporate scandals offer a good illustration of how share value can be destroyed by illegal and unethical corporate behaviour. Enron is a good example. There were obvious losses to shareholders, including those whose pension funds were at stake. However, the direct costs went well beyond the firm and its employees and shareholders. Reputational damage resulted in the collapse of an international accounting firm, Arthur Andersen. A number of financial firms have had to absorb heavy fines for their collaboration in highly questionable financial transactions. Several of the leading players have faced criminal charges, with the consequent destruction of personal reputations.

Failure to meet sound environmental standards of operations have cost corporations in the chemical industry large sums of money by way of fines and clean up costs, to say nothing of the reputational damage experienced.

The list could be extended indefinitely. However, the point is clear. Irresponsible corporate behaviour can generate tangible and direct costs that reduce or destroy share value in the short and the long term.

One indication of the growing significance of the business case for responsible corporate behaviour is the proliferation of codes of conduct, reporting and accountability standards, and the demand for third-party social and environmental audits, all of which provide additional indirect evidence that ethically responsible corporate behaviour or the lack thereof can affect the corporate bottom line. Nonetheless, many institutional investors and managers are largely ignoring the importance of these issues. In the words of one representative publication, 'Markets do not yet fully recognize the importance of new emerging trends, such as the growing pressure on companies to improve corporate governance, transparency and accountability and the increasing importance of reputation risks related to ESG issues' (Global Compact, 2004, p. 3).

In summary, the business case focuses on the financial risks to which investors are exposed when they ignore the importance of responsible business and investment standards and the financial benefits that can accrue to corporations and their shareholders that adhere to sound, socially responsible business practices.

The Ethics Case for Responsible Management

The ethics case for ethically responsible corporate management goes beyond bottom line considerations to include a variable range of what might be described as ethical or moral considerations. Corporations, seen from this perspective, have a moral obligation to act in ethically responsible ways, whether or not doing so can be argued or demonstrated to generate improved short-term or long-term financial returns. This is not to say that ethical considerations are detached from bottom line considerations. None of the business case justifications for responsible corporate behaviour are cancelled or obviated by a focus on the ethics case. Indeed, one would expect all the benefits identified by the business case to flow to firms committed to ethical standards of conduct by virtue simply of their moral or ethical value.

The justification for committing to ethical standards for their own sake, however, does deviate from business case justifications. In addition, as with the business case, it can take a variety of forms. For example, it can be argued that, like individuals, corporations have an obligation to respect sound ethical standards simply by virtue of their membership in the human community. The moral demands made by society on individuals are not dependent on the capacity of society to demonstrate that behaving ethically will always devolve to the individual's benefit. Indeed, we know that respect for and adherence to moral principles and values do not always have this result. Why, it might be argued, should the same not apply to corporations, their employees, managers, and their directors?

What is more, corporations operate with the consent of the societies by virtue of what might be called 'a licence to operate,' which is both in theory and in practice subject to cancellation if the social costs associated with their operations exceed the social benefits. The concept of 'a licence to operate' has literal meaning for the extractive industries, such as mining. However, operating as a metaphor, it illustrates a foundational feature of corporations and their relationship to the societies in which they conduct business (Cragg, 2002).

Finally, corporations receive many of the benefits that accrue to individuals by virtue of their citizenship. Major multinational corporations, for example, benefit from the human rights protections accorded to individuals in the constitutions of liberal democracies where for the most part they are headquartered. They benefit from government infrastructure investments, educational institutions, social welfare systems, public health standards, medical facilities, and law enforcement. As beneficiaries of public goods, they share the same general obligations as citizens. Moreover, like individual citizens, demanding that net benefits be demonstrated before moral standards are incorporated into business operations can be considered self-centred and ethically unjustifiable.

Advocates of the business case frequently eschew arguments based on ethics or values when urging corporations and investors to better integrate EESG factors into their operations. One report urges sustainability advocates to avoid moral arguments and even the use of the term *non-financial* (World Business Council for Sustainable Development, & United Nations Environmental Programme Finance Initiative, 2004). The use of explicitly ethical terminology is often seen as a barrier to the progressive implementation of socially responsible corporate practices (Ambachtsheer, 2005). Nevertheless, the call for responsible business conduct has been historically and still is commonly guided by values and principles that are widely seen as inherently worthy of respect for their own sake and in their own right.

Labour Pension Funds and the Case for Responsible Investment Practices

The case for responsible investment builds on the case for responsible business conduct. Investors have a direct financial stake and a direct responsibility for determining how their money will be invested by themselves or their agents who are, for the most part, institutional investors. It is very unlikely that corporate behaviour will change significantly unless institutional investors take up their responsibilities in this regard more carefully and systematically.

Labour trustees in particular have important reasons to set their approach to investment decision-making within an ethics framework. Unions arose in the industrial age to ensure safe working conditions, reasonable working hours, and liveable wages for workers. Unions were formed, to borrow from the Canadian Auto Workers Union's constitution, to provide workers with 'dignity, a measure of security and a rising standard of living.' In public statements, unions typically ground their demands on the fundamental moral principle that human beings possess an inherent dignity, deserve respect, and are not simply tools whose sole value is their contribution to the enrichment of their employers.

Many of the benefits that organized labour has won for workers have been put in place to ensure that workers are treated fairly and their rights are respected. They have been frequently resisted by employers for financial reasons. Their effect has been to ensure that the economic benefits deriving from business activity are more fairly shared than would otherwise be the case. Perhaps not surprisingly, strengthening the ethical quality of workplace practices and standards has also had, for the most part, the kinds of bottom line benefits that the business case for ethical conduct is built on. This outcome could hardly be thought of as accidental. Ethics lies at the heart of social cooperation. Similarly, the demand that business be conducted in responsible ways has, as its chief motivation, concern for the negative social, environmental, and economic costs of unethical business practices and the positive economic, environmental, and social benefits generated by ethical business practices.

This kind of reasoning is at the heart of labour movement advocacy for the fair treatment of its members. It should apply with equal force to labour pension-fund investment strategies. To be sure, labour trustees face formidable obstacles in undertaking such an approach, due to resistance from other trustees and investment managers and to perceived or real legal constraints. However, bringing the underlying normative issues to the fore and making explicit the linkage with labour's historical role creates an ethical framework that allows the labour pension-fund trustee to assume the important role of champion for sustained, comprehensive, and creative incorporation of ethically sound economic, environmental, social, and governance standards in investment decision-making.

The Role of Standards

We turn now to our second question: How should labour trustees go about incorporating ethically sound principles into the investment strategies and practices of pension funds? A crucial part of the answer to this question lies in the standards that have been articulated by corporations themselves, as well as industry-wide associations, NGOs, international institutions like the Organisation for Economic Cooperation and Development (OECD), and other interested groups and stakeholders. These standards include an array of corporate responsibility instruments including codes, guidelines, principles, and mission and vision statements.

These standards have already played a central role in implementing responsible investing approaches.

• In the 2005 proxy-voting season, the Fonds Bâtirente submitted several shareholder proposals asking companies to report on environmental and social impacts as per the standardized indicators outlined by the Global Reporting Initiative.

- The Vancouver City Savings Union has used the AA1000 Assurance Standard on corporate engagement since 2000.
- The proxy-voting guidelines of the British Columbia Investment Management Corporation includes a requirement that companies adhere to the OECD Guidelines on Multinational Enterprises.
- The New York City Pension Funds are active members on the board of Ceres, an organization that has developed the Ceres Principles and helped launch the Global Reporting Initiative.

Notwithstanding their use to date, it is clear that these standards will have to be further developed and more widely utilized if economic, environmental, social, and governance issues are to be incorporated into corporate decision-making on a systematic and widespread basis. Labour has already played an instrumental role in creating, shaping, and using many of these standards but will have to play a much more active role in their refinement and operationalization.

These standards are crucial to the responsible investment enterprise because they each address one or more of the following:

- *Fairness*: Corporations often contend that the competitive nature of today's economy does not enable them to address EESG issues. The business case for responsible investment brings some of these contentions into doubt, but it is also clear that a corporation that takes the moral high road can be competitively disadvantaged. Standards set benchmarks for issues and/or sectors that can be used by institutional investors in developing responsible investment criteria. Applied consistently, they introduce an element of fairness in the way in which an institutional investor evaluates investment opportunities in a market where corporations are competing for investment dollars. In this way, they help to build pools of capital for corporations that commit to responsible business practices, thus providing the foundation for common global EESG investment criteria. The result is a more level playing field for corporations committed to sound ethical business practices. The consistent use of EESG standards also sends a strong signal to the market that responsible investment standards are being used to make investment decisions. This in turn communicates a message of market support for corporate responsibility.
- *Legitimacy*: To differing degrees, standards are based on widely held values. Many have been negotiated with meaningful input from

groups and individuals representing a variety of corporations, religions, non-governmental organizations, countries, and so forth. Many are based on universal values or hypernorms such as those contained in the Universal Declaration of Human Rights.[10] The existence of international standards of this nature lends a degree of legitimacy to the use of those standards by corporations in global markets and institutional investors who choose those standards to guide investment decisions.

• *Efficiency and effectiveness*: Standards leverage the accumulated experience of the actors that have had input in creating them. Many standards are tailored to a particular industry, sector, or geographic region and provide detailed guidance on implementation. By operationalizing values using best practices, they minimize the costs and time required to effectively incorporate EESG factors into decision-making. Often they provide a level of detailed guidance that legislation typically either does not or cannot provide.

• *Accountability*: Many standards outline reporting and assurance protocols for internal and external uses. Reporting is especially challenging, since many EESG issues are qualitative. Yet reliable measurement is crucial for integrating these issues, or any issue, for that matter. Regular reporting and verification is salient for accountability both within a corporation and for stakeholders. It allows for comparability of performance between and among corporations.

A given standard is not necessarily designed to fulfil all of these quintessential functions. Standards are not created equal; some supply more legitimacy or accumulated experience than others. There is considerable overlap between existing standards. There is clearly much work to be done in creating, improving, and consolidating standards that address EESG issues. What is abundantly apparent now, however, is that international standards have a leading role to play if responsible investing is to be fully integrated into institutional investment practices.

The Evolution of Corporate Responsibility Standards

The plethora of standards that seek to define parameters of corporate responsibility are a recent phenomenon. Although most have been developed since the early 1990s, it is nonetheless instructive to begin with the evolution of the business environment following the Second World War.

Discrimination by states or others based on race, religion, gender, and other morally irrelevant traits and characteristics is not a recent phenomenon. The kinds and nature of the discrimination on the part of national states that preceded, contributed to, and accompanied the Second World War, however, occurred on an unprecedented scale. It is thus unsurprising that the codification of human rights standards by the international community in the aftermath of the war was overwhelmingly focused on the responsibility of national governments to the individuals subject to their jurisdiction. In 1948, the Universal Declaration of Human Rights (UDHR) was adopted by the United Nations General Assembly and has since gained near universal legitimacy.

Although often stalled by Cold War politics, the ensuing years saw the ratification of several other important instruments including the Convention Against Torture and Other Cruel, Inhuman, or Degrading Treatment or Punishment (1949), the International Convention on Civil and Political Rights (1966), and the International Convention on Economic and Social Rights (1966). Urged on by their citizens, the governments of the liberal democracies in large part accepted these responsibilities and enshrined many of these principles as articles in national constitutions and laws. The result was a de facto division of responsibilities between government, to ensure the just treatment of their citizens, and business, which was assumed to be responsible for generating economic wealth within the framework of the law. The corporate codes that evolved during this period focused as a result on the ethical standards corporations required of their employees. The purpose of these and related corporate codes of conduct was to provide an environment where the goal of profit maximization could be pursued efficiently.

THE 1970s

Several developments during the 1970s brought into question the effectiveness of what might be described as a tacit post-war social contract between government and the private sector and thus prompted a gradual re-conceptualization of a corporation's responsibilities. These developments must be understood in the context of the wide-ranging structural changes that became apparent during that period. The early 1970s marked the beginning of a dramatic rise in the pace of globalization and hence of corporate activity outside the developed markets of the United States, Canada, Europe, and Japan. The decade saw the advent of important technological innovations, which led to vastly cheaper communication and transportation costs. These innovations, coupled with the macroeconomic shocks of the oil industry national-izations and the fall of American dollar-gold convertibility, heralded trends that continue to the present day. These trends include a surge in the flows of goods, services, currency, and direct investment across national borders as well as market liberalization and deregulation. The result was the onset of the increasingly profound changes described in the introduction to this chapter.

Against this backdrop, many began to challenge reigning notions of the responsibilities of corporations to the societies within which they operated. In particular, the continued entrenchment of apartheid in South Africa brought into question the role of multinational corpora-tions in propping up that regime. This in turn led many to ask whether corporations operating within a state that was unwilling to fulfil its responsibilities to its citizens as codified in international instruments such as the UDHR had responsibilities stretching beyond mere compli-ance with that state's laws.

Questions about corporate conduct only multiplied as the decade wore on. There were revelations that the International Telephone and Telegraph Corporation (ITT) had offered the Central Intelligence Agency $1 million in 1970 to block the election of Chilean presidential candidate Salvador Allende (Cragg & Woof, 2002, p. 103). A series of bribes by Lockheed Aircraft Corporation to Japanese politicians to secure military contracts was uncovered. The Watergate investigations revealed questionable payments by corporations not only to President Nixon, but also to many foreign parties. Over 400 companies admitted to making upwards of $300 million in such payments (Cragg and Woolf, 2002 p. 105).

It was in this milieu that the first ethics codes addressing corporate activity emerged. In late 1974, a group of 77 developing countries (G77) initiated the creation of the Commission on Transnational Corporations (UNCTC) at the Economic and Social Council of the United Nations in response to what they viewed as the neo-colonialist practices of many multinational corporations (Hummel, 2005, p. 23). Negotiations at the UNCTC regarding a code of conduct for multinational corporations ensued, with many developing countries advocating a legally binding approach. As a result of vociferous opposition from business and devel-oped countries, a code was never agreed upon at the UNCTC. How-ever, it did play a role in prompting developed countries to take some action. In 1976, the OECD, a grouping of developed countries, launched the Guidelines for Multinational Enterprises.

The OECD Guidelines were voluntary and afforded no robust enforcement or review mechanisms. They included a chapter on employment. It is important to note that the Guidelines were part of a recommendation entitled the *Declaration on International Investment and Multinational Enterprises*, whose purpose was to promote foreign investment by multinational enterprises (Salzman, 2005). Corporations' 'licences to operate' under the existing arrangement were increasingly under fire. There were well-founded fears that developing countries would impose restrictions on foreign investors in response to abuses or interference by multinational corporations. The Guidelines were thus intended to 'prevent misunderstandings and build an atmosphere of confidence and predictability among business, labour and governments' (Trade Union Advisory Committee, 1997, ¶14). Indeed, through the OECD Trade Union Advisory Committee (TUAC), the labour movement played a key role in the creation of the Guidelines.

Taking note of the OECD Guidelines, one year later the International Labour Organisation (ILO) adopted the Tripartite Declaration of Principles Concerning Multinational Enterprises and Social Policy. Like the OECD Guidelines, the Tripartite Declaration was voluntary and nonbinding, and relied on a promotional means of enforcement (Alston, 2004). It incorporated all core labour standards and provided guidelines to governments, employers, and workers in the areas of employment, training, work conditions, and industrial relations. As with other ILO instruments, the Tripartite Declaration emerged from a process that included input from governments, employer organizations, and trade union organizations. Challenging what we have described as the post-war social contract's view of corporate responsibility, the Tripartite Declaration urged 'all the parties' to 'respect the Universal Declaration of Human Rights and the corresponding International Covenants.'

In 1977, another voluntary code, the Sullivan Principles, was launched, which was to become almost synonymous with corporate responsibility and responsible investment in the public eye. Unlike the OECD Guidelines and the ILO Tripartite Declaration, which emerged from international organizations, the Sullivan Principles were authored by an individual, Leon Sullivan. The Sullivan Principles enunciated the responsibilities of multinational corporations operating in apartheid South Africa. At the time of their launch, the Sullivan Principles attracted the kind of debate and controversy that continues to swirl around voluntary corporate codes to the present, particularly those that are aspirational. Are voluntary codes effective in changing corporate conduct? Is it realistic to expect companies to play a catalytic role in fostering social change? Do corporations subscribe to codes only to prevent regulation or for public relations?

One notable exception to the attempt to change corporate conduct abroad through voluntary codes was the *Foreign Corrupt Practices Act* passed by the U.S. Congress in 1978. The *Foreign Corrupt Practices Act* criminalized the bribery of foreign public officials by American-based multinationals. Many in Congress argued that the conduct of multinationals abroad was jeopardizing U.S. foreign policy objectives, including the increased liberalization of markets. This attempt at regulating the extra-territorial conduct of multinationals was unique in two senses: it was limited to the corruption issue and, until the late 1990s, had no equivalent in any another country.

THE 1980s AND EARLY 1990s

The 1980s were also a period of heightened concerns regarding corporate conduct in both the developed and developing world. These concerns were tragically confirmed by the 1984 Bhopal disaster. As a result of a poisonous gas leak from a Union Carbide plant, an estimated 15,000 people were killed and between 150,000 and 600,000 injured in Bhopal, India. Subsequent investigations established several causes for the disaster, among them findings that Union Carbide used unproven and untested technologies, had reduced the frequency of safety checks due to cost pressures, and had insufficient contingency planning.

Throughout the decade, there were public calls for reform or divestment from multinationals operating in apartheid South Africa and in Northern Ireland. In 1987, after a decade of buttressing the Sullivan Principles and lobbying corporations to endorse and implement them, Reverend Sullivan urged companies to completely withdraw their operations from South Africa. In response to employment-related discrimination in Northern Ireland, the Irish National Caucus enunciated the MacBride Principles, a code of conduct for multinationals consisting of nine principles.

The grounding of the *Exxon Valdez* off the coast of Alaska in 1989 led to what is still the largest ever oil spill, with its concomitant environmental devastation. In the wake of this disaster, several labour pension funds, including the California Public Employees Retirement System (CalPERS), and the New York City Employees Retirement System (NYCERS), joined in founding the Coalition for Environmentally Responsible Economies (CERES). CERES was developed within a framework of a coalition of investors, unions, pension funds, and other public interest groups. This 10-point code of conduct calls on companies to improve their environmental performance and reporting.

The Caux Round Table Principles for Business were developed by a group of business leaders in 1994. Like several codes of conduct discussed above, they were voluntary and aspirational, but they were unique in that they were a business-led initiative. Their preamble notes that business is becoming increasingly global and that 'law and market forces are necessary but insufficient guides for conduct' (Caux Round Table, 1994, p. 2).

THE LATE 1990s AND BEYOND

The last decade has witnessed exceptionally important developments in the area of non-financial standards. Two trends in particular are worth highlighting. The first is the re-emergence of governments and international organizations as key players. Several examples illustrate this development. In 1998, the ILO issued the Declaration of Fundamental Principles and Rights at Work. The Declaration identified four core labour standards underpinned by eight ILO Conventions that were aimed primarily at member states but also applied to corporations. A substantial revision of the OECD Guidelines in 2000 expanded their applicability to activities of multinational corporations in non-member states and strengthened the settlement mechanism.[11] The OECD also issued the OECD Principles of Corporate Governance in 1999.

Alongside these new and revised initiatives at the ILO and the OECD, two initiatives at the UN addressed corporate conduct at the global level. The Global Compact, a multi-stakeholder voluntary initiative, was launched by Kofi Annan in 1999. Its 10 principles are based on international instruments including the UDHR, the ILO Declaration, and the UN Convention Against Corruption. The Global Compact is aimed at fostering policy dialogue and partnerships between civil society and corporations.

In stark contrast, the draft UN Norms on the Responsibilities of Transnational Corporations and Other Business Enterprises with Regard to Human Rights tabled in 2003 were intended to be legally binding if they are adopted. They formalized the kinds of demands originally made by developing countries at the UN Commission on Transnational Corporations in the mid-1970s. Drawing upon myriad international instruments, the draft Norms proposed that corporations be required to respect human rights within their respective spheres of influence. Although they generated active and often polarized debate and have been largely sidelined by subsequent developments, the draft Norms were seen in some quarters as a basis for addressing the failure of multinational corporations to assume their human rights responsibilities.

The G8 endorsement of the OECD Guidelines, ILO Declaration, and UN Global Compact in 2003 is an indication of renewed governmental involvement in setting standards for corporations in global markets.

The criminalization of the bribery of foreign public officials also illustrates the increased involvement of government and international organizations in setting corporate ethical standards. In 1999, the OECD Convention Against Bribery of Foreign Public Officials in International Business Transactions came into effect. The Convention called on OECD-member countries to adopt legislation similar to *American Foreign Corrupt Practices Act* that criminalized the bribery of foreign public officials by American corporations. Implementation of the Convention was buttressed in late 2000 by an OECD action statement calling on members' export credit agencies to take active measures to ensure that support is withheld for transactions involving corruption or bribery. The UN Convention Against Corruption, adopted by the General Assembly in 2003, goes well beyond the OECD Convention in several areas. A growing number of countries are passing legislation to comply with these two conventions.

The World Bank is similarly involved in standard setting on corporate responsibility, particularly on governance and anti-corruption. For example, in 1998 the World Bank's private-sector arm, the International Finance Corporation (IFC), set environmental, social, labour, and disclosure standards for the projects it helps to finance in developing countries. The IFC standards were subsequently incorporated into the Equator Principles, an initiative launched in 2003 by major banks worldwide engaged in project financing.

Governments have also acted outside the framework of established international organizations to create standards of responsible corporate conduct. In 2000, the U.S. and U.K. governments drafted the Voluntary Principles on Security and Human Rights to guide corporate conduct in the extractive industry in providing security for their personnel and their operations. The governments of Norway and the Netherlands subsequently also entered the process. Another government-driven initiative addressing the extractive industry is the Extractive Industries Transparency Initiative. The Extractive Industries Transparency Initiative was launched by the United Kingdom in 2002 at the World Summit on Sustainable Development in Johannesburg. It is a multi-stakeholder coalition that supports the full disclosure and verification of company payments and government revenues in the oil, gas, and mining sectors. Comprising governments, companies, civil society organizations, and investors, the Extractive Industries Transparency Initiative endeavours to combat corruption in resource-rich countries with developing or undeveloped economies.

The second key trend that has emerged since the late 1990s is the extensive effort to develop instruments that provide standardized reporting and assurance on EESG issues. This trend has been driven by concerns of investors, public interest groups, and other stakeholders that aspirational or promotional instruments such as the CERES Principles, the Caux Round Table Principles, the Sullivan Principles, the MacBride Principles, the Global Compact, and the OECD Guidelines are by themselves insufficient to improve corporate conduct on EESG issues. Few mechanisms had existed to ensure systematic improvement in performance and accountability. The proliferation of social responsibility reports by corporations has been welcomed with some scepticism because of concerns about what the information disclosed actually measured, what its scope was, whether it was systematically collected, and what it meant compared to similar reports by other corporate actors.

Most notable in the effort to standardize EESG reporting is the Global Reporting Initiative (GRI), launched in 1997. The GRI is a multi-stakeholder process and institution that has set out to develop and promote a globally applicable framework for corporate social responsibility and sustainability reporting. The GRI guidelines set out reporting principles and specific indicators to guide the development of sustainability and corporate social responsibility reports. Another effort, the Greenhouse Gas Protocol Initiative, is aimed at the harmonization of global greenhouse gas accounting and reporting standards, launched in 2001.

The other element of this second key trend has been the advent of instruments designed to allow the verification of corporate performance against EESG standards. These efforts have been particularly evident for labour standards in the apparel sector. Several codes of conduct have been launched in recent years that include auditing and verification mechanisms such as SA 8000 (1997), Code of Labour Practices for the Apparel Industry Including Sportswear (1998), Ethical Trading Initiative Base Code (1998), Fair Labor Association Code of Conduct

(1998), Worldwide Responsible Apparel Production (WRAP), Apparel Certification Program (1998), and AVE (German Retail Association for External Trade) (1999).

The coffee and tea industry has similarly seen several assurance and verification initiatives. These typically address both labour and environmental standards and include a labelling scheme. Examples include Utz Kapeh (1997) and the Common Code for the Coffee Community (2004). Certification schemes and codes of conduct for the social and environmental impacts of the broader agricultural industry include EurepGAP (Good Agricultural Practices) (1997), Rainforest Alliance Certification and the Fair Trade Labeling Organizations International (1988).

Some certification standards that are aimed at EESG issues apply generally. These include the AA1000 Assurance Standard, which was launched in 1999 and was developed through an international multi-stakeholder process by AccountAbility, a not-for-profit and member-based organization. The AA1000 Assurance Standard integrates stakeholder engagement into a cycle of planning, auditing, accounting, reporting, and assurance.

This drive to create tools that facilitate the evaluation of corporate conduct against voluntarily endorsed codes of conduct has also included governments and international organizations, as we have already noted. The UN Norms is perhaps the ultimate manifestation, with its attempt to create a legally binding set of standards governing corporate conduct. The Global Compact has set out a complaints procedure, which can potentially lead to withdrawal of a corporation's right to use its logo. The OECD Guidelines also feature a settlement mechanism through the National Contact Point system. The Extractive Industries Transparency Initiative is designed to ensure accountability by requiring the full disclosure and verification of company payments and government revenues in the oil, gas, and mining sectors.

The Future of EESG Standards

Standards addressing the EESG dimensions of corporate conduct have clearly come a long way in the past three decades. Yet if there is to be systemic change in standards of business conduct, they will have to evolve even further still. Two of the leading thinkers in the field, Ernst Ligteringen and Simon Zadek, expect the next five to ten years will be crucial to the prospects of truly mainstreaming corporate responsibility (Ligteringen & Zadek, 2005). To this end, there are at least three strategic priorities for those seeking to mainstream the entrenchment of EESG factors in corporate and investor decision-making.

INTEGRATION

The preceding discussion has underscored the fact that different standards play different roles. These include the roles of providing 'normative frameworks,' 'process guidelines,' and 'management systems' (Ligteringen & Zadek, 2005). Normative frameworks furnish guidance on best practice and acceptable performance. Process guidelines enable a corporation's performance to be measured, assured, and communicated. Management systems guide the integration of corporate codes of conduct in strategic and day-to-day corporate management. All three components must be present and integrated with each other for ongoing performance improvement on these issues.

CONSOLIDATION

With respect to labour standards, John Ruggie, the UN special representative for Business and Human Rights, recently noted the proliferation of initiatives, each with its own audit and compliance requirements: '[It] is hard to imagine achieving major breakthroughs in achieving sustainable compliance until the issues of code and audit proliferation are dealt with' (Ruggie, 2006, p. 5). Especially in the labour arena but also beyond, there is room for consolidation of initiatives to decrease confusion and implementation costs to companies as well as to free up scarce resources of organizations involved in codification and assurance Ligteringen & Zadek, 2005; Waddock, 2003, p. 12).

MOBILIZE GOVERNMENT

As noted, the last few years have seen governments acting within and outside existing international organizations to address corporate conduct. This development is somewhat ironic in that it was governments' inability or unwillingness to regulate corporate conduct that prompted civil society, investors, and even corporations to take the lead in developing the economic, environment, social, and governance standards created over the past three decades. However, it is becoming increasingly clear that governments must be mobilized to take action if the integration of EESG issues into corporate decision-making is to become mainstream.

There are several reasons for this need. Governments are often the largest consumers of corporate products and services – their procurement policies can play a quintessential role in fostering responsible corporate conduct. Effective incorporation of EESG standards into these procurement policies is essential in this regard. In addition, adherence to EESG standards can be a designated criterion of eligibility for corporations receiving governmental benefits such as subsidies, export credits, and grants. For example, the French and Dutch governments require corporations to endorse the OECD Guidelines in order to be eligible to receive taxpayer-funded export credit guarantees.

Moreover, governments are key funders of many non-financial standards initiatives. The organizations to which they contribute funds and the ends to which this support is directed may hold important implications for fulfilling the strategic priorities of EESG integration and consolidation. Governments can also play a direct role in initiating the creation of EESG standards, as with Extractive Industries Transparency Initiative or the Fair Labor Association. Moreover, through securities, pension fund, and other legislation, governments can promote increased corporate and institutional investor transparency on EESG issues. For example, Prime Minister Tony Blair launched the Carbon Disclosure Project, which involves institutional investors collectively requesting corporations to disclose information on their greenhouse gas emissions. Such disclosure can also be promoted through legislation. For example, beginning in 2000, the U.K. government required pension funds to disclose how they account for environmental and social issues in their investment decision-making.

Conclusion: Labour Pension Funds, Responsible Investment, and Standards

The labour trustees of public-sector pension funds should be central players in encouraging socially, environmentally, and economically responsible business practices. Beyond any other institutional investors, except retail ethical funds or mission-based organizations, the labour movement is grounded on values that intersect in very positive ways with calls for principled and responsible investment practices. Moreover, labour funds control some of the largest pools of investment capital and thus harbour substantial potential for making change. In addition, labour trustees can tap into the labour movement's extensive national and international networks of unions and public interest groups. These networks will have to lead in developing and refining standards of corporate responsibility.

To be sure, labour funds have long acted as catalyzing agents for responsible investment. CalPERS, NYCERS, and the Connecticut

Retirement Plans and Trust Funds in particular were indispensable to the creation and/or promotion of initiatives such as the MacBride Principles, the Sullivan Principles, CERES, the GRI, and the SA8000. However, for the most part, as a group, labour pension funds have thus far failed to harness their full potential as active owners. In our view, this should change. The case for the endorsement by the labour movement of socially responsible investment and the use of emerging tools to guide labour pension-fund investment strategies and practices is clear and persuasive.

Notes

1 It should be noted that much recent literature on responsible investment refers to environmental, social, and governance (ESG) issues. Here we use EESG to underscore the point that economic impacts are a central part of the picture and are particularly important to labour union issues. We use the expression *ethical responsibilities* and related phrases as synonymous with EESG responsibilities. Moreover, we use the term *governance* to refer to the process by which a firm recognizes its responsibilities. This definition encompasses issues of 'board process' that reach beyond the current widespread emphasis on board structure issues such as independence. See Leblanc and Gillies (2003).

2 The gross domestic product (GDP) figures used in Figure 9.1 are calculated using market exchange rates. However, many economists argue that this method understates the true size and living standards of developing country economies. Instead they employ an estimation of the purchasing power parity (PPP) exchange rate, which attempts to adjust the official exchange rate to reflect the actual cost of living in a given country. The logic is that a dollar in, for example, the United States is not worth the same as a dollar in China because, although the prices of internationally traded goods (for example, a Nikon digital camera) are roughly similar, non-tradable goods and services (for example, a haircut) are significantly cheaper. A major hurdle in calculating the PPP exchange rate is the thorny task of matching a given basket of goods and services across countries and time. At any rate, the GDP for the countries in the chart using the PPP method as published by the World Bank are: Sweden $232 billion, Indonesia $683 billion, South Africa $467 billion, Bangladesh $230 billion, Ethiopia $53 billion (World Bank, 2004).

3 The Harvard Mouse or Oncomouse was designed by Harvard University and Dupont. It was genetically modified to be susceptible to cancer, thereby

making it useful for cancer research. Several jurisdictions have granted patents for the mouse, with Canada being a notable exception, due to the Supreme Court's holding in *Harvard College v. Canada (Commissioner of Patents)* in 2002.

4 Hannah Arendt describes this as the power to 'act into nature' (Baehr, 2000).
5 For a more detailed discussion of this development, see Peter Muchlinski's (2001) discussion of the evolving understandings of the ethical responsibilities of business.
6 See, for example, Daly and Cobb (1989).
7 For example, Alan Greenspan, former chair of the Federal Reserve Board, has remarked, 'The current CEO-dominant paradigm, with all its faults, will likely continue to be viewed as the most viable form of corporate governance for today's world. The only credible alternative is for large – primarily institutional – shareholders to exert far more control over corporate affairs than they appear to be willing to exercise' (Greenspan, 2002, ¶32).
8 This is not to deny the important roles played by individual labour funds on particular issues.
9 The *Exxon Valdez* oil spill of 1989 is considered by many to be the most devastating environmental disaster ever to have occurred at sea. The tobacco industry's settlements of the late 1990s involve the culmination of dozens of lawsuits by states and individuals based on the industry's decades-long cover-up of tobacco-related health problems. They involve the ultimate payout of hundreds of billions of dollars by the tobacco industry. The Bhopal disaster of 1984, considered by many to be the worst industrial disaster in history, caused over 15,000 deaths and several hundred thousand injuries. Former Disney CEO and chairman Michael Eisner's $565 million stock option payout in 1997 is widely considered to be the most egregious case of excessive executive pay.
10 Hypernorms are defined by Donaldson and Dunfee (1999, p. 265) as 'principles so fundamental to human existence that they serve as a guide in evaluating lower level moral norms.'
11 It should be noted that the OECD Guidelines were also revised in 1979, 1984, and in 1991.

References

Alston, P. (2004). 'Core labour standards' and the transformation of the international labour rights regime. *European Journal of International Law, 15*(3), 457–521.

Ambachtsheer, J. (2005). Report on the evolution of SRI. *Benefits & Compensation International, 35*(1), 1–7.

Anderson, S., & Cavanagh, J. (2000). The rise of corporate power. Retrieved 15 October 2006 from Institute for Policy Studies website: http://www.ips-dc.org/downloads/Top_200.pdf

Baehr, P. (2000). The concept of history, ancient and modern. In P. Baehr (Ed.), *The portable Hannah Arendt*. New York: Penguin Books.

BusinessWeek. (2003). *The Global 1000*. Retrieved 25 June 2004 from http://www.businessweek.com/magazine/content/03_28/b3841013_mz047.htm?chan=search

Caux Round Table. (1994). *Principles for business*. Retrieved 21 February 2007 from Caux Round Table website: http://www.cauxroundtable.org/documents/Principles%20for%20Business.PDF

Central Intelligence Agency (CIA). (2004). The world factbook 2004. Retrieved 23 July 2004 from http://www.cia.gov/ https://www.cia.gov/library/publications/the-world-factbook/

Cragg, W. (2002). Business ethics and stakeholder theory. *Business Ethics Quarterly 12*(2), 113–43.

Cragg, W., & Woof, W. (2002). The U.S. foreign corrupt practices act: A study of its effectiveness. *Business & Society Review, 107*(1), 98–144.

Daly, H.E., & Cobb, J.B. (1989). *For the common good: Redirecting the economy toward community, the environment and a sustainable future*. Boston: Beacon.

Donaldson, T., & Dunfee, T.M. (1999). *Ties that bind*. Boston: Harvard Business School Press.

Global Compact. (2004). Who cares wins: Connecting financial markets to a changing world. Retrieved 21 February 2007 from United Nations Globe Compact website: http://www.unglobalcompact.org/Issues/financial_markets/who_cares_who_wins.pdf

Greenspan, A. (2002). *Corporate governance*. Paper presented at the Stern School of Business, New York University. Retrieved 21 February 2007 from the Federal Reserve Board website: http://www.federalreserve.gov/BoardDocs/Speeches/2002/200203262/default.htm

Harvard College v. Canada (Commissioner of Patents), 4 S.C.R. 45 (SCC 2002).

Hummel, H. (2005). *The United Nations and transnational corporations*. Paper presented at Global Governance and the Power of Business conference, 8–10 December, Witenberg. Retrieved 12 September 2007 from http://www.weltwirtschaft-und-entwicklung.org/cms_en/downloads/hummelunandtncs2005.pdf

Jensen, M.C. (2005). *Agency costs of overvalued equity*. Working paper. Retrieved 21 February 2007 from John F. Kennedy School of Government website:

http://www.ksg.harvard.edu/leadership/Pdf/JensenWorkingPaper
.pdf

Leblanc, R., & Gillies, J. (2003). The coming revolution in corporate governance. *Ivey Business Journal, 68*(1), 1–11.

Ligteringen, E., & Zadek, S. (2005, 20 April). The future of corporate responsibility codes, standards and frameworks. *An executive briefing by the Global
Reporting Initiative and AccountAbility* Retrieved 21 February 2007 from
http://www.resourcesaver.org/file/toolmanager/Custom016C45F63376
.pdf

McKague, K., & Cragg, W. (2005). *Compendium of ethics codes and instruments of
corporate responsibility.* Toronto: Schulich School of Business, York University.

Muchlinski, P.T. (2001). Human rights and multinationals: Is there a problem?
International Affairs, 77(1), 31–47.

Ruggie, J. (2006). *Remarks.* Paper presented at forum on Corporate Social
Responsibility, 14 June 2006. Retrieved 21 February 2007 from Business &
Human Rights Resource Centre website: http://www.reports-and-materials
.org/Ruggie-remarks-to-Fair-Labor-Association-and-German-Network-of-
Business-Ethics-14-June-2006.pdf

Salzman, J. (2005). *Decentralized administrative law in the organization for economic
cooperation and development.* Retrieved 21 February 2007 from Institute for
International Law and Justice website: http://www.iilj.org/papers/
documents/10120507_Salzman.pdf

Trade Union Advisory Committee. (1997). *The multilateral agreement on investment.* Retrieved 21 February 2007 from TUAC website: http://www.tuac
.org/statemen/communiq/maj01.htm

Waddock, S. (2003). *What will it take to create a tipping point for corporate responsibility?* Retrieved 21 February 2007 from Boston College Personal Web Server:
www2.bc.edu/~waddock/TpgPtPpr.doc

World Bank. (2004). PPP GDP 2002 [Electronic Version]. *World Development
Indicators database.* Retrieved 26 June 2006 from http://www.worldbank
.org/data/databytopic/GDP_PPP.pdf

World Business Council for Sustainable Development, & United Nations Environmental Programme Finance Initiative. (2004). *Generation lost: Young financial analysts and environmental, social and governance issues.* Retrieved 21
February 2007 from http://www.unepfi.org/fileadmin/documents/ymt_
summary_2005.pdf

World Economic Forum. (2005). Mainstreaming responsible investment.
Retrieved 4 January 2007 from http://www.weforum.org/pdf/mri.pdf

10 Training for Effective Action: Evaluation of the Quebec Federation of Labour Training Program on the Bargaining and Administration of Pension Plans

ALAIN DUNBERRY

The Quebec Federation of Labour (FTQ) training program on the administration and negotiation of pension plans is the largest of its kind in Canada. After five years of development, the FTQ's Education Department has expressed an interest in a formative evaluation to identify the strengths and weaknesses at each level of the program as well as in the ways they interact with and complement each other.

Evaluative Approach

Given the concerns expressed by the FTQ, it seemed appropriate that we should undertake an evaluative approach based upon Patton (1997). This approach rests on the fundamental principle that evaluation must be judged on its actual usefulness. The role of the evaluator consists not in passing an external, 'objective' judgement on the program but rather in making it easier for this judgement to be expressed and for decisions to be made by the users. Since no evaluation can be value-free, the position that is clearly taken in this model is that the values of the users will form the basis of the evaluative judgement. Other authors (Fitzpatrick, Sanders, & Worthen, 2004; Sonnichsen, 1994) have confirmed the relevance of involving the decision-makers and users with a view to ensuring that the evaluation and recommendations will serve a useful purpose.

User involvement has accordingly made a major contribution, primarily in describing the program and its general and specific goals, defining the major questions of the evaluation and the indicators to be used in responding to it, as well as in interpreting the data and making recommendations. The users were also consulted concerning methodology, in order to ensure that the approach taken would both be realistic and generate results that would be seen to be valid.

Context of the Program

As early as the 1980s, the FTQ considered including preparation for retirement in the training it provided to its members and its affiliated unions. In the following years, threats of substantial reductions in the income security of workers when they retired were increasingly heard. The FTQ therefore extended its strategy and demanded that pension plans no longer remain under the sole control of employers. In Quebec, it was not until 1990 that this legislative reform was achieved. From then on, a pension committee that was independent of the employer would administer each plan and the legislation required at least a minimum representation of workers, both active and retired.

At the same time, the Fonds de Solidarité of the FTQ took innovative action on investment practices and the economic education of workers. Mobilization for the creation of the FTQ's Fonds de Solidarité led to the provision of training sessions in economics designed for these workers. Furthermore, the FTQ has shown over the years that the union movement has the ability to manage capital by attempting to reconcile the objective of achieving adequate returns with economic and social objectives, such as job protection.

From 1991 to 2001, the FTQ's Education Department, in cooperation with the Service aux collectivités at Université du Québec à Montréal (UQAM), developed its first advanced training program on the negotiation and administration of pension plans. It was given two or three times a year over 10 years to the affiliated unions of the FTQ throughout Quebec. During those 10 years, the members who were FTQ delegates in the pension committees and the people responsible for negotiating such plans, together with the other activists, became increasingly aware that many plans still did not meet the minimum standards laid down in Quebec. The committee members felt isolated and out of their depth in their new role as plan administrators. In addition, the permanent staff of the FTQ expressed their own uncertainty in their role in negotiating pension plans. Intimidated by the technical aspects of the subject, they tended to defer to the experts, who were often actuaries with connections to the employers.

At around the same time, proposals for improving the governance of the major banks in this country were submitted to annual meetings of the banks' shareholders and, despite its support for these proposals, the union movement found that the managers entrusted with the assets of pension plans were the first to vote against these proposals. The inaction of the union movement in this situation was a cause for concern.

These concerns led to the establishment of an ambitious training program designed to equip the members of the FTQ and its affiliates with the most up-to-date knowledge and appropriate technical vocabulary. The primary goal was to strengthen and expand the actions taken by pension committee members. This new program resulted in a more proactive approach by the advisers responsible for the renewal of collective agreements, executive committee members, and bargaining committee members. Another concern of the FTQ was to ensure that pension-fund assets were managed in a way that better reflected the interests and values of the members of these plans. In putting this program forward, the FTQ's Service de l'éducation and UQAM's Community Services have combined with a third partner, the Fondation de la formation économique du Fonds de Solidarité de la FTQ, which, armed with its experience in providing workers with economic training, wished to grapple with the challenges of pension plans and the financial power they represent.

In November 2000, at the request of its members, the FTQ organized a major conference on investment management in workers' pension funds. Seven hundred people, far exceeding expectations, took part with interest in presentations focusing on terms and concepts that had become much more technical, and the main issues and challenges of pension-fund investments from a union perspective. At the FTQ Congress in 2001, the central union adopted a policy statement that made it possible for decisions to be made on the importance of providing training for members and enriching the program continuously.

This is how the training activities provided for members of the FTQ and its affiliates on the administration and negotiation of pension funds were gradually strengthened and diversified before the training program that is now offered was developed.

The Program

The general objectives of the training program are as follows:

• To increase the understanding among all interested members of the FTQ of the essential principles and concepts involved in negotiating and administering pension plans in order to provide income security for the members when they retire, in accordance with union values and principles

- To strengthen the ability of the members to act as trustees and nego-tiators on the basis of their increased understanding
- To promote the implementation of a support network for the mem-bers of pension plans in order to overcome their isolation and encourage them to become involved in administering supplemen-tary pension plans
- To increase the training provided and make it accessible in the regions and other unions through a core of trainers, in order to ensure continuity in transferring and updating knowledge
- To define, implement, and promote collective and socially responsi-ble investment strategies that reflect the values of the union move-ment, especially in the exercise of voting rights

This program is geared to four separate client groups:

1. *Pension committee members.* Given the extent of the FTQ's presence in the private sector in Quebec, 1,000 to 1,300 members hold office as trustees in pension committees that are subject to the Quebec legislation. According to a document published by the Régie des Rentes du Québec (2003), pension committee members perform a dual function. They perform financial functions relating to manage-ment of the plan, for example, in ensuring that the fund is invested appropriately and will be able to meet its financial obligations to its members.
2. *Members of bargaining and executive committees.* This group is much larger than that referred to above. However, it accounts for 40% of those taking part in the basic training sessions. The more advanced course is not intended for this group.
3. *Advisers.* These are about 600 employees of the affiliated unions, including the people responsible for negotiating collective agree-ments.
4. *Trainers.* These are 30 experienced activists appointed by the affili-ated unions and trained by the FTQ.

The program comprises five courses:

1. *'Acting as a Union to Take Charge of Our Pension Plans.'* This is the basic course on pension plan administration. It extends over three

days and focuses upon public plans, defined contribution and defined benefit plans, funding and actuarial valuation, governance, organization, and union involvement. It is given to the members of pension committees, bargaining committees, executive committees, and other interested individuals, and is facilitated by two trainers from the pool created by the FTQ.

2. *'Investing Our Funds in Our Members' Interests.'* This course is geared specifically to pension committee members who have already taken the basic course. It is a five-day residential course given three or four times a year. It covers investment policy, the funding of pension plans, the policy on voting rights, and monitoring the investment manager as well as bonds, stocks, and socially responsible investing.

3. *'Negotiating Our Pension Plans and Taking Our Place.'* This is a three-day course given four or five times a year. The content of the basic course was adapted to meet the needs of advisers responsible for negotiating pension plans, among other things. This course includes role-playing exercises focusing on the negotiation of pension plans when collective agreements are renewed. It examines the contribution made by the advisers and the conditions for success within the union. The sections of the first course dealing with administration and information were not included.

4. *'Training the Trainers'* (for the basic first course). The initial training is given over five days, during which time the participants examine the contents of the basic course. They learn about ways to deliver the training so that they become proficient in facilitating the basic training sessions. This initial training is supplemented by the requirement of one day's preparation before each session, during which methods and contents are reviewed and adapted to the group in question. The FTQ's Education Department is responsible for preparing the team of trainers. This course allows participants to update their knowledge of the contents while reviewing teaching methods. The contents are adapted to meet the trainers' needs and any difficulties they have encountered in sessions they have facilitated.

5. *An annual seminar.* This seminar is designed to provide ongoing training for all the client groups involved in the program. It covers new issues relating to pension plans and allows people to update their knowledge. The annual seminar consists of presentations and workshops followed by question periods on topics such as bargaining, legislation, responsible investing, and other relevant union

activities. The management of a pension plan involves three inter-dependent dimensions: benefits, funding, and investment. A union may protect its members through collective bargaining relating to maintenance of the plan and improvements of the benefits, its funding, or its governance. The first and third courses focus prima-rily on benefits and on the funding of these benefits, whereas the second course focuses primarily on investments and funding.

The program's originality rests on three central features. First, it stresses the interdependence among benefits, funding, and investment in order to ensure that plans are viable. Second, the basic course makes it possible to bring together various parties involved in the plan (trust-ees, advisers, members of the executive, or bargaining committee) and promotes exchanges and networking. Third, the second course pro-vides the technical basis to enable people to deal as equals with the employer's representatives while acting on concerns about investing responsibly.

When the evaluation took place, close to 500 people had taken part in the basic course. The training sessions in the third course on negotiating made it possible to bring together some 60 staff members, while approx-imately 200 trustees took the second course on investing. Finally, the annual seminars, which aim to bring together more than 100 people each year, have attracted some 600 participants since 2001.

Main Questions in the Evaluation

Users of the program devised five questions, and the evaluation was structured around them.

1. *To what extent did the members of the pension committee understand at the end of the session some of the essential concepts involved in the administra-tion and negotiation of the pension plans examined during training?*

This question was designed specifically to assess the level of learning achieved at the end of training. This question is relevant because of the level of technical difficulty of some of these concepts and the need for pension committee members to have a sound understanding of them in order to be able to take action. Furthermore, the answer to this question makes it possible to assess in part the extent to which the training allows participants to attain certain objectives relating to understanding.

The assessment of what has been learned has important limitations in itself. In fact, it may not be assumed that it will fully reflect what has been learned by participants, since the assessment (including use of a written examination) is far removed from their basic experience and may cause stress that leads them to underperform (Donaldson, Gooler, & Scriven, 2002).

2. To what extent does the training prepare the participants to act in administering and negotiating pension plans in their various organizations?

This second question is designed to assess what contribution the training has made to help them move into action. For this purpose, it seemed relevant to make use of the concepts of empowerment (Le Bosse & M., 1993; Ninacs, 2003; Ninacs & Leroux, 2002) and self-efficacy (Bandura, 2003). These concepts will be presented in the following section.

3. To what extent did the training help to change the administration and negotiation practices of the participants' pension plans in their various organizations?

This question is designed to determine the impact of the training on the practices of members. It includes the transfer of what was learned in the training to regular practices as well as the new behaviours that have emerged following the training – behaviours that may be attributable, directly or indirectly, to the training. This question is therefore focused essentially on the nature, intensity, and frequency of changes in behaviour resulting from the training in the context of the organizations in which the participants work.

4. Which are the factors that facilitate or impede changes in administration and negotiating practices in the participants' pension plans in their various organizations?

The purpose of this question was to consider in detail the environmental factors that may facilitate or impede changes in practices. The literature on transfer of learning (Baldwin & Ford, 1988) indicates that these factors may be linked to the individual, the training process, or the environment. What seems especially important in the context of this evaluation is to separate the influence of the participants and the training they have received from the influence of the environment in which they work. What, then, are the environmental factors that lead to resistance or alternatively generate change? Furthermore, what are the factors in this same environment that appear to weaken these behaviours?

5. What changes should be made, whether in the training program or the environment of the participants, in order to support and increase their ability to take charge of and make an impact on pension plans?

This final question emerges logically from the previous two questions. Among other things, does the training provide adequate preparation for action? If so, what aspects of this process appear to have made a particular contribution to changing practices? In addition, what additional learning would be required for participants to cope better with the constraints imposed by the environment?

Conceptual Framework

Empowerment may be defined as 'a process by which an individual or a community acquires power and develops the skills to exercise it' (Ninacs, 2003, p. 21). This concept is particularly applicable to the context of this evaluation. In fact, empowerment is not limited solely to the acquisition of skills or increasing awareness of certain problems; its goal is a true appropriation by the participants of the power to act on their reality. This is indeed what the union training aims to achieve: to increase awareness but also to inspire action.

Ninacs (2003) suggests that empowerment has four components and this process is to some extent the outcome of a successful interaction among these four factors: participation, the technical skills required for structuring action in the community, critical awareness that makes it possible to analyse the challenges and to locate any action accordingly, and the self-esteem that allows those involved to believe in their ability to act – a characteristic strengthened by success.

Within this evaluation of the program, self-esteem was replaced by self-efficacy or SE (Bandura, 2003). This concept 'concerns people's belief in their ability to act in such a way as to control the events that affect their existence' (Bandura, 1997, in Carre, 2004, p. 41). This leads, among other things, to an ability to take risks because the individual is confident about making successful changes. Increasingly used as a means of evaluating training programs and regarded as a decisive factor in the transfer of learning (Bandura, 2003; Haccoun, Jeanrie, & Saks, 1997), the concept of self-efficacy makes it possible to show that the performance of learners does not depend solely on objective skills but also on their self-confidence.

Self-esteem and SE are nevertheless two distinct concepts. Indeed, self-esteem concerns the overall personal value of the individual, whereas self-efficacy refers to quite specific skills or abilities. SE is easier to discern, understand, and observe and more likely to vary following a training activity.

As part of this evaluation, the extent to which technical skills are acquired is covered by a learning test administered at the end of the training and by the comments made by the participants in discussion groups concerning the impact of training on their behaviours. Self-efficacy is measured by scales that have been developed specifically for this evaluation. The levels of participation and critical awareness are examined in the group discussions. A synthesis of all these data should give us an appreciation of the level of empowerment achieved by the participants in the training. These results should also answer the first and second questions in this program evaluation.

The components of empowerment essentially focus on the individual and related environment. Thus, Alsop, Bertelsen, and Holland (2006) conceive of empowerment as the outcome of the relationship between agency and the institutional environment ('opportunity structure') in which the individual is located. Agency, defined here as the ability of an actor or a group of actors to make thoughtful ('purposeful') choices, is in an iterative relationship with the environment. This relationship permits a certain degree of empowerment that gives rise to developmental results that act retroactively on agency and the environment. This means therefore that a hostile environment, regardless of the agency of the individuals involved, may compromise the empowerment substantially. As part of this evaluation, the effects of the environment are considered through question 4, while the developmental results are explored in the response to question 3.

Methods

The evaluation was conducted in three main ways: (1) evaluation of the self-efficacy of a large group of activists who have taken the training in recent years; (2) evaluation of pension-fund management and technical skills at the start (control groups) and at the end (experimental groups) of the training, and the self-efficacy of those taking the first and second courses in the spring of 2006; (3) group interviews with members of pension committees, members of union bargaining, and executive committees and trainers, and individual interviews with union advisers.

The training objectives of these courses formed the basis for creating a scale to measure the SE. These objectives were translated into skills by the program designers and were then used to develop a list of items. Participant responses were expressed on a 6-point Likert scale, ranging from *not at all capable* to *very capable*. This test was administered to participants in the annual seminar in 2006 who had received the training earlier. It was accordingly a first evaluation of the impact of training over a period varying from a few months to five years. The size of the group also made it possible to check the reliability of the tool by calculating Cronbach's alpha.

To assess learning, the two tests focused on the technical skills essential to the courses. Multiple-choice questions were used to ensure that the inability to write did not negatively influence the performance of the respondents. Each test involved 11 questions. Given the training activities, the knowledge tests were distributed to two control groups (before the training was given) and two experimental groups (at the end of the training) in the first course, and to one control group and one experimental group in the second course. Participants' self-efficacy in the first course was also assessed in a way that made it possible to consider the effect of the training on this variable. The groups consisted of participants referred to the testers by national and local unions, pension committees, or, to a lesser degree, regional councils. For the second course, the participants had to have previously taken the first course and be members of the pension committee. The number of participants ranged from 10 to 20 for the first course and slightly fewer for the second course.

For both individuals and groups, interview guides were prepared by the technical evaluation committee concerning the effect of the training on participation (question 2), the impact of the training (question 3), the organizational factors that facilitate or impede changes in practices (question 4), and the changes that should be made to the program or the environment of the participants (question 5). Discussion groups with 8 to 12 members each were created through telephone solicitation of participants in training activities over the last three years. Advisers were interviewed individually because of their limited availability. Interviews took place primarily in Montreal, but also in Quebec City and Saguenay.

Results

The analysis of the results is structured around the five questions presented above.

What Participants Learned

Table 10.1 shows the results of the learning tests administered to those who took part in the first two courses. For both courses, there were significant differences between the control group and the experimental

Table 10.1. Comparison Results of the Control and Experimental Groups in Tests of What Was Learned in the First Two Courses.

Item	Results – control group	Results – experimental group	Discrimination index	p
Average – first course	0.458 N = 24	0.675 N = 26	0.22	p < .01*
Average – second course	0.580 N = 8	0.77 N = 10	0.19	p < .05**

*Student's *t*-test. **Mann-Whitney *U*.

group. This means that, on the basis of these limited samples, participation in these training courses seemed to have had a significant impact on participants' level of technical skills regarded as essential.

Participant Empowerment

The methodology allows us to assess the impact of the training on three of the four dimensions of empowerment noted in our conceptual framework. The previous section refers to the results relating to technical skills while this section refers to those relating to self-efficacy and participation.

At the annual seminar, the SE scale was administered to a large group of participants who had taken the first three courses ($N = 66$). It was also administered to the above-mentioned first course control ($N = 24$) and experimental groups ($N = 26$). To check the reliability of the SE measurement scale, Cronbach's alpha was calculated separately for all the items responded to by participants in the first course (questions 1 to 14;[1] $N = 50$) and for all items responded to by participants in the second course (questions 15 to 27; $N = 28$) using the answers given by the group of participants in the annual seminar ($N = 66$). The figures obtained for Cronbach's alpha were .9402 and .9595 respectively, which reflect a very high level of reliability and confirm the quality of the tool.

Participants at the Annual Seminar SE Scale Results

Table 10.2 contains the number of respondents, averages, and standard deviations in the answers on the SE scale for participants in the first

Table 10.2. Results on the SE Measurement Scale for Participants in the First Course.

	Item	N	M	SD
1	Explain to the members the sources of income derived from public and supplementary plans available when they retire.	65	4.82	0.98
2	Communicate to the members the importance of fighting against projects to cut benefits in public and supplementary plans.	66	5.00	0.99
3	Explain to the members the benefits of defined benefit plans as compared with defined contribution plans.	66	5.21	0.80
4a	Explain to the members what benefits are provided by the plan in light of the three major challenges: When? How much? Is it indexed or not?	59	4.85	1.05
4b	Calculate the income replacement rate, including any public plans that may apply, from age 60 or age 65.	59	4.39	1.34
4c	Explain the type of clauses that could be negotiated in the collective agreement to protect the members.	57	4.61	1.08
5	Identify the contribution rate required in order to obtain a minimum income replacement rate.	12	3.58	0.90
6	Explain the personalized statement issued by the pension plan to the members.	66	4.97	0.91
7	Determine the quality of the plan in light of the anticipated replacement rate of 70%.	65	4.63	1.18
8	Recommend improvements in the plan in light of its characteristics and the context.	66	4.62	1.09
9	Provide arguments for the position that the fund, including its surpluses, represents a deferred salary for the benefit of its members.	64	4.42	1.28
10	Explain to the members which persons ('the successors') are entitled as a matter of priority to benefits in the event of the member's death.	65	4.37	1.33
11	Explain in simple terms to the members how the pension plan portion of a family patrimony is divided in the event of divorce or legal separation.	65	4.23	1.30
12	What would you say to the pension committee to explain the duties and rights of the committee's members?	65	4.49	1.42
13	Develop good communications with the members concerning the pension plan.	66	4.95	0.89
14	Propose or develop strategies involving the union structures to meet the priority needs that are identified.	62	4.37	1.09

course who attended the annual seminar. It should be noted that the responses to each item were expressed on a 6-point Likert scale ranging from *not at all capable* (1) to *very capable* (6).

Note that the average lies between 3.58 for item 5 and 5.21 for item 3.

If we exclude item 5, which relates to a dimension of defined contribution plans on which the training did not focus, the responses indicated that, overall, the participants felt capable, within their community and with the resources at their disposal, of reproducing the behaviours referred to in the items. A post hoc analysis using the Tukey test shows primarily that item 3, which relates to the ability to explain the advantages of defined benefit plans over defined contribution plans, produces a significantly higher score than all the items except item 2.

Table 10.3 contains the number of respondents, averages, and standard deviations in the responses to the SE measurement scale for participants in the second course who attended the annual seminar. Note that the averages lie between 3.87 for item 27 and 4.91 for item 23. Once again, the responses indicated that overall, the participants felt capable of reproducing the behaviours indicated by the items. The results of the post hoc analysis using the Turkey test confirm for us that the averages for items 23 and 16 were higher and this causes them to stand out significantly from a number of other items. Items 26 and 27, which relate to responsible investing, also stand out, but in the reverse. The respondents therefore felt less capable of taking action in connection with responsible investing.

Comparison of Groups before and after the Training on the SE Scale

A comparative analysis of the SE test results for the control and experimental groups shows that the average for the experimental group for all the items relating to the first course is significantly higher than the figure for the control group ($t = -3.502$, $df = 32$, $p < .01$). This result seems to indicate that overall, the participants who receive the training felt better able to reproduce the behaviours covered in that course than those who had not yet taken it. This significant difference at thresholds of .05 and .01 can be observed for all the items except items 4c and 5. These items involve, respectively, the ability to explain the kind of clauses that could be negotiated in a collective agreement in order to protect members, and the ability to identify the level of contribution required to produce a minimum replacement rate within a defined contribution plan. Note that the highest average for the control group was in item 4c.

Participation

The effect of the training on participation can be measured by the results of the group and individual interviews with the pension com-

284   Alain Dunberry

Table 10.3. Results on the SE Measurement Scale for Participants in the Second Course.

Item		N	M	SD
15	Read an actuarial valuation to determine the pension plan's capitalization, solvency, and normal cost and the employer contribution to be paid.	30	4.77	1.04
16	Ask the actuary all the necessary questions to obtain an idea of the plan's financial situation.	31	4.65	1.02
17	Determine whether the changes made by the actuary in his or her assumptions are in the members' interests.	30	4.53	1.07
18	Understand and follow a presentation using the concepts of average, mean, quartiles, standard deviation, and correlation.	32	4.41	1.27
19	Understand and follow a presentation by bond managers.	32	4.28	1.11
20	Understand the link between the duration of the bond portfolio and changes in interest rates.	32	4.09	1.25
21	Understand and follow a presentation by an equities manager.	32	4.19	1.28
22	Ask the pension committee questions to determine whether the investment policy reflects factors such as the percentage of retirees or the employer's ability to absorb an increase in contributions.	31	4.32	1.17
23	Argue in favour of the need for the committee to hold a meeting at least every quarter.	32	4.91	1.20
24	Act to ensure that the agenda for meetings with the manager includes an examination of his or her performance and an explication of his or her investment strategies.	31	4.39	1.26
25	Act to require the manager to file a report on the exercise of voting rights in the last year.	29	4.24	1.35
26	Reply to the statement that socially responsible investing will necessarily result in lower returns and is thus in breach of our fiduciary duties.	30	3.93	1.36
27	Act as a trustee to ensure that social and environmental factors are taken into account.	30	3.87	1.14

mittee members (five groups; $N = 19$); members of bargaining committees (one group; $N = 3$); and advisers (three individual interviews). Pension committee members in four of the five groups acknowledged that the training improved their understanding and gave them a greater awareness of aspects of pension-fund administration. In all the groups, participants attributed their ability to ask questions or take action to the training they received. They stated that they could not have engaged in these behaviours earlier because they had insufficient understanding of the subject and/or lacked confidence. Participants in two groups said that they now obtain more information, meetings, and transparency from the employer. In four of the five groups, reference was made to an impact on fund management and participation in decision-making. Two participants in two different groups claimed that the training had affected bargaining. One participant said that 'when all is said and done, substantial'[2] improvement in the fund occurred during the latest negotiations, while another established a link with the recent negotiations that enabled him to move back to a defined benefit plan.

Bargaining committee participants admitted that they had a better understanding of and were more comfortable with their duties. The three advisers who were interviewed said they had a better understanding of the technical aspects of pension-fund administration. Two of them said that they were better able to deal with their members, while three claimed that the training had positively affected their bargaining activities.

Overall, we find that the training seems to have had an impact on the level of participation. It seems at the very least that the training helps individuals to move from silent attendance to exercising their right to speak and, in many cases, to involvement in debates and even in decision-making. However, the small number of participants does not allow us to clearly determine the magnitude of this impact on participation.

Assessment of Participants' Empowerment

The observed effects of the level of learning, participation, and self-efficacy suggest that participation in the training program has an impact on participants' empowerment. They have learned about technical skills considered essential in the administration and negotiation of pension plans; their level of participation has increased to include participation in discussions and, in some cases, in decision-making; and their self-efficacy supports their perception that they can reproduce the training behaviours. However, these results do not allow us to include responsible investing with respect to participant empowerment.

Changes in Participant Practice Following Training

On the basis of results of the discussion groups, it seems that the training helps to change participants' administrative and bargaining practices. Committee members had a better understanding of pension issues, which appeared to increase their participation, their active search for information, their involvement in decision-making and better bargaining, as well as improved relations with the bargaining committee. The training apparently improved the quality of meetings with union members, who in some cases showed more trust in their representatives. Finally, it was also noted that some employers modified their behaviour, knowing that the new committee members were better trained.

The bargaining advisers, for their part, had a better understanding, were more comfortable in their functions, and were better able to negotiate. Training of staff advisers resulted in greater understanding and more information about pensions, which had an effect on bargaining activities and relations with members. It seems, therefore, that the effects of the training were not limited to the acquisition of knowledge or essential concepts but were also reflected in the acquisition of actual technical skills that increase participants' ability to act within their environment.

Factors That Facilitate or Impede Changes in Practices

Factors that facilitate or impede changes in practice may be analysed in three related areas: the factors directly linked to training, to the program as a whole, and to the environment in which the members and advisers do their work.

With respect to the training, the course content and the pedagogical approach were frequently viewed in a positive light by the participant groups. However, these same participants were less pleased with the fact that they were exposed to a great deal of content in a short time.

The program as a whole also supports an annual seminar and training for the trainers. The annual seminars evoked a positive assessment from four of the five groups of pension committee members, especially for the fact that they provided a forum where people could meet, discuss, or make contacts. Some groups, however, noted that the content could be too technical and that large groups may not be the best venue for exchange of this type of information or knowledge.

The training given to the trainers consisted of the first course offered in depth and supplemented with basic pedagogical training. Trainers also took part in an annual professional development session and an annual seminar, which enabled them to meet approximately every six months. The course and the proposed approach were viewed by the trainers in a very positive light. The annual professional development meetings were also highly appreciated by the trainers. These meetings provided an opportunity to obtain updates on changes in the subject and enabled people to stay in touch with one another. They provided a venue for informal exchanges, which the participants found important.

Participants with whom we met noted few factors in the environment that made a positive contribution to changed practices. Only two groups of pension committee members mentioned some support, in one case from a resource in the metalworkers' union and, in the other case, from the local executive. Two groups of pension committee members and two advisers referred more to isolation or a lack of supportive resources that could be easily accessed in the event that problems arose.

The minority position of the pension committee members and the lack of interest among plan members were the reasons given by most of the groups of pension committee members. They were followed by three other factors: the employer's conduct or attitude, isolation, lack of support and follow-up, and of opportunity to apply the newly acquired knowledge. The bargaining committee members mentioned the defensive attitude of the employer, isolation, and lack of technical resources, which did not always allow them to demand the maximum. The advisers referred primarily to the same two factors. Differences in training among the various people involved in the system and the lack of co-ordination among the bodies they represent were other possible blocking factors that should be explored.

Improving the Program and the Environment

Among the recommendations made by the pension committee members, three in particular stood out, as all three groups mentioned them. The recommendations were to train more members so that they will be more interested in the administration of their pension plan, provide easy access to a technical resource that they can use when complex problems arise, sometimes even before the training, and facilitate discussions among peers or establish a network of contacts, either in real mode (occasional meetings) or in virtual mode (over the Internet).

The recommendations of the participants in the trainers' group were to change the title so that people have a better understanding of the course objectives and so that more of them register, expand the program to include bargaining issues and union actions, and train more union activists (for example, the presidents of the executive and nego-tiators). Further recommendations were to provide follow-up on the training through a team of intermediaries who can help people to be more certain about their role, encourage pension committee members to provide training for their members, and include the pensions issue in other areas of FTQ training. It should be added that legislative changes to the *Supplemental Pension Plans Act* enacted in December 2006 could significantly improve the governance of pension commit-tees and therefore the environment in which labour trustees have to operate in. Some of the key changes include enshrining the trustees' right to all the 'documents and information needed to administer the pension plan' (a. 151.3; see also 154.2 and 154.3), the recognition that trustee education is an admissible 'administration cost' (a. 162) and the requirement that all pension committees must, in their by-laws, specify 'the measures to be taken to provide professional development to com-mittee members' (a. 151.1), the requirement that all pension committees must have by-laws covering at least 10 issues (a. 151.1), and much greater accountability and transparency from service providers and delegates (a. 153 to 154.4).

The bargaining committee members made several recommenda-tions. The first was to lighten the content of the courses and make members more aware of retirement and prepare them for it. The FTQ should also provide more information, among other things, about the dates on which the courses are to be given. It should promote exchanges among members, train replacements in order to ensure that they do not start from scratch each time a new team is elected, and pro-vide technical support to ensure that demands are checked prior to the negotiations.

A single individual made the advisers' recommendations, which were to give a course on actuarial concepts; encourage pension commit-tee members to raise awareness in their constituency; leave more time for practical exercises; have the unions provide greater access to expert technical resources; network the officers so that they can share experi-ence and expertise on the subject; and have a long-term vision that does not jeopardize the viability of the undertaking.

There is accordingly a certain consensus that more members need to be reached so that they become more aware of their interests and thus become involved. Technical resources need to be placed at the disposal of those involved so that they can be used for support and troubleshooting in the event that problems occur. Networking was also mentioned as a support mechanism.

Conclusion

In short, the program fully attains most of its training objectives, and this accomplishment appears to contribute to increased involvement and empowerment of the people immersed in the field of pensions. However, it would perhaps be advantageous to intervene more on the environment in which these activities take place if we wish to continue developing the capacity of unions to deal with the administration and negotiation of pension plans and socially responsible investing. Indeed, the best training alone is inadequate to strengthen the capacity for action. The people who are trained must also be located in a fostering environment that facilitates the immediate and ongoing transfer of what has been learned. If the opposite is the case, there is a strong likelihood that over a certain period of time what has been learned will gradually be lost. Pension committee members and other union members with responsibility in this area noted that if the union movement wishes to develop and maintain individual and collective empowerment among the union officials involved with pension issues, it might consider developing a true community of practice to support people in an environment that may be hostile to desired change.

In other words, it seems relevant to ensure better support and follow-up of participants after the training has been given. Alternating between training and practice – an approach that is praised in professional training – is an approach also very relevant in this situation. Participants would benefit if they could receive training, return to the situation where they practise what they have learned, and then return for more training to discuss with one another the problems experienced in transferring what they have learned and possible solutions that have proved effective, and to develop other approaches on the basis of their experience.

What is more, integrated training and consultation strategies at the local level need to be promoted to advisers and executives in order to ensure more widespread involvement of the people concerned (including the plan members) and greater synergy between the bodies involved (pension committee, bargaining committee, and local executive). The identification and distribution of participants among the training activities in line with their functions and the offices they hold is strategically essential for this purpose.

Notes

1 Question 5 had to be withdrawn for this analysis since there were too few respondents ($N = 6$). This question was intended exclusively for the members of defined contribution plans, who are very few in number.
2 Groupe de membres de comités de retraite, Quebec City, 15 May 2006.

References

Alsop, R., Bertelsen, M., & Holland, J. (Eds.). (2006). *Empowerment in practice: From analysis to implementation*. Washington DC: World Bank.

Baldwin, T.T., & Ford, J.K. (1988). Transfer of training: A review and directions for future research. *Personnel psychology 41*(1), 63–105.

Bandura, A. (2003). *Auto-efficacité. Le sentiment d'efficacité personnelle*. Paris: De Boeck Diffusion.

Carre, P. (2004). Bandura: une psychologie pour le XXIe siècle? *Savoirs* (hors-série 2004), 9–50.

Donaldson, S.I., Gooler, L.E., & Scriven, M. (2002). Strategies for managing evaluation anxiety: Toward a psychology of program evaluation. *American Journal of Evaluation, 23*(3), 261–73.

Fitzpatrick, J.L., Sanders, J.R., & Worthen, B.R. (2004). *Program evaluation: Alternative approaches and practical guidelines* (3rd ed.). Boston: Allyn and Bacon.

Haccoun, R.R., Jeanrie, C., & Saks, A.M. (1997). Concepts et pratiques contemporaines en évaluation de la formation: Vers un modèle de diagnostic des impacts. *Gestion, 22*(3), 108–13.

Le Bosse, Y.D., & Lavallee, M. (1993). Empowerment et psychologie communautaire. *Les cahiers internationaux de psychologie sociale, 18*(2), 7–20.

Ninacs, W. (2003). *L'empowerment et l'intervention sociale*: Document d'accompagnement, Centre de documentation sur l'éducation des adultes et la condition féminine.

Ninacs, W., & Leroux, R. (2002). *Intervention et empowerment*: Formation à l'institut de dévelopement communautaire, Université de Concordia.

Patton, M.Q. (1997). *Utilization-focused evaluation: The new century text* (3rd ed.). Thousand Oaks, CA: Sage.

Régie des rentes du Québec. (2003). *Supplemental Pension Plans: Guide for Pension Committee Members*. Quebec: Author.

Sonnichsen, R.C. (1994). Evaluators as change agents. In J.S. Wholey, H.P. Hatry, & K.E. Newcomer (Eds.), *Handbook of practical program evaluation* (pp. 534–48). San Francisco: Jossey-Bass.

Supplemental Pension Plans Act, R.S.Q., ch. R-15.1 (2006).